Who's Afraid of Java?

LIMITED WARRANTY AND DISCLAIMER OF LIABILITY

Who's Afraid of Java?

Steve Heller

AP Professional

AP Professional is a division of Academic Press

Boston   San Diego   New York
London   Sydney   Tokyo   Toronto

AP PROFESSIONAL
1300 Boylston Street, Chestnut Hill, MA 02167
An Imprint of Academic Press
A Division of Harcourt Brace & Company
World Wide Web site at http://www.apnet.com

United Kingdom Edition published by
ACADEMIC PRESS LIMITED
24-28 Oval Road, London NW1 7DX

ISBN 0-12-339101-6

Printed in the United States of America
97 98 99 00 IP 9 8 7 6 5 4 3 2 1

Contents

Figures

Dedication

This book is dedicated to Susan Patricia Caffee Heller, the light of my life. Without her, this book would not be what it is; even more important, I would not be what I am: a happy man.

Acknowledgements

I'd like to thank my test readers Fred Ballard, Chic Barna, Mike Kelleghan, John Kottal, and Bruce Ordway, for pointing out typos and the like, as well as for their general feedback on my writing.

The often heated discussions on the JAVAUSER forum of Compuserve have given me some insight into the "true believer" mentality too often associated with any new language, Java not excluded. I suppose it's too much to ask that technical topics be discussed with reason and cordiality, but I refuse to give up hope.

Of course, I'm deeply indebted to Eric Raymond for his wonderful foreword; I can only hope that you and my other readers like this book as well as he does!

My editors at AP Professional, Chuck Glaser and Jeff Pepper, have both been everything that a technical author could hope for (and most don't get).

Besides those who have directly helped me with this book, I'd like to acknowledge two of the greatest benefactors of mankind in general and myself in particular. The first of these is the greatest writer I know, Ayn Rand. She had the ability to explain complex philosophical concepts in language so simple that anyone could understand them; if I can explain programming half as clearly, I will consider myself a great success. Even more important, she laid the foundation for solving what is possibly the greatest conundrum of philosophy: how to connect what is with what ought to be.

Finally, I want to thank L. Ron Hubbard for his discoveries and inventions in the field of the mind and spirit. Even a small fraction of his myriad contributions to knowledge would qualify him for the first rank of friends of mankind; in total, they elevate him without question to the top of the list.

Preface

Is this book for you? If you're a programmer in a language other than Java™, and want to upgrade your skills, then the answer is yes.[1] But what if you have no previous programming experience? In that case, here's a little quiz that may help you decide:

1. Do you want to know how the programs in your computer work inside, and how to write some of your own?
2. Are you willing to exert yourself mentally to learn a complex technical subject?
3. Do you have a sense of humor?

If you've answered yes to these questions and follow through with the effort required, then you will get a lot out of this book.

The common wisdom states that programming is a difficult subject that should be reserved for a small number of specialists. One of the main reasons that I have written this book is that I believe this attitude is wrong; it is possible, and even desirable, for you to learn how programs work and how to write them. Those who don't understand how computers perform their seemingly magical feats are at an increasing disadvantage in a society ever more dependent on these extraordinary machines.

Regardless of the topic, I can see no valid reason for a book to be stuffy and dry, and I've done everything possible to make this one approachable. However, don't let the casual tone fool you into thinking that the subject is easy; there is no "royal road" to programming, any more than there is to geometry. Especially if you have no prior experience in programming, this book will stretch your mind more than virtually any other subject you could study.

One important reason why this book is different from other books is the participation of Susan, my primary "test reader", whose

---

1. If you are a C++ programmer, you might want to read Appendix B, which describes the most important differences between that language and Java before reading the rest of the book.

account of her involvement in this project immediately follows this preface. I recommend that you read that account before continuing with the technical material following it, as it explains how and why she contributed to making your task easier and more enjoyable.

Speaking of Susan, here is a bit of correspondence between us on the topic of how one should read this book, which occurred after her first reading of what is now Chapters 2 and 3:

> **Susan**: Let me say this: to feel like I would truly understand it, I would really need to *study* this about two more times. Now, I could do this, but I am not sure you would want me to do so. I think reading a chapter once is enough for most people.

> **Steve**: As a matter of fact, I would expect the reader of my book to read and study this chapter several times if necessary; for someone completely new to programming, I imagine that it **would** be necessary. Programming is one of the most complex human disciplines, although it doesn't take the mathematical skills of a subject such as nuclear physics, for example. I've tried to make my explanations as simple as possible, but there's no way to learn programming (or any other complex subject) without investing a significant amount of work and thought.

After she had gone through the text a number of times and had learned a lot from the process, we continued this discussion as follows:

> **Susan**: Well then, maybe this should be pointed out in a preface or something. Of course, it would eventually be obvious to the reader as it was to me, but it took me a while to come to that conclusion. The advantage of knowing this in advance is that maybe I would not be so discouraged that I was not brilliant after one read of a chapter.

> **Steve**: I will indeed mention in the preface that the reader shouldn't be fooled by the casual tone into thinking that this is going to be a walk in the park. In any event, please don't be discouraged. It seems to me that you have absorbed a fair amount of very technical material with no previous background; that's something to be proud of!

We'll be hearing from Susan many more times in the course of the book. She will be checking in frequently in the form of extracts from the e-mail discussion we engaged in during the testing and revising process. I hope you will find her comments and my replies add a personal touch to your study of this technical material.

While we're on the topic of your studying, this would be a good time to tell you how to get updates and help with any errors you might find in the book or any other questions you might have. The best way is to visit my WWW page:

http://www.websurfer.net/personal/technovelist/homepage.htm

If you don't have WWW access, you can write to me in care of my publishers at the following address:

Steve Heller
c/o AP Professional
1300 Boylston Street
Chestnut Hill, MA 02167

I should also tell you how the various typefaces are used in the book. HelveticaNarrow is used for program listings, for terms used in programs, and for words defined by the Java language. *Italics* are used primarily for technical terms that are found in the glossary, although they are also used for emphasis in some places. The first time that a particular technical term is used, it is in **bold** face; if it is a term defined in the Java language, it will be in **HelveticalNarrowBold**.

The next voice you will hear is that of Susan, my test reader. I hope you get as much out of her participation in this book as I have.

Letter from a Novice

As a famous frog once said, "It's not easy being green".

Yet being new at programming languages seems to be my forte these days, at least according to Steve Heller, who, after one tumultuous effort in the production of his book *Who's Afraid of C++?* found me indispensable enough to employ my lack of knowledge once again in the making of *Who's Afraid of Java?*.

After being a "professional novice" for 2 years now I still can't get used to the idea of my ignorance as being an important commodity. Sometimes I wonder why I so foolishly spent nearly 5 years in college. Perhaps if I had not done that I could be in huge demand as one of the world's greatest "know-nothings". It really is a difficult position to rationalize, and creates a very odd slant to my reality system.

However once again I have been prevailed upon to apply my expertise of knowing nothing to learning the Java programming language. And once again Steve and I went full circle, asking and answering questions concerning his writing until I felt comfortable enough with each concept that I could move on to the next. To do this has been and still is an exercise in extremes, emotionally and intellectually. But once again I sincerely hope that, for those of you totally new to programming, our efforts will make the road to learning Java a little less rocky for you because we tried to think like you do, and give you explanations that you will be able to understand.

This book, based on the same general outline as *Who's Afraid of C++?*, gives a novice reader the basics of programming and then leads up to some rather advanced concepts that even experienced programmers in other languages might find a bit of a stretch. This is because Java quickly incorporates what is considered a higher level of complexity in other languages.

I must admit that there was one unexpected oversight on our part concerning my commission as the resident know-nothing. I suddenly realized not too far into the Java book that my career as a professional novice might be in jeopardy, as we overlooked one minor detail, that is <ahem>, I know C++.[1] That is, I know enough about C++ to make comparisons of the two languages, which came up many times in the reading of the book. That fact made it in some cases easier for me to read this book, but in some cases harder. While I must consider that in all fairness I might be suffering from "first language chauvinism", the differences in the two languages forced me to make side by side comparisons and it didn't take me long to start to complain about what I disliked in Java.[2]

Even though my days of absolute novicehood may be over, I am sure that Steve will be imploring me to apply my relative lack of knowledge to yet another of his many book ideas. Since each new language will be just that (new) to me, I think I will be able to keep my status as a novice for quite some time to come. However, I have already put him on alert that there is at least one subject I won't suffer through: there will be *no* book called *Who's Afraid of Assembly Language?* with my name in it. I have seen the stuff, and I am certain about this: I am afraid of *that*!

---

1. When you get further along in the book, you may wonder on occasion how I could ask such basic questions if I already have knowledge of another language such as C++. The answer is simple: those questions are transplanted from our previous book, *Who's Afraid of C++?*. Of course, they have been edited to fit into a discussion of Java, but they are essentially the same questions I asked when I was first learning about programming.

2. You can find some of these complaints in Appendix B, which discusses the differences between C++ and Java.

Foreword

Steve and Susan Heller have given a new meaning to the cliche "labor of love". By the time you read this book, I expect to have danced at their wedding. That ceremony will make a perfect symbol of what this book is and why I care about it — and why I think you will, too.

The best technical books marry the expertise of a technical expert with the curiosity and eagerness of a novice. Books like this do not merely recite facts and approaches; they challenge. They motivate. They are even (what a concept!) *fun to read*. Because so much technical tutorial writing is boring, pretentious, and constipated in style, it is easy to forget these books exist.

But every once in a while a book like *Who's Afraid of Java?* comes along and reminds us that the very best technical books are discoveries in both knowledge and joy.

Tutorial books this good are very hard to write. The people who write them are, after all, experts. It takes a very difficult mental effort to abandon that expertise, to see their fields through a novice's eyes. It takes an even more taxing effort to hold the expert and novice viewpoints in one mind simultaneously. The wonder isn't that really good technical tutorials by one author are so rare, it's that they exist at all.

Perhaps the ideal team for a good technical book is one expert and one highly motivated novice. But collaboration has its own perils. The partners have to be compatible. They have to understand each other. They have to work to resolve differences. They have to be committed to making the relationship work. It's not unlike being...married.

Susan was Steve's novice. They collaborated on this book as they did on *Who's Afraid of C++?*. Her questions in the text are lucid, penetrating, unafraid. They're the *right* questions to support a novice reader struggling through the unavoidable complexities of the exposition.

The dialogue between them — both intelligent, both able writers, gives this book an almost unique strength. Susan stimulates Steve to address the novice viewpoint without ever having to abandon his natural voice as an expert. The sympathy between them shows; and it invites the reader almost irresistibly into the conversation and the sense of intellectual intimacy it creates.

(Oh, yes. If it's not obvious from the foregoing, this book works technically, too. It's a thorough and concise treatment of its topics. I differ with Steve's opinions about Java sometimes, but his facts are reliable.)

Steve and I have been friends since long before either of us were successful authors; we know each other well. After *Who's Afraid of Java?* I feel like I know Susan's personality nearly as well. What they've done together is a delight and an astonishment.

I look forward to more books from these two, perhaps *Who's Afraid of the World Wide Web*? I look forward to meeting Susan at their wedding in June 1997. And I'll have just two things to say to Steve as I shake his hand afterwards:

1. Keep this one, she's good for you!
2. Are you going to put her name on the cover next time?

Eric Raymond
Malvern, Pa.
May 1997

About the Author

Steve Heller had always been fascinated by writing. In his childhood days in the 1950s and 1960s, he often stayed up far past his bedtime reading science fiction. Even in adulthood, if you came across him in his off-hours, he was more likely to be found reading a book than doing virtually anything else.

After college, Steve got into programming more or less by accident; he was working at an actuarial consulting firm and was selected to take charge of programming on their time-sharing terminal, because he was making much less than most of the other employees. Finding the programming itself to be more interesting than the actuarial calculations, he decided to become a professional programmer.

Until 1984, Steve remained on the consuming side of the writing craft. Then one day he was reading a magazine article on some programming-related topic and said to himself, "I could do better than that". With encouragement from his wife of the time, he decided to try his hand at technical writing. Steve's first article submission — to the late lamented *Computer Language Magazine* — was published, as were a dozen more over the next ten years.

But although writing magazine articles is an interesting pastime, writing a book is something entirely different. Steve got his chance at this new level of commitment when Harry Helms, then an editor for Academic Press, read one of his articles in *Dr. Dobb's Journal* and wrote him a letter asking whether he would be interested in writing a book for AP. He answered, "Sure, why not?", not having the faintest idea of how much work he was letting himself in for.

The resulting book, *Large Problems, Small Machines*, received favorable reviews for its careful explanation of a number of facets of program optimization, and sold a total of about twenty thousand copies within a year after publication of the second edition, entitled *Efficient C/C++ Programming*.

By that time, Steve was hard at work on his next book, *Who's Afraid of C++*, which is designed to make object-oriented programming intelligible to anyone from the sheerest novice to the programmer with years of experience in languages other than C++. To make sure that his exposition was clear enough for the novice, he posted a message on CompuServe requesting the help of someone new to programming. The responses included one from a woman named Susan Spino, who ended up contributing a great deal to the book. Her contribution was wonderful, but not completely unexpected.

What *was* unexpected was that Steve and Susan would fall in love during the course of this project, but that's what happened. Since she lived in Texas and he lived in New York, this posed some logistic difficulties. The success of his previous book now became extremely important, as it was the key to Steve's becoming a full-time writer. Writers have been "telecommuting" since before the invention of the telephone, so his conversion from "programmer who writes" to "writer" made it possible for him to relocate to her area, which he promptly did.

Since his move to Texas, Steve has been hard at work on his writing projects, including *Introduction to C++*, a classroom text that covers more material in the same space as *Who's Afraid of C++?* at the expense of the email exchanges in the latter book, followed by the book you are now reading.

Steve and Susan were married in June of 1997.

Chapter 1

Prologue

Introduction to Programming

"Begin at the beginning, and go on till you come to the end: then stop." This method of telling a story is as good today as it was when the King of Hearts prescribed it to the White Rabbit in *Alice in Wonderland*. In this book, we must begin with you, the reader, since my job is to explain a technical subject to you. It might appear that I'm at a severe disadvantage; after all, I've never met you.

Nevertheless, I can make some pretty good guesses about you. You almost certainly own a computer and know how to use its most common application, word processing. If you use the computer in business, you probably also have an acquaintance with spreadsheets and perhaps some database experience as well. Now you have decided to learn how to program the computer yourself rather than relying completely on programs written by others. On the other hand, you might be a student using this book as a text in an introductory course on programming. In that case, you'll be happy to know that this book isn't written in the dry, overly academic style employed by many textbook writers. I hope that you will enjoy reading it, as my "test readers" have.

Whether you are using this book on your own or in school, there are many good reasons to learn how to program. You may have a problem that hasn't been solved by commercial software; you may want a better understanding of how commercial programs function so you can figure out how to get around their shortcomings and peculiarities; or perhaps you're just curious about how computers perform their seemingly magical feats. Whatever the initial reason, I

1

hope you come to appreciate the great creative possibilities opened up by this most ubiquitous of modern inventions.[1]

Before we begin, however, we should agree on definitions for some fundamental words in the computing field. Susan had some incisive observations about the power of words. Here is our exchange on that issue:

> **Susan**: I will read something usually at face value, but often there is much more to it; that is why I don't get it. Then, when I go back and really think about what those words mean, it will make more sense. This book almost needs to be written in ALL CAPS to get the novice to pay closer attention to each and every word.

> **Steve**: IMAGINE WRITING A BOOK IN ALL CAPS! THAT WOULD BE VERY DIFFICULT TO READ, DON'T YOU THINK?

Many of the technical words used in this book are in the Glossary at the end of the book; it is also very helpful to have a good technical dictionary of computer terms, as well as a good general dictionary of English.

Of course, you may not be able to remember all of these technical definitions the first time through. If you can't recall the exact meaning of one of these terms, just look up the word or phrase in the index, and it will direct you to the page where the definition is stated. You could also look in the Glossary, at the end of the book. Definitions of key technical terms are listed there in alphabetical order.

Before we continue, let's check in again with Susan. The following is from her first letter to me about the contents of this book:

> **Susan**: I like the one-on-one feel of your text, like you are just talking to me. Now you did make a few references to how simple some things were that I didn't catch on to, so it kinda made me feel I was not too bright for not seeing how apparently simple those things were. . . .
>
> I think maybe it would have been helpful if you could have stated from the onset of this book just what direction you were taking, at least chapter by chapter. I would have liked to have seen a goal stated or at least a summary of objectives from the beginning. I often would have the feeling I was just suddenly thrown into something as I was reading

---

1. Of course, it's also possible that you already know how to program in another language and are using this book to learn how to do so in Java. If so, you'll have a head start; I hope that you'll learn enough to make it worth your while to wade through some material you already know.

along. Also (maybe you should call this *Java for Dummies*, or is that taken already?)[2], you might even *define* what programming is! What a concept! Because it did occur to me that since I have never seen it done, or a language or anything, I really don't know what programming *is*! I just knew it was something that nerds do.

Susan's wish is my command, so I have provided a list of objectives at the beginning of each chapter after this one. I've also fulfilled her request for a definition of some programming terms, starting as follows:

An **algorithm** is a set of precisely defined steps to calculate an answer to a problem or set of problems, which is guaranteed to arrive at such an answer eventually. As this implies, a set of steps that might never end is *not* an algorithm.

Programming is the art and science of solving problems by the following procedure:[3]
1.   Find or invent a general solution to a class of problems.
2.   Express this solution as an algorithm or set of algorithms.
3.   Translate the algorithm(s) into terms so simple that a stupid machine like a computer can follow them to calculate the specific answer for any specific problem in the class.

At this point, let's see what Susan had to say about the above definition and my response:

> **Susan**: Very descriptive. How about this definition: "Programming is the process of being creative using the tools of science, such as incremental problem solving, to make a stupid computer do what you want it to"? That I understand!
>   Your definition is just fine. A definition has to be concise and descriptive and that you have done and covered all the bases. But you know what is lacking? An example of what it looks like. Maybe just a little statement that really looks bizarre to me and then say that by the end of the chapter you will actually know what this stuff really means! Sort of like a coming attraction type of thing.

---

2. As it happens, that title is indeed taken, as is *Java Programming for Dummies*!

3. This definition is possibly somewhat misleading since it implies that the development of a program is straightforward and linear, with no revisions required. This is known as the "waterfall model" of programming, since water going over a waterfall follows a preordained course in one direction. In real-life, however, programming doesn't usually work this way; rather, most programs are written in an incremental process as assumptions are changed and errors are found and corrected.

> **Steve**: I understand the idea of trying to draw the reader into the "game"; however, I think that presenting a bunch of apparent gibberish with no warning could frighten readers as easily as it might intrigue them. I think it's better to delay showing examples until they have some background.

Now let's return to our list of definitions.

Hardware refers to the physical components of a computer, the ones you can touch. Examples include the keyboard, the monitor, the printer.

Software refers to the other, nonphysical components of a computer, the ones you cannot touch. If you can install it on your hard disk, it's software. Examples include a spreadsheet, a word processor, a database program.

A **source-code program** is a program in a form suitable for reading and writing by a human being.

A **byte-code program** is a Java program in a form suitable for running (by an interpreter) on a user's computer.

A **byte-code instruction** is one of the fundamental operations that a *Java interpreter* can perform. Some examples of these operations are addition, subtraction, or other arithmetic operations; other possibilities include operations that control what instruction will be executed next. All Java programs must be converted into byte-code instructions by a *compiler* before they can be executed by the Java interpreter.

Compilation, in Java, is the process of translating *source code* into a *byte-code program*, which is composed of *byte-code instructions* along with the data needed by those instructions. We have to compile Java programs before we can use them, because the Java interpreter (see following definition) doesn't know how to deal with source-code instructions, only with byte-code instructions.

A Java **compiler** is a program that performs compilation as defined above.

An **interpreter** is a program that controls the execution of another program.

The **Java interpreter** is the program that controls the execution of your Java programs.

How to Write a Program

Now you have a definition of programming. Unfortunately, however, this doesn't tell you how to write a program. The process of solving a problem by programming in Java follows these steps:

Problem: After discussions between the user and the programmer, the programmer defines the problem precisely.

Algorithms: The programmer finds or creates algorithms that will solve the problem.

Java: The programmer implements these algorithms as source code in Java.

Compiler: The programmer runs the Java compiler, which must already be present on the programmer's machine, to translate the source code into a byte-code program.

Interpreter: The user uses a Java interpreter to run the resulting byte-code program on his or her computer.

```
Problem
Algorithms
Java
Interpreter
Hardware
```

These steps advance from the most abstract to the most concrete, which is perfectly appropriate for an experienced Java programmer. However, if you're using this book to learn how to program in Java, you're obviously not an experienced Java programmer, so before you can follow this path to solving a problem, you're going to need a fairly thorough grounding in all of these steps. It's not really feasible to discuss each step exhaustively before going to the next one, so I've created a little "step indicator" that you'll see on each page of the text, with the currently active step shown in bold. For example, when we're discussing algorithms, the indicator will display the word **Algorithms** in bold.

The five steps of this indicator correspond to the five steps in problem solving just defined. I hope this device will make it easier for you to follow the sometimes tortuous path to programming knowledge. Let's see what Susan thinks of it.

> **Susan**: With all the new concepts and all the new language and terms, it is so hard to know what one thing has to do with the other and where things are supposed to fit into the big picture. With the key, you can see

how these things all fit as logical steps to an end. Now I know it isn't going to be easy, but at least I know what my destination is before I board the plane. Anyway, you have to understand; for someone like me, this is an enormous amount of new material to be introduced to all at once. When you are bombarded with so many new terms and so many abstract concepts, it is a little hard to sort out what is what. Will you have guidelines for each of the steps? Since I know a little about this already, the more I look at the steps, I just know that what is coming is going to be a big deal. For example, take step 1: you have to give the ingredients for properly defining a problem. If something is left out, then everything that follows won't work.

Steve: I hope you won't find it that frustrating, because I explain all of the steps carefully as I do them. Of course, it's possible that I haven't been careful enough, but in that case you can let me know and I'll explain it further.

Unfortunately, it's not possible for me to provide a thorough guide to all of those steps, as that would be a series of books in itself. However, there's a wonderful small book called *How to Solve It* by G. Polya that you should be able to get at your local library. It was written to help students solve geometry problems, but the techniques are applicable in areas other than geometry. I'm going to recommend that readers of my book read it if they have any trouble with general problem solving.

```
Problem
Algorithms
Java
Interpreter
Hardware
```

The steps for solving a problem via programming might sound reasonable in the abstract, but that doesn't mean that you can follow them easily without practice. Assuming that you already have a pretty good idea of what the problem is that you're trying to solve, the Algorithms step is likely to be the biggest stumbling block. Therefore, it might be very helpful to go into that step in a bit more detail.

Baby Steps

If we already understand the problem we're going to solve, the next step is to figure out a plan of attack, which we will then break down into small enough steps to be expressed in Java. This is called **stepwise refinement**, since we start out with a "coarse" solution and refine it until the steps are within the capability of the Java language. For a complex problem, this may take several intermediate steps, but let's start out with a simple example. Say that we want to know how much older one person is than another. We might start with the following general outline:

1. Get ages from user.
2. Calculate difference of ages.
3. Print the result.

This can in turn be broken down further as follows:

1. Get ages from user.
   a. Ask user for first age.
   b. Ask user for second age.
2. Subtract second age from first age.
3. Print the result.

This looks okay, except that if the first person is younger than the second one, then the result will be negative. That may be acceptable. If so, we're just about done, since these steps are simple enough for us to translate them into Java fairly directly. Otherwise, we'll have to modify our program to do something different depending on which age is higher. For example,

1. Get ages from user.
   a. Ask user for first age.
   b. Ask user for second age.
2. Compute difference of ages.
   a. If first age is greater than second, subtract second age from first age.
   b. Otherwise, subtract first age from second age.
3. Print result.

Problem
Algorithms
Java
Interpreter
Hardware

You've probably noticed that this is a much more detailed description than would be needed to tell a human being what you want to do. That's because the computer is extremely stupid and literal: it does only what you tell it to do, not what you meant to tell it to do. Unfortunately, it's very easy to get one of the steps wrong, especially in a complex program. In that case, the computer will do something ridiculous, and you'll have to figure out what you did wrong. This "debugging", as it's called, is one of the hardest parts of programming. Actually, it shouldn't be too difficult to understand why that is the case. After all, you're looking for a mistake you've made yourself. If you knew exactly what you were doing, you wouldn't have made the mistake in the first place.

I hope that this brief discussion has made the process of programming a little less mysterious. In the final analysis, it's basically just logical thinking.[4]

On with the Show

Now that you have some idea how programming works, it's time to see exactly how the computer actually performs the steps in a program, which is the topic of Chapter 2.

```
Problem
Algorithms
Java
Interpreter
Hardware
```

---

4. Of course, the word *just* in this sentence is a bit misleading; taking logical thinking for granted is a sure recipe for trouble.

Chapter 2

Hardware Fundamentals

Getting Started

Like any complex tool, the computer can be understood on several levels. For example, it's entirely possible to learn to drive an automobile without having the slightest idea of how it works. The analogy with computers is that it's relatively easy to learn how to use a word processor without having any notion of how such programs work. On the other hand, programming is much more closely analogous to designing an automobile than it is to driving one; therefore, we're going to have to go into some detail about the internal workings of a computer, not at the level of electronic components, but at the lowest level important to a Java programmer.

This is a book on learning to program in Java, not on how a computer works. Therefore, it might seem better to start there and eliminate this detour, and indeed many (perhaps most) books on Java do exactly that. However, in working out in detail how I'm going to explain Java to you, I've come to the conclusion that it would be virtually impossible to explain *why* certain features of the language exist and how they actually work, without your understanding *how* they relate to the underlying computer hardware.

I haven't come to this position by pure logical deduction, either. In fact, I've worked backward from the concepts that you will need to know to program in Java to the specific underlying information that you will have to understand first. I'm thinking in particular of one specific concept, the *reference*, which is supposed to be extremely difficult for a beginning programmer in Java to grasp. With the approach we're taking, you shouldn't have much trouble understanding this concept by the time you get to it in Chapter 6; it's noted as such in the discussion there. I'd be interested to know how you find my explanation there, given the background that you'll have by that point; don't hesitate to e-mail me about this topic (or any other, for that matter).

On the other hand, if you're an experienced programmer, a lot of this will be just review for you. Nonetheless, it can't hurt to go over the basics one more time before diving into the ideas and techniques that make Java different from other languages.

Now let's begin with some definitions and objectives for this chapter.

Definitions

A **digit** is one of the characters used in any positional number system to represent all numbers starting at 0 and ending at one less than the base of the number system. In the decimal system, there are ten digits, 0–9, and in the hexadecimal system there are sixteen digits, 0–9 and a–f.

A **binary** number system is one that uses only two digits, 0 and 1.

```
Problem
Algorithms
Java
Interpreter
Hardware
```

A **hexadecimal** number system is one that uses 16 digits, 0–9 and a–f.

A **variable** is a programming construct that represents a specific item of data that we wish to keep track of in a program. Some examples are the weight of a pumpkin or the number of cartons of milk in the inventory of a store.

Objectives for This Chapter

By the end of this chapter, you should:

1. Understand the programmer's view of the most important pieces of hardware in your computer.
2. Understand the programmer's view of the most important pieces of software in your computer.
3. Be able to solve simple problems using both the binary and hexadecimal number systems.
4. Understand how whole numbers are stored in the computer.

Behind the Curtain

First we'll need to expand on the definition of *hardware*. As noted earlier, *hardware* means the physical components of a computer, the ones you can touch.[1] Examples are the monitor, the keyboard, the printer, and all of the interesting electronic and electromechanical components inside the case of your computer.[2]

Right now we're concerned with the Java programmer's view of the hardware. The hardware components of a computer with which you'll be primarily concerned are the disk, RAM (short for Random Access Memory), and the CPU (short for Central Processing Unit).[3] We'll take up each of these topics in turn.

Disk

When you sit down at your computer in the morning, before you turn it on, where are the programs you're going to run? To make this more specific, suppose you're going to use a word processor to revise a letter you wrote yesterday before you turned the computer off. Where is the letter, and where is the word processing program?

You probably know the answer to this question: They are stored on a disk inside the case of your computer.[4] Disks use magnetic recording media, much like the material used to record speech and music on cassette tapes, to store information in a way that will not be lost when the power is turned off. How exactly is this information

Problem
Algorithms
Java
Interpreter
Hardware

---

1. Whenever I refer to a *computer*, I mean a modern microcomputer capable of running MS-DOS™; these are commonly referred to as *PCs*. Most of the fundamental concepts are the same in other kinds of computers, but the details differ.

2. Although it's entirely possible to program without ever seeing the inside of a computer, you might want to look in there anyway, just to see what the CPU, RAM chips, disk drives, etc., look like. Some familiarization with the components would give you a head start if you ever want to expand the capacity of your machine.

3. Other hardware components can be important to programmers of specialized applications; for example, game programmers need extremely fine control on how information is displayed on the monitor. However, we have enough to keep us busy learning how to write general data-handling programs; you can always learn how to write games later, if you're interested in doing so.

4. Technically, this is a hard disk, to differentiate it from a floppy disk, the removable storage medium often used to distribute software or transfer files from one computer to another. Although at one time many small computers used floppy disks to store data, the tremendous decrease in hard disk prices means that today even the most inexpensive computer stores programs and data on a hard disk.

(which may be either executable programs or data such as word processing documents) stored?

We don't have to go into excruciating detail on the storage mechanism, but it is important to understand some of its characteristics. A disk consists of one or more circular *platters*, which are extremely flat and smooth pieces of metal or glass covered with a material that can be very rapidly and accurately magnetized in either of two directions, "north" and "south". To store large amounts of data, each platter is divided into many millions of small regions, each of which can be magnetized in either direction independent of the other regions. The magnetization is detected and modified by *recording heads*, similar in principle to those used in tape cassette decks. However, in contrast to the cassette heads, which make contact with the tape while they are recording or playing back music or speech, the disk heads "fly" a few millionths of an inch away from the platters, which rotate at very high velocity.[5]

The separately magnetizable regions used to store information are arranged in groups called *sectors*, which are in turn arranged in concentric circles called *tracks*. All tracks on one side of a given platter (a *recording surface*) can be accessed by a recording head dedicated to that recording surface; each sector is used to store some number of *bytes* of the data, generally a few hundred to a few thousand. "Byte" is a coined word meaning a group of 8 *bi*nary digi*ts*, or *bits* for short.[6] You may wonder why the data aren't stored in the more familiar decimal system, which of course uses the digits from 0 through 9. This is not an arbitrary decision; on the contrary, there are a couple of very good reasons that data on a disk are stored using the binary system, in which each digit has only two possible states, 0 and 1. One of these reasons is that it's a lot easier to determine reliably whether a particular area on a disk is magnetized "north" or "south" than it is to determine 1 of 10 possible levels of magnetization. Another reason is that the binary system is also the natural system for data storage using electronic circuitry, which is used to store data in the rest of the computer.

Problem
Algorithms
Java
Interpreter
Hardware

---

5. The heads have to be as close as possible to the platters because the influence of a magnet (called the *magnetic field*) drops off very rapidly with distance. Thus, the closer the heads are, the more powerful the magnetic field is and the smaller the region that can be used to read and write data reliably. Of course, this leaves open the question of why the heads aren't in contact with the surface; that would certainly solve the problem of being too far away. Unfortunately, this seemingly simple solution would not work at all. There is a name for the contact of heads and disk surface while the disk is spinning: *head crash*. The friction caused by such an event destroys both the heads and disk surface almost instantly.

6. In some old machines, bytes sometimes contained more or less than 8 bits, but the 8-bit byte is virtually universal today.

Although magnetic storage devices have been around in one form or another since the very early days of computing, the advances in technology just in the last dozen years have been staggering. To comprehend just how large these advances have been, we need to define the term used to describe storage capacities: the Megabyte. The standard engineering meaning of *Mega* is "multiply by one million", which would make a Megabyte equal to one million (1,000,000) bytes. As we have just seen, however, the natural number system in the computer field is binary. Therefore, "one Megabyte" is often used instead to specify the nearest "round" number in the binary system, which is 2^{20} (2 to the 20th power), or 1,048,576 bytes.[7] This wasn't obvious to Susan, so I explained it some more, as you can see here:

> **Susan**: Just how important is it to really understand that the Megabyte is 2^{20} (1,048,576) bytes? I know that a meg is not really a meg; that is, it's more than a million. But I don't understand 2^{20}, so is it enough to just take your word on this and not get bogged down as to why I didn't go any further than plane geometry in high school? You see, it makes me worry and upsets me that I don't understand how you "round" a binary number.

> **Steve**: The ^ symbol is a common way of saying "to the power of", so 2^{20} would be 2 to the power of 20; that is, twenty 2s multiplied together. This is a "round" number in binary just as 10 * 10 * 10 (1000) is a "round" number in decimal.

Problem
Algorithms
Java
Interpreter
Hardware

1985, a Space Odyssey

With that detail out of the way, we can see just how far we've come in a short period of time. In 1985, I purchased a 20 Megabyte disk for $900 ($45 per Megabyte); its **access time**, which measures how long it takes to retrieve data, was approximately 100 milliseconds (milli = 1/1000, so a millisecond is one thousandth of a second). In April 1997, a 6510 Megabyte disk cost as little as $449, or approximately 7 *cents* per Megabyte; in addition to delivering 650 times as much storage per dollar, this disk had an access time of 14 milliseconds, which is approximately 7 times as fast as the old disk. Of course, this

---

7. In case you're not familiar with the ^ notation, the number on its right indicates how many copies of the number to the left have to be multiplied together to produce the final result. For example, $2^5 = 2 * 2 * 2 * 2 * 2$, whereas $4^3 = 4 * 4 * 4$. Of course, I've just introduced another symbol you might not be familiar with: the * is used to indicate multiplication in programming.

significantly understates the amount of progress in technology in both economic and technical terms. For one thing, a 1997 dollar is worth considerably less than a 1985 dollar. In addition, the new drive is superior in every other measure as well: It is much smaller than the old one, consumes much less power, and has many times the projected reliability of the old drive.

This tremendous increase in performance and price has prevented the long-predicted demise of disk drives in favor of new technology. However, the inherent speed limitations of disks still require us to restrict their role to the storage and retrieval of data for which we can afford to wait a relatively long time.

You see, while 14 milliseconds isn't very long by human standards, it is a long time indeed to a modern computer. This will become more evident as we examine the next essential component of the computer, the *RAM*.

RAM

Problem
Algorithms
Java
Interpreter
Hardware

The working storage of the computer, where data and programs are stored while we're using them, is called **RAM**, which is an acronym for Random Access Memory.[8] For example, your word processor is stored in RAM while you're using it. The document you're working on is likely to be there as well unless it's too large to fit all at once, in which case parts of it will be retrieved from the disk as needed. Since we have already seen that both the word processor and the document are stored on the disk in the first place, why not leave them there and use them in place, rather than copying them into RAM?

The answer, in a word, is *speed*. RAM is physically composed of millions of microscopic switches on a small piece of silicon known as a *chip*: a 4 Megabit RAM chip has approximately four million of them.[9] Each of these switches can be either on or off; we consider a switch that is "on" to be storing a 1, and a switch that is "off" to be storing a 0. Just as in storing information on a disk, where it was easier to magnetize a region in either of two directions, it's a lot easier to make a switch that can be turned on or off reliably and quickly than one that can be set to any value from 0 to 9 reliably and

---

8. *RAM* is sometimes called "internal storage", as opposed to "external storage", that is, the disk.

9. Each switch is made of several transistors. Unfortunately, an explanation of how a transistor works would take us too far afield. Consult any good encyclopedia, such as the *Encyclopedia Britannica*, for this explanation.

quickly. This is particularly important when you're manufacturing millions of them on a silicon chip the size of your fingernail.

A main difference between disk and RAM is what steps are needed to access different areas of storage. In the case of the disk, the head has to be moved to the right track (an operation known as a *seek*), and then we have to wait for the platter to spin so that the region we want to access is under the head (called *rotational delay*). On the other hand, with RAM, the entire process is electronic; we can read or write any byte immediately, as long as we know which byte we want. To specify a given byte, we have to supply a unique number called its **memory address** or just **address** for short.

Return to Sender, Address Unknown

What is an address good for? Let's see how my discussion with Susan on this topic started.

> **Susan**: About memory addresses: Are you saying that each little itty bitty tiny byte of RAM is a separate address? Well, this is a little hard to imagine.
>
> **Steve**: Actually, each byte of RAM *has* a separate address, which doesn't change, and a value, which does.

Problem
Algorithms
Java
Interpreter
Hardware

In case the notion of an address of a byte of memory on a piece of silicon is too abstract, it might help to think of an address as a set of directions as to how to find the byte being addressed, much like directions to someone's house. For example, "Go three streets down, then turn left. It's the second house on the right". With such directions, the house number wouldn't need to be written on the house. Similarly, the memory storage areas in RAM are addressed by position; you can think of the address as telling the hardware which street and house you want, by giving directions similar in concept to the preceding example. Therefore, it's not necessary to encode the addresses into the RAM explicitly.

Susan wanted a better picture of this somewhat abstract idea.

> **Susan**: Where are the bytes on the RAM, and what do they look like?
>
> **Steve**: Each byte corresponds to a microscopic region of the RAM chip. As to what they look like, have you ever seen a printed circuit board such as the ones inside your computer? Imagine the lines on that circuit

board reduced thousands of times in size to microscopic dimensions, and you'll have an idea of what a RAM chip looks like inside.

Since it has no moving parts, storing and retrieving data in RAM is much faster than waiting for the mechanical motion of a disk platter turning.[10] As we've just seen, disk access times are measured in milliseconds, or thousandths of a second. RAM access times, however, are measured in *nanoseconds* (abbreviated *ns*); *nano* means one billionth. In early 1997, a typical speed for RAM was 70 ns, which means that it is possible to read a given data item from RAM about 200,000 times as quickly as from a disk with an access time of 14 milliseconds. In that case, why not use disks only for permanent storage, and read everything into RAM in the morning when we turn on the machine?

The reason is cost. In early 1997, the cost of 16 Megabytes of RAM was approximately $80. For that same amount of money, you could have bought over 1100 Megabytes of disk space![11]! Therefore, we must reserve RAM for tasks where speed is all-important, such as running your word processing program and holding a letter while you're working on it. Also, since RAM is an electronic storage medium (rather than a magnetic one), it does not maintain its contents when the power is turned off. This means that if you had a power failure while working with data only in RAM, you would lose everything you had been doing.[12] This is not merely a theoretical problem, by the way; if you don't remember to save what you're doing in your word processor once in a while, you might lose a whole day's work from a power outage of a few seconds.[13]

Problem
Algorithms
Java
Interpreter
Hardware

---

10. There's also another kind of electronic storage, called **ROM**, for Read-Only Memory; as its name indicates, you can read from it, but you can't write to it. This is used for storing permanent information, such as the program that allows your computer to read a small program from your *boot disk*; that program, in turn, reads in the rest of the data and programs needed to start up the computer. This process, as you probably know, is called *booting* the computer. In case you're wondering where that term came from, it's an abbreviation for *bootstrapping*, which is intended to suggest the notion of pulling yourself up by your bootstraps.

You may have noticed that the terms RAM and ROM aren't symmetrical; why isn't RAM called RWM, Read-Write Memory? Because that's too hard to pronounce.

11. To be sure, an 1100 Megabyte disk cost more than $80 in April 1997, but 1100 Megabytes of space on the 6510 Megabyte drive I mentioned earlier would represent a little less than $80 of its total price of $449.

12. The same disaster would happen if your system were to crash, which is not that unlikely if you're using certain popular PC graphically oriented operating environments whose names start with "W".

13. Most modern word processors can automatically save your work once in a while, for this very reason. I heartily recommend using this facility; it's saved my bacon more than once.

Before we get to how a program actually works, we need to develop a better picture of how RAM is used. As I've mentioned before, you can think of RAM as consisting of a large number of bytes, each of which has a unique identifier called an *address*. This address can be used to specify which byte we mean, so the program might specify that it wants to read the value in byte 148257, or change the value in byte 66666.

Susan wanted to make sure she had the correct understanding of this topic.

> **Susan**: Are the values changed in RAM depending on what program is loaded in it?

> **Steve**: Yes, and they also change while the program is executing. RAM is used to store both the program itself and the values it manipulates.

This is all very well, but it doesn't answer the question of how we actually use the data in RAM. The answer is by means of **variables**, which represent specific items of data that we wish to keep track of in our programs, such as weights and numbers of items.

You can put something in a variable, and it will stay there until you store something else there; you can also look at it to find out what's in it. As you might expect, several types of variables are used to hold different kinds of data; the first ones we will look at are variables representing whole numbers (the so-called **integer variables**), which are a subset of the category called **numeric variables**. As this suggests, there are also variables that represent numbers that can have fractional parts. We'll look at these so-called floating-point variables briefly in a later chapter.

Problem
Algorithms
Java
Interpreter
Hardware

Different types of variables require different amounts of RAM to store them, depending on the amount of data they contain; a very common type of numeric variable, known as a short, requires 16 bits (that is, 2 bytes) of RAM to hold any of 65536 different values, from −32768 to 32767, including 0. These odd-looking numbers are the result of using the binary system. To make this number system more intelligible, I have written the following little fable.

Odometer Trouble

Once upon a time, the Acme company had a factory that made golf carts. One day, Bob, the president of Acme, decided to add an odometer to the carts, so that the purchaser of the cart could estimate when to recharge the battery. To save money, Bob decided to buy the little numbered wheels for the odometers and have his employees put the odometers together. The minimum order was a thousand odometer wheels, which was more than he needed for his initial run of 50 odometers. When he got the wheels, however, he noticed that they were defective: Instead of the numbers 0–9, each wheel had only two numbers, 0 and 1. Of course, he was quite irritated by this error, and attempted to contact the company from which he had purchased the wheels, but it had closed down for a month for summer vacation. What was he to do until it reopened?

While he was fretting about this problem, the employee who had been assigned to the task of putting the odometers together from the wheels came up with a possible solution. This employee, Jim, came into Bob's office and said, "Bob, I have an idea. Since we have lots of orders for these odometer-equipped carts, maybe we can make an odometer with these funny wheels and tell the customers how to read the numbers on the odometer."

Bob was taken aback by this idea. "What do you mean, Jim? How can anyone read those screwy odometers?"

Problem
Algorithms
Java
Interpreter
Hardware

Jim had given this some thought. "Let's take a look at what one of these odometers, say with five wheels, can display. Obviously, it would start out reading 00000, just like a normal odometer. Then when one mile has elapsed, the right-most wheel turns to 1, so the whole display is 00001; again, this is no different from a normal odometer."

"Now we come to the tricky part. The right-most wheel goes back to 0, not having any more numbers to display, and pushes the 'tens' wheel to 1; the whole number now reads 00010. Obviously, one more mile makes it 00011, which gives us the situation shown in the following diagram:

```
Normal odometer     Funny odometer

     00000               00000
     00001               00001
     00002               00010
     00003               00011
```

Figure 2.1: The first few numbers

Jim continued, "What's next? This time, the right-most wheel turns over again to 0, triggering the second wheel to its next position. At this point, however, the second wheel is already at its highest value, 1; therefore, it also turns over to 0 and increments the third wheel. It's not hard to follow this for a few more miles, as illustrated in Figure 2.2.

```
Normal odometer      Funny odometer

    00004                00100
    00005                00101
    00006                00110
    00007                00111
```

Figure 2.2: The next few numbers

Bob said, "I get it. It's almost as though we were counting normally, except that you skip all the numbers that have anything but 0s or 1s in them."

"That's right, Bob. So I suppose we could make up a list of the 'real' numbers and give it to the customers to use until we can replace these odometers with normal ones. Perhaps they'll be willing to work with us on this problem."

"Okay, Jim, if you think they'll buy it. Let's get a few of the customers we know the best and ask them if they'll try it; we won't charge them for the odometers until we have the real ones, but maybe they'll stick with us until then. Perhaps any odometer would be better than no odometer at all."

Jim went to work, making some odometers out of the defective wheels; however, he soon figured out that he had to use more than five wheels, because that allowed only numbers from 0 to 31. How did he know this?

Each wheel has two numbers, 0 and 1. So with one wheel, we have a total of two combinations. Two wheels can have either a 0 or a 1 for the first number, and the same for the second number, for a total of four combinations. With three wheels, the same analysis holds: 2 numbers for the first wheel * 2 for the second wheel * 2 for the third wheel = 8 possibilities in all; actually, they are the same 8 possibilities we saw in Figures 2.1 and 2.2.

A pattern is beginning to develop: For each added wheel, we get twice as many possible combinations. To see how this continues, take a look at Figure 2.3, which shows the count of combinations versus the number of wheels for all wheel counts up to 16 (i.e., 16-bit quantities).

Problem
Algorithms
Java
Interpreter
Hardware

```
Number of wheels      Number of combinations14

        1                          2
        2                          4
        3                          8
        4                         16
        5                         32
        6                         64
        7                        128
        8                        256
        9                        512
       10                       1024
       11                       2048
       12                       4096
       13                       8192
       14                      16384
       15                      32768
       16                      65536
```

Figure 2.3: How many combinations?

Jim decided that 14 wheels would do the job, since the life span of the golf cart probably wouldn't exceed 16,383 miles, and so he made up the odometers. The selected customers turned out to be agreeable and soon found that having even a weird odometer was better than none, especially since they didn't have to pay for it. However, one customer did have a complaint: The numbers on the wheels didn't seem to make sense when translated with the chart supplied by Acme. The customer estimated that he had driven the cart about 9 miles, but the odometer displayed the following number:

11111111110111

which, according to his translation chart, was 16,375 miles. What could have gone wrong?

Jim decided to have the cart brought in for a checkup, and what he discovered was that the odometer cable had been hooked up backwards. That is, instead of turning the wheels forward, they were going backwards. That was part of the solution, but why was the value 16375?

Just like a car odometer, in which 99999 (or 999999, if you have a six-wheel odometer) is followed by 0, going backwards from 0 reverses that progression. Similarly, the number 11111111111111 on

Problem
Algorithms
Java
Interpreter
Hardware

---

14. If you think that last number looks familiar, you're right: It's the number of different values that I said could be stored in a type of numeric variable called a short. This is no coincidence; read on for the detailed explanation.

the funny odometers would be followed by 00000000000000, since the "carry" off the left-most digit is lost. Therefore, if you start out at 0 and go backward one mile, you'll get

11111111111111

The next mile will turn the last digit back to 0, producing

11111111111110

What happens next? The last wheel turns back to 1, and triggers the second wheel to switch as well:

11111111111101

The next few "backward" numbers look like this:

11111111111100
11111111111011
11111111111010
11111111111001
11111111111000
11111111110111

Problem
Algorithms
Java
Interpreter
Hardware

and so on. If you look at the right-hand end of these numbers, you'll see that the progression is just the opposite of the "forward" numbers.

As for the customer's actual mileage, the last one of these is the number the customer saw on his backward odometer. Apparently, he was right about the distance driven, since this is the ninth "backward" number. So Jim fixed the backward odometer cable and reset the value to the correct number, 00000000001001, or nine miles.

Eventually, Acme got the right odometer wheels with 0–9 on them, replaced the peculiar ones, and everyone lived happily ever after.

THE END

Back to the Future

Of course, the wheels that made up the funny odometers contain only two digits, 0 and 1, so the odometers use the binary system for counting. Now it should be obvious why we will see numbers like

65536 and 32768 in our discussions of the number of possible different values that a variable can hold: Variables are stored in RAM as collections of bytes, each of which contains 8 bits. As the list of combinations indicates, 8 bits (1 byte) provide 256 different combinations, while 16 bits (2 bytes) can represent 65,536 different possible values.

But what about the "backward" numbers with a lot of 1s on the left? As the fable suggests, they correspond to "negative" numbers. That is, if moving two miles forward from 0 registers as 00000000000010, and moving two miles backward from 0 registers as 11111111111110, then the latter number is in some sense equivalent to –2 miles. In Java, all integer variables can store either positive or negative values, and this "backward" representation is the way that negative integers are represented in a Java variable.

Over-Hexed

Problem
Algorithms
Java
Interpreter
Hardware

You may have noticed that it's tedious and error prone to represent numbers in binary; a long string of 0s and 1s is hard to remember or to copy. For this reason, the pure binary system is hardly ever used to specify numbers in computing. However, we have already seen that binary is much more "natural" for computers than the more familiar decimal system. Is there a number system that we humans can use a little more easily than binary, while retaining the advantages of binary for describing internal events in the computer?

As it happens, there is. It's called **hexadecimal**, which means "base 16". As a rule, the term *hexadecimal* is abbreviated to *hex*. Since there are 16 possible combinations of 4 bits (2*2*2*2), hexadecimal notation allows 4 bits of a binary number to be represented by one hex digit. Unfortunately, however, there are only 10 "normal" digits, 0–9.[15] To represent a number in any base, you need as many different digit values as the base, so that any number less than the base can be represented by one digit. For example, in base 2, you need only two digits, 0 and 1. In base 8 (*octal*), you need eight digits, 0–7.[16] So far, so good. But what about base 16? To use this base, we need 16 digits. Since only 10 numeric digits are available, hex notation needs a source for the other six digits.

---

15. Paging Dr. Seuss. . .

16. In the early days of computing, base 8 was sometimes used instead of base 16, especially on machines that used 12-bit and 36-bit registers; however, it has fallen into disuse because almost all modern machines have 32-bit registers.

Because letters of the alphabet are available and familiar, the first six letters, a–f, were adopted for this service.[17]

Although the notion of a base 16 number system doesn't seem strange to people who are familiar with it, it can really throw someone who learned normal decimal arithmetic solely by rote, without understanding the concepts on which it is based. This topic of hexadecimal notation occupied Susan and me for quite awhile; here's some of the discussion we had about it:

Susan: I don't get this at all! What is the deal with the letters in the hex system? I guess it would be okay if 16 wasn't represented by 10!

Steve: Well, there are only 10 "normal" digits, 0–9. To represent a number in any base, you need as many "digits" as the base, so that any number less than the base can be represented by one "digit". This is no problem with a base less than ten, such as octal, but what about base 16? To use this base we need 16 digits, 0–9 and a–f. One way to remember this is to imagine that the "hex" in "hexadecimal" stands for the six letters a–f and the "decimal" stands for the 10 digits 0–9.

Susan: OK, so a hex digit represents 16 bits? So then is hex equal to 2 bytes? According to the preceding, a hex digit is 4 bits.

Steve: Yes, a hex digit represents 4 bits. Let's try a new approach. First, let me define a new term, a *hexit*. That's short for "hex digit", just like "bit" is short for "binary digit". Now let's look at the answers to the following questions.

Problem
Algorithms
Java
Interpreter
Hardware

1. How many numbers can be represented with no more than one decimal digit?
2. How many numbers can be represented with no more than two decimal digits?
3. How many numbers can be represented with no more than three decimal digits?
4. How many numbers can be represented with no more than four decimal digits?
5. How many numbers can be represented with no more than one bit?
6. How many numbers can be represented with no more than two bits?
7. How many numbers can be represented with no more than three bits?

---

17. Either upper or lower case letters are acceptable to most programs (and programmers). I'll use lower case because such letters are easier to distinguish than upper case ones; besides, I find them less irritating to look at.

8. How many numbers can be represented with no more than four bits?
9. How many numbers can be represented with no more than one hexit?
10. How many numbers can be represented with no more than two hexits?
11. How many numbers can be represented with no more than three hexits?
12. How many numbers can be represented with no more than four hexits?

The answers are:

1. 10
2. 100
3. 1000
4. 10000
5. 2
6. 4
7. 8
8. 16
9. 16
10. 256
11. 4096
12. 65536

Problem
Algorithms
Java
Interpreter
Hardware

What do all these answers have in common? Let's look at the answers a little differently, in powers of 10, 2, and 16, respectively:

1. $10 = 10^1$
2. $100 = 10^2$
3. $1000 = 10^3$
4. $10000 = 10^4$
5. $2 = 2^1$
6. $4 = 2^2$
7. $8 = 2^3$
8. $16 = 2^4$
9. $16 = 16^1$
10. $256 = 16^2$
11. $4096 = 16^3$
12. $65536 = 16^4$

That is, a number that has one digit can represent "base" different values, where "base" is two, ten, or sixteen (in our examples). Every time we increase the size of the number by one more digit, we can represent "base" times as many possible different values, or in other words, we multiply the range of values that the number can represent by the base. Thus, a two-digit number can represent any of "base*base" values, a three-digit number can represent any of "base*base*base" values, and so on. That's the way positional number systems such as decimal, binary, and hex work. If you need a bigger number, you just add more digits.

Okay, so what does this have to do with hex? If you look at the above table, you'll see that 2^4 (16) is equal to 16^1. That means that 4 bits are exactly equivalent to one hexit in their ability to represent different numbers: Exactly 16 possible numbers can be represented by four bits, and exactly 16 possible numbers can be represented by one hexit.

This means that you can write one hexit wherever you would otherwise have to use four bits, as illustrated in Figure 2.4.

```
4-bit value   1-hexit value

0000              0
0001              1
0010              2
0011              3
0100              4
0101              5
0110              6
0111              7
1000              8
1001              9
1010              a
1011              b
1100              c
1101              d
1110              e
1111              f
```

Figure 2.4: Binary to hex conversion table

```
Problem
Algorithms
Java
Interpreter
Hardware
```

So an 8-bit number, such as:
0101 1011
can be translated directly into a hex value, like this:
5   b

For this reason, binary is almost never used. Instead, we use hex as a shortcut to eliminate the necessity of reading, writing, and remembering long strings of bits.

Susan: A hex digit or hexit is like a four-wheel odometer in binary. Since each wheel is capable of only one of two values, being either (1) or (0), then the total number of possible values is 16. Thus your 2*2*2*2 = 16. I think I've got this down.

Steve: You certainly do!

Susan: If it has 4 bits and you have 2 of them, then won't there be eight "wheels" and so forth? So 2 hex would hold XXXXXXXX places and 3 hex would hold XXXXXXXXXXXX places.

Steve: Correct. A one-hexit number is analogous to a one-digit decimal number. A one-hexit number contains 4 bits and therefore can represent any of 16 values. A two-hexit number contains 8 bits and therefore can represent any of 256 values.

Now that we've seen how each hex digit corresponds exactly to a group of four binary digits, here's an exercise you can use to improve your understanding of this topic: Invent a random string of four binary digits and see where it is in Figure 2.4. I guarantee it'll be there somewhere! Then look at the "hex" column and see what "digit" it corresponds to. There's nothing really mysterious about hex; since we have run out of digits after 9, we have to use letters to represent the numbers 'ten', 'eleven', 'twelve', 'thirteen', 'fourteen', and 'fifteen'.

Here's a table showing the correspondence between some decimal, hex, and binary numbers, with the values of each digit position in each number base indicated, and the calculation of the total of all of the bit values in the binary representation, as shown in Figure 2.5.

Problem
Algorithms
Java
Interpreter
Hardware

Decimal Place Values 10 1	Hexadecimal Place Values 16 1	Binary Place Values 16 8 4 2 1		Sum of Binary Digit Values
0	0 0	0 0 0 0 0	=	0 + 0 + 0 + 0 + 0
1	0 1	0 0 0 0 1	–	0 + 0 + 0 + 0 + 1
2	0 2	0 0 0 1 0	=	0 + 0 + 0 + 2 + 0
3	0 3	0 0 0 1 1	=	0 + 0 + 0 + 2 + 1
4	0 4	0 0 1 0 0	=	0 + 0 + 4 + 0 + 0
5	0 5	0 0 1 0 1	=	0 + 0 + 4 + 0 + 1
6	0 6	0 0 1 1 0	=	0 + 0 + 4 + 2 + 0
7	0 7	0 0 1 1 1	=	0 + 0 + 4 + 2 + 1
8	0 8	0 1 0 0 0	=	0 + 8 + 0 + 0 + 0
9	0 9	0 1 0 0 1	=	0 + 8 + 0 + 0 + 1
1 0	0 a	0 1 0 1 0	=	0 + 8 + 0 + 2 + 0
1 1	0 b	0 1 0 1 1	=	0 + 8 + 0 + 2 + 1
1 2	0 c	0 1 1 0 0	=	0 + 8 + 4 + 0 + 0
1 3	0 d	0 1 1 0 1	=	0 + 8 + 4 + 0 + 1
1 4	0 e	0 1 1 1 0	=	0 + 8 + 4 + 2 + 0
1 5	0 f	0 1 1 1 1	=	0 + 8 + 4 + 2 + 1
1 6	1 0	1 0 0 0 0	=	16 + 0 + 0 + 0 + 0
1 7	1 1	1 0 0 0 1	=	16 + 0 + 0 + 0 + 1
1 8	1 2	1 0 0 1 0	=	16 + 0 + 0 + 2 + 0
1 9	1 3	1 0 0 1 1	=	16 + 0 + 0 + 2 + 1

Figure 2.5: Different representations of the same numbers

Another reason to use hex rather than decimal is that byte values expressed as hex digits can be combined directly to produce larger values, which is not true with decimal digits. In case this isn't obvious, let's go over it in more detail. Since each hex digit (0–f) represents exactly 4 bits, two of them (00–ff) represent 8 bits, or one byte. Similarly, 4 hex digits (0000–ffff) represent 16 bits, or a short value; the first two digits represent the first byte of the 2-byte value, and the last two digits, the second byte. This can be extended to any number of bytes. On the other hand, representing 4 bits requires two decimal digits, as the values range from 00–15, whereas it takes three digits (000–255) to represent one byte. A 2-byte value requires five decimal digits, since the value can be from 00000 to 65535. As you can see, there's no simple relationship between the decimal digits representing each byte and the decimal representation of a 2-byte value.

Susan had some more thoughts on the hexadecimal number system. Let's listen in.

> **Susan**: I think you need to spend a little more time reviewing the hex system, like an entire chapter.<G> Well, I am getting the impression that we are going to be working with hex, so I am trying to concentrate my understanding on that instead of binary. I think this all moves a little too fast for me. I don't know what your other reviewers are saying but I just feel like I get a definition of a abstract concept, and the next thing I know I am supposed to be doing something with it, like make it work. Ha! I personally need to digest new concepts, I really need to think them over a bit, to take them in and absorb them. I just can't start working with it right away.

```
Problem
Algorithms
Java
Interpreter
Hardware
```

As usual, I've complied with her request; the results are immediately ahead.

Exercises

Here are some exercises that you can use to check your understanding of the binary and hexadecimal number systems.[18] I've limited the examples to addition and subtraction, as that is all that you're ever likely to have to do in these number systems. These operations are exactly like their equivalents in the decimal system, except that as we have already seen, the hexadecimal system has six

---

18. Please note that the ability to do binary or hexadecimal arithmetic, although valuable in a number of applications, is *not* essential to further reading in this book.

extra digits after 9: a, b, c, d, e, and f. We have to take these into account in our calculations: for example, adding 9 and 5, rather than producing 14, produces e.

1. Using the hexadecimal system, answer these problems:
    a.   1a + 2e = ?
    b.   12 + 18 = ?
    c.   50 – 12 = ?
2. In the binary system, answer these problems:
    a.   101 + 110 = ?
    b.   111 + 1001 = ?
    c.   1010 – 11 = ?

    Let's suppose that x is a short, currently holding the value 32767, or 7fff in hex. What is the result of adding 1 to x, in both decimal and hex?

Answers to exercises can be found at the end of the chapter.

Problem
Algorithms
Java
Interpreter
Hardware

The CPU

There's one point we haven't covered yet: how these variables are actually referred to and modified. The ultimate answer to that question is that every action in the computer is performed by another piece of hardware: the **CPU** (Central Processing Unit). Like RAM, it is physically composed of millions of microscopic transistors on a chip; however, the organization of these transistors in a CPU is much more complex than on a RAM chip, as the latter's functions are limited to the storage and retrieval of data. The CPU, on the other hand, is capable of performing dozens or hundreds of different fundamental operations called *machine instructions*, or just *instructions* for short. While each instruction performs a very simple function, the tremendous power of the computer lies in the fact that the CPU can perform (or *execute*) tens or hundreds of millions of these instructions per second.[19]

---

19. Each type of CPU has a different set of instructions, so that programs intended for one CPU cannot in general be run on a different CPU. Some CPUs, such as the very popular 80x86 ones from Intel, fall into a "family" of CPUs in which each new CPU can execute all of the instructions of the previous family members. This allows upgrading to a new CPU without having to throw out all of your old programs, but correspondingly limits the ways in which the new CPU can be improved without affecting this "family compatibility".

These instructions fall into a number of categories: instructions that perform arithmetic operations such as adding, subtracting, multiplying, and dividing; instructions that move information from one place to another in RAM; instructions that compare two quantities to help make a determination as to which instructions need to be executed next and instructions that implement that decision; and other, more specialized types of instructions.

With most languages, the programs you write are translated into machine instructions for a specific CPU. However, one of the design goals of Java was to allow the same translated program to work on any machine. To facilitate this task, the process of making your programs runnable works differently in Java: Instead of your programs being translated into a form designed to be executed on a specific CPU, they are translated into a form that can be executed on any CPU with the intervention of a special program called an **interpreter**. We'll go into how this works in great detail in the next chapter; for now, just keep in mind that Java programs aren't tied to a specific type of computer.

You've just been subjected to a barrage of information on how a computer works. Let's go over it again briefly before continuing.

Review

Problem
Algorithms
Java
Interpreter
Hardware

Two main components of the computer hardware are of most significance to Java programmers: disk and RAM. Both of these store programs and data for use by Java programs.

Computers represent pieces of information (or data) as binary digits, universally referred to as *bits*. Each bit can have the value 0 or 1. The binary system is used instead of the more familiar decimal system because it is much easier to make devices that can store and retrieve 1 of 2 values than 1 of 10. Bits are grouped into sets of eight, called *bytes*.

The disk uses magnetic recording heads to store and retrieve groups of a few hundred bytes on rapidly spinning platters in a few milliseconds. The contents of the disk are not lost when the power is turned off, so it is suitable for more or less permanent storage of programs and data.

RAM, which is an acronym for Random Access Memory, is used to hold programs and data while they're in use. It is made of millions of microscopic transistors on a piece of silicon called a *chip*. Each bit is stored using a few of these transistors. RAM does not retain its contents when power is removed, so it is not good for permanent storage. However, any byte in a RAM chip can be accessed in about 70 nanoseconds (billionths of a second), which is hundreds of thousands of times as fast as accessing a disk. Each byte in a RAM chip can be independently stored and retrieved without affecting other bytes, by providing the unique memory address belonging to the byte you want to access.

The binary system is the most fundamental number system in the computer, but it is not very convenient for people, especially when dealing with large numbers. For this purpose, the hexadecimal number system is considerably more convenient, as the representations of large numbers are much shorter and easier to remember.

Unlike most other computer languages, Java was designed to allow the same program to be run on various kinds of computers, with the intervention of a special kind of program called an interpreter.

Conclusion

Problem
Algorithms
Java
Interpreter
Hardware

In this chapter, we've covered a lot of material on how a computer actually works. As you'll see, this background is essential if you're going to understand what really happens inside a program. In the next chapter, we'll get to the "real thing": how to write a program to make all this hardware do something useful.

Answers to Exercises

1. Hexadecimal arithmetic
    a.   48
        You probably won't be surprised to hear that Susan didn't care much for this answer originally. Here's the discussion on that topic:

> **Susan**: Problem 1a. My answer is 38. Why? My own personal way of thinking: If a = 10, right? and if e = 14 and if 1 * 10 = 10 and if 2 * 14 = 28, then if you add 10 + 28 you get 38. So please inform me how you arrived at 48? I didn't bother with the rest of the problems. If I couldn't get the first one right, then what was the point?
> **Steve**: Here's how you do this problem, with the letter "h" indicating a hex number:
>   10h(1 * 16) + ah(10 * 1)

20h(2 * 16) + eh(14 * 1)

30h(3 * 16) + 18h(24 * 1 = 1 * 16 + 8 * 1)

Carry the 1 from the low digit to the high digit of the answer, to produce:

40h(4 * 16) + 8h(8 * 1), or 48 hex, which is the answer.

b.   2a

c.   3e

2.   Binary arithmetic

a.   1011

b.   10000

c.   111

3.   −32768, or 8000 in hex

In case you got this wrong, you should remember that the range of short values is −32768 to +32767, with 0000h to 7fffh being considered positive, and 8000h to ffffh considered negative.

Problem
Algorithms
Java
Interpreter
Hardware

Chapter 3

Basics of Programming

Creative Programming?

After that necessary detour into the workings of the hardware, we can now resume our regularly scheduled explanation of the creative possibilities of computers. It may sound odd to describe computers as providing grand scope for creative activities: Aren't they monotonous, dull, unintelligent, and extremely limited? Yes, they are. However, they have two redeeming virtues that make them ideal as a canvas of invention: They are extraordinarily fast and amazingly reliable. These characteristics allow the creator of a program to weave intricate chains of thought and have a fantastic number of steps carried out without fail. We'll begin to explore how this is possible after we go over some definitions and objectives for this chapter.

Definitions

A **keyword** is a word defined in the Java language, such as if and while.

An **identifier** is a user-defined name; variable names are identifiers. Identifiers must not conflict with keywords such as if and while; for example, you cannot create a variable with the name while.

An **operator** is one of the facilities of Java that is built into the language rather than being added on later, and therefore can have a name that does not conform to the rules for *identifiers*. Examples are +, -, and =.

A **statement** is a complete operation understood by the Java compiler. Each statement is ended with a semicolon (;).

A **token** is a part of a program that the *compiler* treats as a separate unit. It's analogous to a word in English; a *statement* is more like a sentence. For example, String is a token, as is (. On the other hand, x = 5; is a statement.

An **expression** is one of the units of which a *statement* is made. It is made up of one or more *tokens*. In the statement i = k + 3;, "k + 3" is an expression composed of the three tokens k, +, and 3.

An **if statement** is a *statement* that causes its *controlled statement* to be executed if the condition specified in the if statement is true.

A **while statement** is a *statement* that causes its *controlled statement* to be executed while a specified condition is true.

A **block** is a group of *statement*s that are considered one logical statement. A block is delimited by the "curly braces", { and }; the first of these symbols starts a block, and the second one ends the block. A block can be used anywhere that a statement can be used, and is treated in exactly the same way as if it were one statement.

```
Problem
Algorithms
Java
Interpreter
Hardware
```

Objectives for This Chapter

By the end of this chapter, you should:

1. Understand what a program is and have some idea how one works.
2. Understand how to get information into and out of a Java program.
3. Understand how to use if and while to control the execution of a Java program.[1]
4. Understand how to tell the compiler to treat a section of a Java program as one unit.
5. Be able to understand a simple program I've written in Java.
6. Be able to write a simple program in Java.

---

1. Please note that capitalization counts in Java, so IF and WHILE are not the same as if and while. You have to use the latter versions.

Speed Demon

The most impressive attribute of modern computers is, of course, their speed; as we have already seen, this is measured in MIPS (millions of instructions per second).

Of course, raw speed is not very valuable if we can't rely on the results we get. ENIAC, one of the first electronic computers, had a failure every few hours on the average; since the problems it was used to solve took about that much time to run, the likelihood that the results were correct wasn't very high. Particularly critical calculations were often run several times, and if the users got the same answer twice, they figured it was probably correct. By contrast, modern computers are almost incomprehensibly reliable. With almost any other machine, a failure rate of one in every million operations would be considered phenomenally low, but a computer with such a failure rate would make dozens or hundreds of errors per second.[2]

Blaming It on the Computer

Problem
Algorithms
Java
Interpreter
Hardware

On the other hand, if computers are so reliable, why are they blamed for so much that goes wrong with modern life? Who among us has not been the victim of an erroneous credit report, or a bill sent to the wrong address, or been put on hold for a long time because "the computer is down"? The answer is fairly simple: It's almost certainly not the computer that is really at fault. It may be the software, other equipment such as telephone lines, tape or disk drives, or any of the myriad "peripheral devices" that the computer uses to store and retrieve information and interact with the outside world. Usually, it's the software; when customer service representatives tell you that they can't do something obviously reasonable, you can bet that the problem is the software. For example, I once belonged to a 401K plan whose administrators provided statements only every three months, about three months after the end of the quarter; in other words, in July I found out how much my account had been worth at the end of March. To estimate how much I had in the meantime, I had to look up the share values in the newspaper and multiply by the

---

2. However, we haven't yet eliminated the possibility of hardware errors, as the floating-point flaw in early versions of the Pentium™ processor illustrates. In rare cases, the result of the divide instruction in those processors was accurate to only about 5 decimal places rather than the normal 16 to 17 decimal places.

number of shares. Of course, the mutual fund that issued the shares could tell its shareholders their account balances at any time of the day or night; however, the company that administered the 401K plan didn't bother to provide such a service, as it would have required doing some work.[3] Needless to say, whenever I hear that "the computer can't do that" as an excuse for such poor service, I reply "Then you need some different programmers."

That Does Not Compute

All of this emphasis on computation, however, should not blind us to the fact that computers are not solely arithmetic engines. The most common application for which PCs are used is word processing, which is hardly a hotbed of arithmetical calculation. While we have so far considered only numeric data, this is a good illustration of the fact that computers also deal with another kind of information, which is commonly referred to by the imaginative term **non-numeric variables**. Numeric variables are those suited for use in calculations, such as in totalling a set of weights. On the other hand, non-numeric data are items that are not used in calculations like adding, multiplying, or subtracting: Examples are names, addresses, telephone numbers, Social Security numbers, bank account numbers, or drivers license numbers. Note that just because something is called a *number*, or even is composed entirely of the digits 0–9, does not make it numeric data by our standards. The question is how the item is used. No one adds, multiplies, or subtracts drivers license numbers, for example; they serve solely as identifiers and could just as easily have letters in them, as indeed some do.

Problem
Algorithms
Java
Interpreter
Hardware

For the present, though, let's stick with numeric variables. We've already discussed the short, but in the rest of this book we'll be using its big brother, the int, which is 4 bytes long and therefore can represent numbers from -2147483648 (-2^31) to 2147483647 (2^31-1). What can we do with variables of this type?

To do anything with them, we have to write a Java program, which consists primarily of a list of operations to be performed by the computer, along with directions that influence how these operations are to be translated into a form called "byte-code instructions", or just "byte codes" for short.

This raises a couple of interesting points:

---

3. This was apparently against the plan administrator's principles.

1. What are byte codes, anyway?
2. Why does our Java program have to be translated into byte codes?

Before we can answer these questions, we have to consider a more general notion, that of a "virtual computer". We'll discuss this immediately after adding some more terms to our vocabulary.

The Man behind the Curtain

Unlike many words in the vocabulary of computing, *virtual* has more or less retained its standard English definition: "That is so in essence or effect, although not formally or actually; admitting of being called by the name so far as the effect or result is concerned."[4] In other words, a virtual computer would be something that acts just like a computer, but really isn't one. Who would want such a thing?

Apparently everyone, since *virtual computer* is just another name for what we have been calling *software*. This may seem a rash statement, but it really isn't. One of the most important mathematical discoveries (inventions?) of the twentieth century was Alan Turing's demonstration that it was possible to create a fairly simple computing device (called a *Turing machine* for some reason) that could imitate *any* other computing device. This machine works in the following way: You provide it with a description of the other computer you want it to imitate, and it follows those directions. Suppose we want a computer that calculates only trigonometric functions. Then we could theoretically write a set of instructions as to how such a computer would behave, feed it into a Turing machine, and have the Turing machine imitate the behavior of this theoretical "trigonometric computer".

This is undoubtedly interesting, but you may be wondering what it has to do with programming. Well, what we're actually doing when we write a Java program is creating instructions to be used by another program called the **Java interpreter,** describing the actions that would be taken by a hypothetical specialized computer that would solve the problem our program is designed to solve. When we run the program, the Java interpreter simulates these actions. In other words, our program is the definition of a particular virtual computer.

Of course, the Java interpreter can't really simulate *any* possible program, because there are limits in the amount of memory or disk

Problem
Algorithms
Java
Interpreter
Hardware

---

4. *Oxford English Dictionary*, first current definition (4).

space it has available, as well as limits on the speed of its execution. However, for problems that can be solved within those limits, it is a general-purpose computing facility that can be tailored to a particular problem by programming.

In the particular case of Java, there are actually two levels of virtuality; whereas your Java program is executed by the Java interpreter, the Java interpreter itself is executed by a real, physical computer component. As we've seen in the previous chapter, that component, the **CPU** (for **C**entral **P**rocessing **U**nit), is the active ingredient inside a computer; the RAM and disk are merely the tools that it uses to store and retrieve data. In other words, the Java interpreter is a "virtual computer" that is simulated by the CPU, whereas a Java byte-code program is a "virtual computer" that can be simulated by the Java interpreter.

So now we can answer the question of what a byte-code instruction is: It's the primitive unit of computation in the Java interpreter, just as a machine instruction is the primitive unit of computation in a physical CPU.

```
Problem
Algorithms
Java
Interpreter
Hardware
```

Lost in Translation

Now we're ready to answer those questions that we put on hold for our little excursion into virtual reality. First, let's discuss byte codes in some more detail.

Like a physical CPU, the Java interpreter understands a limited set of instructions, each of which does a very simple task such as adding two numbers together or comparing two numbers to see which is greater. These are much simpler than the source-code statements that we write in our Java programs. Therefore, our source-code programs have to go through an intermediate step, called **compilation**, which converts them from source code to byte codes so that they can be executed by the Java interpreter.

It may not be obvious why we need both an interpreter and a compiler. It wasn't to Susan.

> **Susan**: Can you have just an interpreter and no compiler? Do all interpreted languages then need a compiler?

> **Steve**: Yes, you can have an interpreter without a compiler, but that's not very common because it is so inefficient; you don't want to do all the work to find out what each statement means every time you look at

it, so virtually all interpreted languages translate the source code into a form that is easier to interpret at run time.

Susan: The interpreter doesn't work until run time?

Steve: Right.

The most basic tasks that the Java compiler performs are:[5]

1. Converting variable names to numbers that will refer to areas of memory when the program is running. This allows us to use names for variables in our Java programs, while keeping the byte-code instructions simpler and easier to execute.
2. Translating arithmetic and other operations (such as +, −, etc.) into the equivalent byte codes, including references to variables assigned in the previous step.

Susan had some questions about what the compiler actually does for us.

Susan: A byte-code instruction is in binary?

Steve: Yes, or hex.

Susan: So it attaches instructions to the variables?

Steve: Not exactly. We'll see shortly how it translates the named variables that we use in writing source code so they can be used when we're running a program.

Problem
Algorithms
Java
Interpreter
Hardware

This is probably a bit too abstract to be easily grasped, so let's look at an example. Figure 3.1 shows some sample statements that do arithmetic calculations.

---

5. The compiler also does a lot of other work for us, which we'll get into later.

```
int i;
int j;
int k;
int m;

i = 5;
j = i * 3;              // j is now 15[6]
k = j - i;              // k is now 10
m = (k + j) / 5;        // m is now 5
i = i + 1;              // i is now 6
```

Figure 3.1: A little numeric calculation

To enter such statements in the first place, follow the instructions in the "readme.txt" file on the CD in the back of the book.[7]

Once we have entered the statements for our program, we use the compiler to translate the programs we write into a form that the Java interpreter can perform; as defined in Chapter 1, the form we create is called *source code*, since it is the source of the program logic, whereas the form of our program that the Java interpreter can execute is called a *byte-code program*.

Problem
Algorithms
Java
Interpreter
Hardware

As I've mentioned previously, there are several types of variables, the int being only one of these types. Therefore, the compiler needs some explanatory material so that it can tell what types of variables you're using; that's what the first four lines of our little sample program fragment are for. Each line tells the compiler that the type of the variable i, j, k, or m is int, which specifies the range of values it can hold.[8]

After this introductory material, we move into the list of operations to be performed. This is called the *executable* portion of the program, as it actually causes the Java interpreter to do something when the program is executed; the operations to be performed, as mentioned previously, are called **statements**. The first one, i = 5;, sets the

---

6. The // marks the beginning of a *comment*, which is a note to you or another programmer; it is ignored by the compiler. For those of you with BASIC experience, this is just like REM (the "remark" keyword in that language); anything after it on a line is ignored.

7. By the way, blank lines are ignored by the compiler; in fact, you can even run all the statements together on one line if you want to. That won't confuse the compiler. but it *will* make it much harder for someone reading your code later to understand what you're trying to do. Programs aren't written just for the compiler but also for other people; therefore, it is important to write them so that they can be understood by those other people. One very good reason for this is that more often than you might think, those "other people" turn out to be *you*, six months later.

8. Other kinds of variables can hold different ranges of values; we'll go over them in some detail in future chapters.

variable i to the value 5. A value such as 5, which doesn't have a name, but represents itself in a literal manner, is called (appropriately enough) a **literal** value.

This is as good a time as any for me to mention something that experienced programmers, especially C programmers, take for granted but has a tendency to confuse novices. This is the choice of the = sign to indicate the operation of setting a variable to a value, which is known technically as **assignment**. As far as I'm concerned, an assignment operation would be more properly indicated by some symbol suggesting movement of data, such as 5 => i;, meaning "store the value 5 into variable i". Unfortunately, it's too late to change the notation for the **assignment statement**, as such a statement is called, so you'll just have to get used to it. The = in a statement such as i = 5; means "set the variable on the left (in this case, i) to the value on the right (in this case, 5)".[9]

Now that I've warned you about that possible confusion, let's continue looking at the operations in the program. The next one, j = i * 3;, specifies that the variable j is to be set to the result of multiplying the current value of i by the literal value 3. The one after that, k = j − i;, tells the Java interpreter to set k to the amount calculated by subtracting i from j; that is, j − i. The most complicated line in our little program fragment, m = (k + j) / 5;, calculates m as the sum of adding k and j and dividing the result by the literal value 5. Finally, the line i = i + 1; sets i to the value of i plus the literal value 1.

Problem
Algorithms
Java
Interpreter
Hardware

This last may be somewhat puzzling; how can i be equal to i + 1? The answer is that an assignment statement is *not* an algebraic equality, no matter how much it may resemble one. It is a command telling the Java interpreter to assign a value to a variable. Therefore, what i = i + 1; actually means is "take the current value of i, add 1 to it, and store the result back into i." In other words, a Java variable is a place to store a value; the variable i can take on any number of values, but only one at a time; any former value is lost when a new one is assigned.

This notion of assignment was the topic of quite a few messages with Susan. Let's go to the first round.

---

9. At the risk of boring experienced programmers, let me reiterate that = *does not mean* "is equal to"; it means "set the variable to the left of the = to the value of the expression to the right of the =." In fact, there is *no* equivalent in Java to the mathematical notion of equality. We have only the assignment operator = and the comparison operator ==, which we will encounter later in this chapter. The latter is used in if statements to determine whether two expressions have the same value. All of the valid comparison operators are listed in Figure 4.5.

Susan: I am confused with the statement i = i + 1;, when you have stated previously that i = 5;. So which one is it? How can there be two values for i?

Steve: There can't; that is, not at one time. However, i, like any other variable, can take on any number of values, one after another. First, we set it to 5; then we set it to 1 more than it was before (i + 1), so it ends up as 6.

Susan: Well, the example made it look as if the two values of i were available to be used by the Java interpreter at the same time. They were both lumped together as executable material.

Steve: After the statement i = 5;, and before the statement i = i + 1;, the value of i is 5. After the statement i = i + 1;, the value of i is 6. The key here is that a variable such as i is just our name for some area of memory that can hold only one value at one time. Does that clear it up?

Susan: So it is not like algebra? Then i is equal to an address of memory and does not really equate with a numerical value? Well, I guess it does when you assign a numerical value to it. Is that it?

Problem
Algorithms
Java
Interpreter
Hardware

Steve: Very close. A variable in Java isn't really like an algebraic variable, which has a value that has to be figured out and doesn't change in a given problem. A programming language variable is just a name for a storage location that can contain a value.

With any luck, that point has been pounded into the ground, so you won't have the same trouble that Susan did. Now let's look at exactly what an assignment statement does. If the value of i before the statement i = i + 1; is 5 (for example), then that statement will cause the Java interpreter to perform the following steps:[10]

1. Take the current value of i (5).
2. Add one to that value (6).
3. Store the result back into i.

After the execution of this statement, i will have the value 6.

---

10. If you have any programming experience whatever, you may think that I'm spending too much effort on this very simple point. I can report from personal experience that it's not necessarily easy for a complete novice to grasp. Furthermore, without a solid understanding of the difference between an algebraic equality and an assignment statement, that novice will be unable to understand how to write a program.

What's Going on Underneath?

In a moment we're going to dive a little deeper into how the Java interpreter accomplishes its task of manipulating data, such as we are doing here with our arithmetic program. First, though, it's time for a little pep talk for those of you who might be wondering exactly why this apparent digression is necessary. It's because if you don't understand what is going on under the surface, you won't be able to get past the "Sunday driver" stage of programming in Java. A good Java programmer needs to know a fair amount about the internal workings of the language, for reasons which will become very apparent later in the book. For the moment, you'll just have to take my word that working through these intricacies is essential; the payoff for a thorough grounding in these fundamental concepts of computing will be worth the struggle.

Underware?

I can almost hear the wailing and tooth gnashing out there. Do I expect you to deal with byte codes by yourself? You'll undoubtedly be happy to learn that this isn't necessary, as the compiler and the interpreter take care of these details. On the other hand, if you don't have some idea of how these programs work, you'll be at a disadvantage when you're trying to figure out how to make Java do what you want. Therefore, we're going to spend some time "playing compiler"; that is, I'll examine each statement and indicate what action the compiler might take as a result. I'll simplify the statements a bit to make the explanation simpler; you should still get the idea (I hope). Figure 3.5 illustrates the set of statements that I'll compile.[11]

```
Problem
Algorithms
Java
Interpreter
Hardware
```

However, before we start to analyze how the compiler does its job, we'll need to go over one of the fundamental methods that the Java interpreter and compiler use to organize their data: the **stack**.

Stacking the Deck

Variables in the program fragment we'll be considering are stored in a data structure called a **stack**; the name is intended to suggest the notion of stacking clean plates on a spring-loaded holder such as you

---

11. As I've mentioned previously, blank lines are ignored by the compiler; you can put them in freely to improve readability.

might see in a cafeteria. The last plate deposited on the stack of plates will be the first one to be removed when a customer needs a fresh plate.

But what does this have to do with programming? I think this will become clearer when we see some examples. First, though, we'll need some new terms to describe the behavior of a stack.

1. **Push** means to add a new item to the stack, causing the previously stored items to move down one location in the stack; that is, the item that was in slot 1 goes to slot 2, the entry in slot 2 goes to slot 3, and so on.
2. **Pop** means to remove an item from the stack and store it in a specified destination, causing the other items in the stack to move up one location toward the top; that is, the item that was in slot 2 moves to slot 1, the one in slot 3 moves to slot 2, and so on.

A stack with one entry might look something like Figure 3.2.

Problem
Algorithms
Java
Interpreter
Hardware

1	1234

Figure 3.2: A stack with one entry

If we add (or **push**) another value on to the stack, say 999, the result would look like Figure 3.3.

1	999
2	1234

Figure 3.3: A stack with two entries

If we were to push one more item, this time with the value 1666, the result would look like Figure 3.4.

1	1666
2	999
3	1234

Figure 3.4: A stack with three entries

Now, if we retrieve (or **pop**) a value, we'll get the one on top; namely, 1666. Then the stack will look like it did in Figure 3.3. The next value to be popped off the stack will be the 999, leaving us with the situation in Figure 3.2 again. If we continue for one more round, we'll get the value 1234, leaving us with an **empty stack**.

As we'll see, the actual way that a stack is implemented is a bit different than is suggested by the "stack of plates" analogy, although the effect is exactly the same. Rather than keeping the top of the stack where it is and moving the data (a slow operation), the data are left where they are and the address stored in a **stack pointer** is changed, which is a much faster operation. In other words, whatever address the stack pointer is pointing to is by definition the "top of the stack".[12]

The idea of a stack led to some discussions with Susan. Here's the first installment:

Problem
Algorithms
Java
Interpreter
Hardware

Susan: Where is the stack?

Steve: The actual memory locations used to hold the items in the stack are just like any other locations in RAM; what makes them part of the stack is how they are used. As always, one memory location can hold only one item at a given time, so the locations used to hold entries on the stack cannot be simultaneously used for something else, like byte codes.

Susan: Where you say "what makes them part of the stack is how they are used." How is that?

Steve: RAM is RAM. It can be used to store programs, data on the stack, or other types of data that we'll get to later. What distinguishes these is how the memory is used, not what it's physically made of.

---

12. Please note that the address that the stack occupies in the following diagrams is arbitrary. The actual address where the stack is located in your program is determined by the interpreter in combination with the operating system.

Susan: Yes, but what is different about the use of the RAM used in the stack?

Steve: It's used to hold the data in the stack, rather than byte codes or other kinds of data.

Susan: Then how does the stack pointer "talk" to the stack to change what it is pointing to?

Steve: It doesn't have to. Whatever the stack pointer is pointing to is by definition the top of the stack; therefore, changing the contents of the stack pointer changes the top of the stack.

Susan: So what makes the stack pointer change?

Steve: The interpreter, as it is executing the program. Each byte code instruction has a defined effect on the stack pointer (pushing one or more values, popping one or more values, doing both, or doing neither.

Susan: What do you mean as the interpreter is executing the program? Do you mean that it doesn't work until run time?

Problem
Algorithms
Java
Interpreter
Hardware

Steve: Yes.

Susan: Okay, then if this is what the interpreter does, what does the compiler do? Does it just compile the program into byte-codes that the interpreter can read?

Steve: Yes.

Susan: Then on stacks, is it like this? The stack stays still, and the pointer to the value's address moves.

Steve: The data stays where it is in memory, and the stack pointer points to different places in memory. Whatever it points to is the top of the stack.

Susan: Where is the stack pointer relative to the stack?

Steve: It isn't relative to the stack. It's a register, which doesn't have a memory address.

Susan: I don't get that.

Steve: A register is a storage area that is on the same chip as the CPU. Programs use registers to hold data items that are actively in use; data in registers can be accessed much faster than if it had to be retrieved from RAM every time it was needed.

Susan: But I thought that the stack was in the registers.

Steve: No, the stack is in RAM. The stack pointer is the register that indicates exactly where the top of the stack is in RAM.

Susan: Put that in the book again, darling. Repeat this many times, and then maybe I will remember it.

Steve: It's worth a try.

Compiler's-Eye View

Now we're just about ready to start analyzing a small program fragment to see how it is actually represented in Java byte codes. Here are the rules of this "game":

1. All numbers in the Java program are decimal; all addresses of the byte codes are hexadecimal.
2. Calculations use the stack to store intermediate values.
3. Byte codes are stored at (hexadecimal) addresses starting at 0.
4. All local variables are stored in a series of "local variable slots" in a reserved area of the stack.

Problem
Algorithms
Java
Interpreter
Hardware

Figure 3.5 shows the program fragment that we're going to compile.

```
int i;
int j;

i = 5;
j = i + 3;
```

Figure 3.5: A really little numeric calculation

Now we're ready to start compiling. The first statement, int i;, tells me to allocate storage for an int variable called i; since i is an int, it takes up 4 bytes of memory, which corresponds to one "slot" on the stack. Therefore, the "memory map" at the beginning of our program fragment will look like Figure 3.6 so far, with the ?s indicating that the variable i hasn't been initialized yet; that will happen before the program fragment starts.

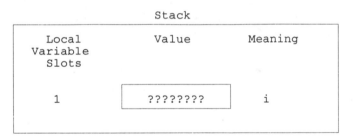

Figure 3.6: Compiling, part 1

As you might have guessed, this exercise was the topic of a considerable amount of discussion with Susan. Here's how it started:

> **Susan**: So the first thing we do with a variable is to tell the address that its name is i, but no one is home, right? It has to get ready to accept a value. Could you put a value in it without naming it, just saying that the first entry on the stack has a value of 5? Why does it have to be called i first?

> **Steve**: The reason that we use names instead of addresses is because it's much easier for people to keep track of names than it is to keep track of addresses. Thus, one of the main functions of a compiler is to allow us to use names that are translated into addresses for the computer's use.

> **Susan**: What are those local variable slots?

> **Steve**: They're the part of the stack that is used to store local variables.

> **Susan**: So is the stack where the compiler puts the variables?

> **Steve**: Yes, the compiler puts them in the local variable part of the stack.

> **Susan**: Are those the places in the stack that do the arithmetic?

> **Steve**: Close, but not quite: The compiler puts the variables in the local variable part of the stack and generates byte codes to transfer them from and to the active part of the stack, where the arithmetic byte codes can access them.

Problem
Algorithms
Java
Interpreter
Hardware

The second statement, int j;, tells me to allocate storage for an int variable called j. Just as with i, j takes 4 bytes of storage, or one slot position on the stack. As before, the ?s indicate that no value has been assigned to this variable yet; it will also be initialized to 0 at run time, so the resulting "memory map" as of the beginning of our program fragment will look like Figure 3.7.

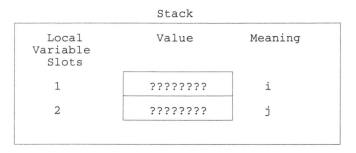

```
                            Stack
    ┌─────────────────────────────────────────────────────┐
    │   Local              Value            Meaning        │
    │  Variable                                            │
    │   Slots                                              │
    │                  ┌───────────────┐                   │
    │     1            │   ???????     │       i           │
    │                  ├───────────────┤                   │
    │     2            │   ???????     │       j           │
    │                  └───────────────┘                   │
    └─────────────────────────────────────────────────────┘
```

Figure 3.7: Compiling, part 2

The next line is blank, so we skip it. This brings us to the statement i = 5; which is an executable statement, so we need to generate one or more byte codes to execute it. Figure 3.8 shows what the code for this program fragment looks like so far, with the statement being compiled listed as a comment before the byte codes that are responsible for executing it.

```
                            Stack
    ┌─────────────────────────────────────────────────────┐
    │   Local              Value            Meaning        │
    │  Variable                                            │
    │   Slots                                              │
    │                  ┌───────────────┐                   │
    │     1            │   ???????     │       i           │
    │                  ├───────────────┤                   │
    │     2            │   ???????     │       j           │
    │                  └───────────────┘                   │
    └─────────────────────────────────────────────────────┘
```

Problem
Algorithms
Java
Interpreter
Hardware

```
                            Code
    ┌─────────────────────────────────────────────────────┐
    │  Address           Byte Code        Description      │
    │                                                      │
    │  // i = 5;                                           │
    │  00000000          iconst_5         Push 5           │
    │  00000001          istore_1         Pop into i       │
    └─────────────────────────────────────────────────────┘
```

Figure 3.8: Compiling, part 3

I'm sure you're wondering what those iconst_5 and istore_1 instructions mean. Susan certainly did.

Susan: What is "iconst"?

Steve: A byte code instruction that pushes a (specified) constant on the stack. For example, iconst_5 means to push the value 5.

Susan: So "push 5" means it puts 5 to the top of the stack?

Steve: Right. The rest of the items on the stack stay on the stack, logically moving down one position.

As soon as we compile the rest of the code, we'll see how the Java interpreter performs arithmetic operations.

The last statement, j = i + 3;, is the most complicated statement in our program, and it's not that complicated. As with the previous statement, it's executable, which means we need to generate byte codes to execute it. The byte codes with addresses 2 through 5 are responsible for this operation, as we'll see in gory detail as soon as we get done compiling.

Figure 3.9 shows what the "memory map" looks like now.

```
Problem
Algorithms
Java
Interpreter
Hardware
```

Stack

Local Variable Slots	Value	Meaning
1	00000000	i
2	00000000	j

Code

Address	Byte Code	Description
// i = 5;		
00000000	iconst_5	Push 5
00000001	istore_1	Pop into i
// j = i + 3;		
00000002	iload_1	Push i
00000003	iconst_3	Push 3
00000004	iadd	Pop top two stack entries, push the sum
00000005	istore_2	Pop into j

Figure 3.9: Compiling, part 4

Here's the next installment of the byte-code discussion with Susan:

Susan: So iload_1 is putting i into the local variable slot #1.

Steve: That's pretty close, but not exactly right. Actually, the iload_1 instruction gets the value of the local variable in slot #1 (in this case, i) and pushes it onto the stack.

Susan: Then iload_1 is a retrieving function?

Steve: Yes, it retrieves the value of the local variable in slot #1 and makes it available for calculation (by pushing it on the stack).

Susan: What are the exact functions of iadd and istore and how do they do that?

Steve: I'm glad you asked me that question. First, iadd is the "integer add" instruction. It pops the top two entries off the stack, adds them together, and pushes the result back on the stack.

The istore instruction is sort of the opposite of iload; it pops a value from the stack and stores it in a local variable. In our example program, we're using the istore_2 instruction to store the result of our calculation into local variable #2 (that is, j).

Problem
Algorithms
Java
Interpreter
Hardware

How It All Stacks Up

Having examined what the compiler does at **compile time** with the preceding little program fragment, the next question is what happens when the compiled program is interpreted. When we start out, the stack and code areas of memory we're concerned with will look like Figure 3.10.[13]

---

13. The next byte code to be executed will be **bold**.

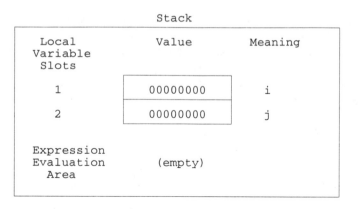

Stack

Local Variable Slots	Value	Meaning
1	00000000	i
2	00000000	j
Expression Evaluation Area	(empty)	

Code

Address	Byte Code	Description
// i = 5;		
00000000	**iconst_5**	**Push 5**
00000001	istore_1	Pop into i
// j = i + 3;		
00000002	iload_1	Push i
00000003	iconst_3	Push 3
00000004	iadd	Pop top two stack entries, push the sum
00000005	istore_2	Pop into j

Problem
Algorithms
Java
Interpreter
Hardware

Figure 3.10: Execution, part 1

First of all, you should note that the variables i and j have been set to the default value for an int, namely, 0. This is guaranteed by the Java language specification.

Now we're just about ready to examine what all those byte codes do when we execute the program. Let's start at the beginning, with the two common ways that electronic calculators do arithmetic operations. The first, used by most calculators except for those made by Hewlett-Packard, is called **algebraic** operation. This method, as the name implies, works in a way similar to how we write arithmetic expressions in Java. For example, to calculate the average of two variables, i and j, we would write the expression (i + j)/2. At run time, the code would add i and j, then divide by 2 to get the answer.

While this method of evaluating arithmetic expressions is seemingly natural for humans, it is not the way that byte code programs work in Java. Instead, the Java compiler converts such expressions into a form similar to the one used by Hewlett-Packard™ calculators. This form is called RPN (for **R**everse **P**olish **N**otation, because it was invented by the Polish logician Jan Lukasiewicz); it uses a stack to store values during the evaluation of an expression. The area of the stack used for this purpose is labeled as the "expression evaluation area" in the figures illustrating the execution of our program fragment.

As you might not be surprised to hear, Susan had some questions about this method of calculating arithmetic expressions.

Susan: What is the "expression evaluation area"?

Steve: The part of the stack used to store intermediate values during execution of the byte codes.

Susan: I need some more explanation of this.

Steve: The expression evaluation area is a part of the stack used during the calculation of an arithmetic expression. For example, in the statement "j = i + 3", the value of the expression "i + 3" is calculated in a couple of steps. First, the value of i is pushed onto the stack; then 3 is pushed onto the stack; finally the "add" instruction adds the top two elements of the stack (i and 3). Now that we have the value of i + 3 on the top of the stack, that value is stored into j. Does that help?

Susan: So the expression evaluation area is like your desktop? A place to work?

Steve: Possibly, but maybe a better analogy would be a blackboard that you calculate something on, but clean off once you have the final result.

Susan: How do I know which byte codes push and which ones pop?

Steve: You can look it up in *The Java Virtual Machine Specification*, by Tim Lindholm and Frank Yellin (Addison-Wesley, 1997). However, you won't normally need to do this, because the compiler will take care of it for you.

```
Problem
Algorithms
Java
Interpreter
Hardware
```

Now let's see exactly how the evaluation of our statements works. Starting out with an empty expression evaluation area, we execute the iconst_5 byte code, which pushes the constant int value 5 onto the stack. This leaves us with the situation in Figure 3.11.

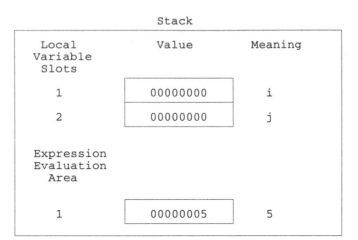

Stack

Local Variable Slots	Value	Meaning
1	00000000	i
2	00000000	j

Expression
Evaluation
Area

1	00000005	5

Code

Address	Byte Code	Description
// i = 5;		
00000000	iconst_5	Push 5
00000001	**istore_1**	**Pop into i**
// j = i + 3;		
00000002	iload_1	Push i
00000003	iconst_3	Push 3
00000004	iadd	Pop top two stack
		entries, push the sum
00000005	istore_2	Pop into j

Problem
Algorithms
Java
Interpreter
Hardware

Figure 3.11: Execution, part 2

The next step is to execute the istore_1 byte code, which pops the value from the top of the stack into local variable 1 (i); that is, it sets i to the value on the top of the stack, and removes that value from the stack. This leaves us with the situation in Figure 3.12. Note that the value of i has been changed to 5, and the expression evaluation area of the stack is empty.

Stack

Local Variable Slots	Value	Meaning
1	00000005	i
2	00000000	j
Expression Evaluation Area	(empty)	

Code

Address	Byte Code	Description
// i = 5;		
00000000	iconst_5	Push 5
00000001	istore_1	Pop into i
// j = i + 3;		
00000002	**iload_1**	**Push i**
00000003	iconst_3	Push 3
00000004	iadd	Pop top two stack entries, push the sum
00000005	istore_2	Pop into j

Problem
Algorithms
Java
Interpreter
Hardware

Figure 3.12: Execution, part 3

Next, we start on the statement j = i + 3;. The Java interpreter will perform this operation by reloading the value of i (variable 1), pushing a literal 3 onto the stack, adding the top two elements of the stack, and finally storing the result into variable 2 (j). Let's go over that step by step, starting with the byte code iload_1, which pushes the value of local variable 1 (i) onto the stack. This leaves us with the situation in Figure 3.13.

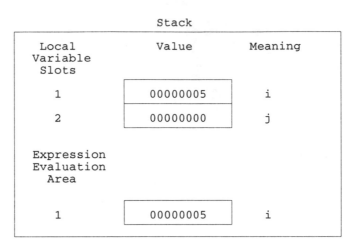

Figure 3.13: Execution, part 4

Next, we execute the byte code iconst_3, which pushes the value 3 onto the stack. This leaves the situation shown in Figure 3.14.

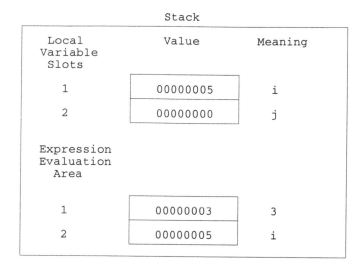

```
                            Stack
      Local            Value           Meaning
      Variable
      Slots

        1            00000005             i

        2            00000000             j


      Expression
      Evaluation
        Area


        1            00000003             3

        2            00000005             i
```

```
                            Code
  Address            Byte Code       Description

  // i = 5;
  00000000           iconst_5        Push 5
  00000001           istore_1        Pop into i

  // j = i + 3;
  00000002           iload_1         Push i
  00000003           iconst_3        Push 3
  00000004           iadd            Pop top two stack
                                     entries, push the sum
  00000005           istore_2        Pop into j
```

Problem
Algorithms
Java
Interpreter
Hardware

Figure 3.14: Execution, part 5

Next, we execute the iadd byte code, which pops the top two entries in the stack, adds them together, and pushes the sum. This leaves the situation shown in Figure 3.15.

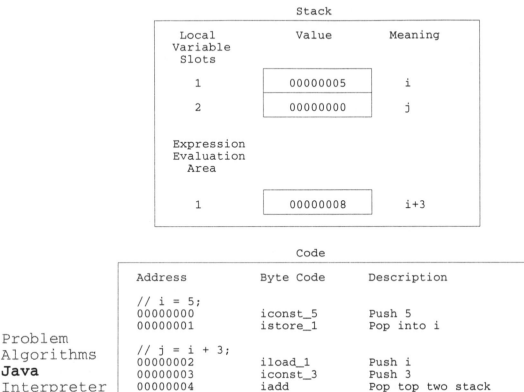

Figure 3.15: Execution, part 6

Finally, we execute the istore_2 byte code, which stores the top entry in the stack into local variable 2 (j). This leaves the situation shown in Figure 3.16.

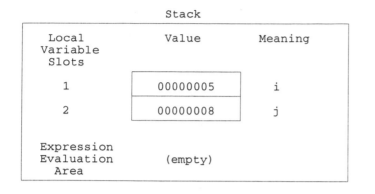

Stack

Local Variable Slots	Value	Meaning
1	00000005	i
2	00000008	j
Expression Evaluation Area	(empty)	

Code

Address	Byte Code	Description
// i = 5;		
00000000	iconst_5	Push 5
00000001	istore_1	Pop into i
// j = i + 3;		
00000002	iload_1	Push i
00000003	iconst_3	Push 3
00000004	iadd	Pop top two stack entries, push the sum
00000005	istore_2	Pop into j

Problem
Algorithms
Java
Interpreter
Hardware

Figure 3.16: Execution, part 7

The difference between this situation and the last one is that the expression evaluation area of the stack is empty and the value of j has been set to 8.

Here's the next installment of my discussion with Susan on this topic:

Susan: Now this may sound like a very dumb question, but please tell me where 5 comes from? I mean if you are going to move the value of 5 onto the stack, where is 5 hiding to take it from and to put it in the stack? Is it stored somewhere in memory that has to be moved, or is it simply a function of the user just typing in that value?

Steve: No, it's not a dumb question at all. The 5 is part of the byte code iconst_5. You see, because small numbers (0 through 5 and minus 1) are so common in Java programs, the Java interpreter has special byte codes to push those values onto the stack. If the number were greater than 5, it would be stored as a literal value immediately following a byte code that means "push a literal value".

By the way, don't be misled by this example into thinking that all byte codes are 1 byte in length. It's just a coincidence that all of the ones I've used here are of that length. The actual size of a byte-code instruction can vary considerably; in fact, some byte-code instructions can be virtually unlimited in length. Most byte codes, however, take from 1 to 3 bytes.

A Cast of Characters

This should give you some idea of how numeric variables and values work. But what about non-numeric ones?

This brings us to the subject of two new variable types and the values they can contain. These are the **char** and its relative, the **String**. What are these good for, and how do they work?[14]

A variable of type char corresponds to 1 character of text, which in Java occupies 2 bytes (16 bits) of storage. Since a char has 16 bits, it can hold any of 65536 (2^{16}) values, which is the same number of values that a short can hold. So what's the difference between these two types?

Problem
Algorithms
Java
Interpreter
Hardware

The main purpose of a char is to represent an individual letter, digit, punctuation mark, "special character" (e.g., $, #, %, and so on), or one of the other "printable" and displayable units from which words, sentences, and other textual data such as this paragraph are composed.[15] We don't need anywhere near 65,536 possibilities to represent any character in English, as well as a number of European languages; in fact 256 possibilities is enough to handle all of the characters in those languages, so in most programming languages other than Java a char is only 1 byte long.

However, the written forms of "ideographic" languages such as Chinese and Korean consist of far more than 256 characters, so 1 byte isn't going to do the trick for these languages. While they have been supported to some extent by schemes that switch among a number of sets of 256 characters each, such clumsy approaches to the

---

14. In case you were wondering, the most common pronunciation of char has an *a* like the a in "married", while the *ch* sounds like "k".

15. As we will see shortly, not all characters have visible representations; some of these "nonprintable" characters are useful in controlling how our printed or displayed information looks.

problem made programs much more complicated and error prone. As the international market for software is increasing rapidly, it has become more important to have a convenient method of handling large *character sets*. To solve this problem, the *Unicode standard*, which uses 2 bytes per character, has been developed. This is the representation that Java uses for its chars.[16]

Even in an ideographic language, one char isn't good for much by itself, so we often use groups of them, called Strings, to represent a significant amount of text. Just as with numeric values, these variables can be set to literal values, which represent themselves. Figure 3.17 is an example of how to specify and use each of these types we've just encountered.

```
public class Basic00
{
    public static void main( String args[ ] )
    {
        char c1;
        char c2;
        String s1;
        String s2;
        String s3;

        c1 = 'A';
        c2 = c1;

        s1 = "Congratulations! ";
        s2 = "You got an ";
        s3 = " on the test.";

        System.out.println( s1 + s2 + c2 + s3);
    }
}
```

Problem
Algorithms
Java
Interpreter
Hardware

Figure 3.17: Some real characters and Strings (code\basic00\basic00.java)

This file, basic00.java, is the source code for the first complete program we've seen, so there are a couple of new constructs that I'll have to explain to you. Before we get to the explanation, however, I should mention that one of the reasons that Java currently doesn't run under DOS or Windows 3.1 is that it requires long filenames, that is,

---

16. The Unicode standard is actually a "small" version of a standard that uses 32 bits per character, for the day when Unicode doesn't have sufficient capacity; that should take care of any languages that alien civilizations might introduce to our planet.

ones that have more than 8 characters before the period or more than three characters after the period. In this case, of course, it is the extension, .java, that is not legal under DOS or Windows 3.1.

By the way, in case the program in Figure 3.17 doesn't seem very useful, that's because it isn't; it's just an example of the syntax of defining and using variables and literal values. However, we'll use these constructs to do useful work later, so going over them now isn't a waste of time.

The first construct we have to examine is the line public class basic00, which has three components. The first component of this line is the keyword public, which means that we're defining something that is generally available to any program that wants to use it. The particular kind of "something" that we're making available is specified by the second component of this line: the keyword class, which tells the Java compiler that we are beginning the definition of a class. What is a class? That's a very good question, because every program in Java is composed of the definitions of one or more classes. This is obviously a very important part of the language; however, you'll need a significant amount of background in other aspects of the Java language before its explanation is likely to mean very much to you, so I'm deferring that discussion until Chapter 6. For now, just take my word that every Java program has to start with a line telling the compiler the name of the class that we're defining.

As this brief explanation suggests, the third component of this line is basic00, which is the name of the particular class we're defining in this program. We could call it whatever we wanted, but since it's the first example program in this chapter on the basics of programming, I named it basic00 so that you and I could keep track of it more easily.

Once we have specified the name of the class that we're creating, we can define the piece of code that is going to actually do the work for us. That's the job of the next line:

```
public static void main( String args[ ] )
```

This will be the first line of every main function that we will examine in this book. Eventually I'll be able to explain exactly what every part of this line means, but you don't have enough background yet. Therefore, you'll have to take my word that everything on that line will eventually mean something.

However, there is one thing I can explain: the meaning of main. Java has a rule that execution always starts at the place called main. Since this is where we want our program to start executing, we have

Problem
Algorithms
Java
Interpreter
Hardware

to call it by that name; marking the place where we want to start is the main purpose of the line we're discussing.

You may also be puzzled by the function of the other statements in this program. If so, you're not alone. Let's see the discussion that Susan and I had about that topic.

> **Susan**: Okay, in the example *why* did you have to write c2 = c1;? Why not B? Why make one thing the same thing as the other? Make it different. Why would you even want c2=c1; and not just say c1 twice, if that is what you want?

> **Steve**: It's very hard to think up examples that are both simple enough to explain and realistic enough to make sense. You're right that this example doesn't do anything useful; I'm just trying to introduce what both the char type and the String type look like.

> **Susan**: Come to think of it, what does c1='A'; have to do with the statement s1= "Congratulations! ";? I don't see any relationship between one thing and the other.

> **Steve**: This is the same problem as the last one. They have nothing to do with one another; I'm using an admittedly contrived example to show how these variables are used.

> **Susan**: I am glad now that your example of chars and Strings (put together) didn't make sense to me. That is progress; it wasn't supposed to.

Problem
Algorithms
Java
Interpreter
Hardware

What does this useless but hopefully instructive program do? As is always the case, we have to tell the compiler what the types of our variables are before we can use them. In this case, c1 and c2 are of type char, whereas s1, s2, and s3 are Strings. After taking care of these formalities, we can start to use the variables. In the first executable statement, c1 = 'A';, we set the char variable c1 to a literal value, in this case a capital *A*; we need to surround this with single quotation marks (') to tell the compiler that we mean the letter *A* rather than a variable named A. In the next line, c2 = c1;, we set c2 to the same value as c1 holds, which of course is 'A' in this case. The next executable statement, s1 = "Congratulations! ";, as you might expect, sets the String variable s1 to the value "Congratulations! ", which is a String literal.[17] A String literal is a type of literal that we use to assign values to variables of type String. In the statement s1 = "Congratulations! "; we use a

---

17. Please note that there is a *space* (blank) character at the end of that String literal, after the exclamation point (!). That space is part of the literal value.

quotation mark, in this case the double quote ("), to tell the compiler where the literal value starts and ends.

You may be wondering why we need two different kinds of quotes in these two cases. There really isn't a very good reason that I can think of other than to allow the compiler to tell whether we're using a compatible type of literal for a char or a String variable. As far as I can tell, this distinction is left over from C and C++, where it made more sense, but for reasons that aren't relevant here.

The Right Type

As the above discussion suggests, every variable in Java has a type. While some languages allow the same variable to be used in different ways at different times, in Java any given variable always has the same type; for example, a char variable can't change into an int. At first glance, it seems that it would be much easier for programmers to be able to use variables any way they like; why is Java so restrictive?

The Java **type system**, as this feature of a language is called, is specifically designed to minimize the risk of misinterpreting or otherwise misusing a variable. It's entirely too easy in some languages to change the type of a variable without meaning to; the resulting bugs can be very difficult to find, especially in a large program. In Java, the usage of a variable can be checked by the compiler. This **static type checking** allows the compiler to tell you about many errors that otherwise would not be detected until the program is running (**dynamic type checking**). This is particularly important in systems that need to run continuously for long periods of time. While you can reboot your machine if your word processor crashes due to a run-time error, this is not acceptable as a solution for errors in the telephone network, for example.

Of course, you probably won't be writing programs demanding the degree of reliability that the telephone network requires any time soon, but strict static type checking is still worthwhile in helping eliminate errors at the earliest possible stage in the development of our programs.

You might get the impression from this discussion that Java is suitable for developing large applications that have to run indefinitely. Is this true?

Problem
Algorithms
Java
Interpreter
Hardware

Reality Check

Most other books I've seen on Java contain a statement something like the following, often at roughly this point in the exposition:

> Java is the be-all and end-all of computer languages. It is infinitely superior to every other language, especially C++, which has served its purpose now that its obvious successor, Java, has been invented. Java is suitable for every possible application, and most impossible ones. Furthermore, Java is a very simple language that you can learn in a few minutes, probably in your sleep.[18]

This is considerably at variance with the truth. Java has some advantages over other languages, including C++. It also has some serious drawbacks that make it eminently *un*suitable for many types of applications, especially large ones that have to operate for a long time without fail; for example, it would *not* be a good idea to write programs to control the telephone network in Java. I'll explain some of these drawbacks as we run across them in this book.

As for the claim of how simple Java is: I can't agree with that either. Java is not significantly simpler than other computer languages, and in particular it's not any simpler than the part of C++ that you should use to design new programs (as contrasted with the "dark corners" of C++ that you can stumble into when dealing with old programs). However, you don't have to take my word for the complexity of Java; you should have a pretty good idea of how complex it is by the time you get through this book!

```
Problem
Algorithms
Java
Interpreter
Hardware
```

Some Strings Attached

After that info-mercial for the advantages of static type checking (and deflation of some of the hype about Java), we can resume our examination of Strings. You may have noticed that there's a **space** character at the end of the String "Congratulations! ". That's another reason why we have to use a special character like " (the double quote) to mark the beginning and end of a String; how else would the compiler know whether that space is supposed to be part of the String or not? The space character is one of the **non-printing characters** (or **non-display characters**) that controls the format of our displayed or printed information; imagine how hard it would be to read this

---

18. I know I left out the part about its curing cancer, but I don't want to go overboard.

book without space characters! While we're on the subject, I should also tell you about some other characters that have special meaning to the compiler. They are listed in Figure 3.18.

Name	Graphic	Use
single quote	'	surrounds a single-character value
double quote	"	surrounds a multi-character value
semicolon	;	ends a statement
curly braces	{ }	groups statements together
parentheses	( )	surrounds part of a statement[19]
backslash	\	tells the compiler that the next character should be treated differently from the way that it would normally be treated[20]

Figure 3.18: Special characters for program text

I compiled Figure 3.18 at the instigation of guess who.

Problem
Algorithms
Java
Interpreter
Hardware

Susan: How about you line up all your cute little " ' \ ; things and just list their meanings? I forget what they are by the time I get to the next one. Your explanations of them are fine, but they are scattered all over the place; I just want one place that has all the explanations.

Steve: That's a good idea; I think I will.

Our next task will be to see how we get the values of our Strings and chars to show up on the screen.

In and Out

Most programs need to interact with their users, both to ask them what they want and to present the results when they are available. The computer term for this topic is **I/O** (short for "input/output"). We'll start by getting information from the keyboard and displaying

---

19. I'll be more specific later, when we have seen some examples.

20. For example, if you wanted to insert a " in a String, you would have to use \", because just a plain " would indicate the end of the String. That is, if you were to set a String to the literal "This is a \"String\".", it would display as: This is a "String".

it on the screen; later, we'll go over the more complex I/O functions that allow us to read and write data on the disk.

The final line of code in Figure 3.17, System.out.println(s1 + s2 + c2 + s3);, displays information on the screen. In this case, the output will be "Congratulations! You got an A on the test.". How does this occur exactly?

The first construct on this line is System.out, which is a predefined Java variable that is "connected" to the screen. This variable has several built-in ways to display information; the one we're using here is called println, which is short for "print and move to the next line". The value of the expression inside the parentheses after println will be displayed on the screen (the print part of println), and the cursor will be moved to the beginning of the next line (the ln part of println).println

That explains why we'll see some output on the screen, but it doesn't explain the exact output that we'll see, which depends on what's inside the parentheses. In this case, that's s1 + s2 + c2 + s3. I don't blame you if you have some trouble understanding how we can "add" Strings and chars together; that's not exactly intuitively obvious to the casual observer.

What the + means here actually is something like "add", but more precisely it means "add some text data to the end of some other text data". In the current case, that whole expression produces the following sequence of events:

Problem
Algorithms
Java
Interpreter
Hardware

1. Take the contents of s2, and add that to the end of the contents of s1. Since s1 contains "Congratulations! " and s2 contains "You got an ", the result will be the value "Congratulations! You got an ".
2. Take the results of the previous operation and add the contents of c1 ('A') to its end, resulting in the value "Congratulations! You got an A".
3. Take the results of the previous operation and add the contents of s3 (" on the test") to its end, resulting in the value "Congratulations! You got an A on the test."

Finally, the resulting value will be displayed on the screen and the cursor will be moved to the next line.

Susan had an incisive observation about this example program.

Susan: What if the student got a 'B'? Then the second sentence would read "You got an B", which is incorrect.

Steve: That's a good point. I think I'll make fixing that problem into an exercise.

So much for (simple) output. Input from the keyboard is almost as simple. Let's modify our little sample to use it, as shown in Figure 3.19.

```
import WAJ.*;

public class Basic02
{
    public static void main( String args[ ] )
    {
        char c1;
        char c2;
        String s1;
        String s2;
        String s3;
        String s4;

        System.out.print("What is your name? ");
        s4 = RWVar.readString(System.in);

        c1 = 'A';
        c2 = c1;

        s1 = "Congratulations, ";
        s2 = "! You got an ";
        s3 = " on the test.";

        System.out.println( s1 + s4 + s2 + c2 + s3);
    }
}
```

```
Problem
Algorithms
Java
Interpreter
Hardware
```

Figure 3.19: Simple input (code\basic00\basic02.java)

There are a couple of new things in this program. Let's start at the top with the line import WAJ.*;. I'll explain exactly what that line means later, but for now it's sufficient to know that this tells the Java compiler where to find some code that I've written to make it easier for you to write simple Java programs.

The line System.out.print("What is your name? "); is almost like the simple output statement we've seen before, with two exceptions. First, it displays a constant String value on the screen ("What is your name? "), rather than the calculated value we saw earlier. Second, instead of using the println operation, it uses print. The difference between these two is simply that print doesn't move the cursor to the next line, as println does. In the current case, we want to let the user of the program type his or her answer in on the same line as the question rather than on the next line, so this is appropriate.

The next line that has anything unfamiliar is the one that says s4 = RWVar.readString(System.in);. You should be able to guess that the first part of that line, s4 =, sets the String variable s4 to some value, but what value is that exactly?

It's whatever you type in when you see the question What is your name? on the screen. That's what RWVar.readString is for: It takes input up to the next ENTER, and turns it into a String. In this case, we use that String to set the value of the String variable on the left of the equals sign. There are similar ways to read other kinds of variables, like ints, as we'll see later.

But what about System.in? As its name suggests, this is the counterpart to System.out; it supplies characters from the keyboard rather than writing characters to the screen.

Susan had some questions about these little programs, beginning with the question of case sensitivity.

Susan: Are the words such as char and public case sensitive? I had capitalized a few of them just out of habit because they begin the sentence and I am not sure if that was the reason the compiler gave me so many error messages. I think after I changed them I reduced a few messages.

Steve: *Everything* in Java is case sensitive. That includes keywords like char, public, and so on, as well as your own variables. That is, if you have a variable called Name and another one called name, those are completely different and unrelated to one another. This also applies to System.in and System.out; you have to write them just as they appear here, or the compiler won't be able to figure out what you mean.

Susan: What does RWVar stand for?

Steve: "Reading and writing variables".

Susan: Why is the word System used?

Steve: Because those variables (System.out and System.in) are supplied by the system.

Susan: The WAJ.* is confusing to me; what does it do?

Steve: It tells the compiler that we want to be able to use some facilities that are stored under the name WAJ (which is short for "Who's Afraid of Java?"). That's where I've put RWVar, so if we hadn't included the line

Problem
Algorithms
Java
Interpreter
Hardware

import WAJ.*, we wouldn't be able to use RWVar.readString and the other RWVar facilities.

If Only You Knew

In our examples so far, the program always executes the same statements in the same order. However, any real program is going to need to alter its behavior according to the data it is processing. For example, in a banking application, it might be necessary to send out a notice to a depositor whenever the balance in a particular account drops below a certain level; or perhaps the depositor would just be charged some exorbitant fee in that case. Either way, the program has to do something different depending on the balance. In particular, let's suppose that the "Absconders and Defaulters National Bank" has a minimum balance of $10,000. Furthermore, let's assume that if you have less than that amount on deposit, you are charged a $20 "service charge". However, if you are foolish enough to leave that ridiculous amount of money on deposit, then they will graciously allow you to get away with not paying them for the privilege of lending them your money (without interest, of course). To determine whether or not you should be charged for your checking account, the bank can use an if **statement**, as shown in Figure 3.20.

Problem
Algorithms
Java
Interpreter
Hardware

```java
import WAJ.*;

public class Basic03
{
    public static void main( String args[ ] )
    {
        int balance;

        System.out.print("Please enter your bank balance: ");
        balance = RWVar.readInt(System.in);

        if (balance < 10000)
            System.out.println("Please remit $20 service charge.");
        else
            System.out.println("Have a nice day!");
    }
}
```

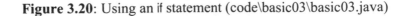

Figure 3.20: Using an if statement (code\basic03\basic03.java)

This program starts by displaying the line

Please enter your bank balance:

on the screen. Then it uses the line balance = RWVar.readInt(System.in); to allow you to type in your balance, followed by the ENTER key (so it knows when you're done). This RWVar.readInt facility is similar to our previous use of RWVar.readString, except that it read an int rather than a String value. Of course, System.in still supplies data from the keyboard.

Next, the conditional statement checks whether you're a "good customer". If your balance is less than $10,000, the next statement is executed, which displays the line

Please remit $20 service charge.[21]

If the condition is **false** (that is, you have at least $10,000 in the bank), the computer skips the statement that asks you to remit $20; instead, it executes the one after the else, which tells you to have a nice day. That's what **else** is for; it specifies what to do if the condition specified in the if statement is false (that is, not true). If you typed in a number 10000 or higher, the program would display the line[22]

Have a nice day!

You don't have to specify an else if you don't want to. In that case, if the if condition isn't **true**, the program just goes to the next statement as though the if had never been executed.

Problem
Algorithms
Java
Interpreter
Hardware

While We're on the Subject

The while statement is another way of affecting the order of program execution. This conditional statement executes the statement under its control as long as a certain condition is true. Such potentially repeated execution is called a **loop**; a loop controlled by a **while** statement is called, logically enough, a while *loop*. Figure 3.21 is a

---

21. This explanation assumes that the "10000" is the balance in dollars. Of course, this doesn't account for the possibility of balances that aren't a whole number of dollars. I'll mention a possible solution to this problem later.

22. Please note that you cannot include the "," in a number in your programs, whether you're writing the program or entering data when it runs. You have to type "10,000" as "10000" or you'll get an error either at compile time or when the program is running.

program that uses a while loop to challenge the user to guess a secret number from 0 to 9, and keeps asking for guesses until the correct answer is entered.

```java
import WAJ.*;

public class Basic04
{
    public static void main( String args[ ] )
    {
        int Secret;
        int Guess;

        Secret = 3;

        System.out.println("Try and guess my number. Hint: It's from 0 to 9");
        Guess = RWVar.readInt(System.in);

        while (Guess != Secret)
        {
            System.out.println("Sorry, that's not correct.");
            Guess = RWVar.readInt(System.in);
        }

        System.out.println("You guessed right!");
    }
}
```

Problem
Algorithms
Java
Interpreter
Hardware

Figure 3.21: Using a while statement (code\basic04\basic04.java)

There are a few wrinkles here that we haven't seen before. Although the while statement itself is fairly straightforward, the meaning of its condition != isn't intuitively obvious. However, if you consider the problem we're trying to solve, you'll probably come to the (correct) conclusion that != means "not equal", since we want to keep asking for more guesses while the Guess is not equal to our Secret number.[23] Since there is a comparison operator that tests for "not equal", you might want to know how to test for "equal" as well. The answer is that you can test whether two int values are equal by using the == operator; we'll see in the next chapter why we can't use = for this task.

---

23. You may be wondering why we need parentheses around the expression Guess != Secret. The conditional expression has to be in parentheses so that the compiler can tell where it ends and the statement to be controlled by the while begins.

Would an if statement with an else clause would serve as well as the while? After all, if is used to select one of two alternatives, and the else could select the other one. The answer is that this would allow the user to take only one guess; the while loop lets the user try again as many times as needed to get the right answer.

Now you should have enough information to be able to write a simple program of your own, as Susan asked to do at this point.

> **Susan**: Based on what you have presented in the book so far, send me a setup, an exercise for me to try to figure out how to program, and I will give it a try. I guess that is the only way to do it. I can't even figure out a programmable situation on my own. So if you do that, I will do my best with it, and that will help teach me to think. (Can that be?) Now, if you do this, make it simple, and no tricks.

Of course, I did give her the exercise she asked for (exercise 1), but also of course, that didn't end the matter. She decided to add her own flourish, which resulted in exercise 2.

Separate but Possibly Equal

It would be convenient to compare two variables of any type by just using == or !=, the former to tell whether they are equal and the latter whether they are unequal. Unfortunately, this won't work. As we'll see in much more detail later, most types of variables in Java fall in one of two categories: **primitive** (sometimes called **native**) and **user-defined**. Strings are an exception, being sort of a cross between these two types, acting more like the latter. You can indeed compare primitive variables such as ints and chars by using the == or != operators; however, to compare non-primitive variables, including Strings, you have to use the equals facility. In particular, to compare whether two Strings, a and b, have the same value, you have to write if (a.equals(b)).

Does this seem much clumsier than just writing if (a == b), as you would do to compare two ints? Many diehard Java supporters claim that it's much better to have two different ways to compare variables, depending on whether they are actually part of the language (primitive) or are added on afterwards (user-defined and Strings). Personally, I think it would be better to be able to treat all types of variables in the same way, but maybe I'm missing something here.[24]

Problem
Algorithms
Java
Interpreter
Hardware

---

24. And maybe pigs can fly.

How to Do the Exercises

We're ready for the exercises that Susan asked for, along with some others of the same general level of difficulty. To write programs to solve these exercises, see the section titled "Writing and compiling your own programs" in the file "\readme.txt" on the CD in the back of the book.

Once you have followed those instructions to write and run a program, it may work the first time you try them. However, if it doesn't (which is quite likely), you will need more information about what's happening in the program. Fortunately, Java compilers come with a **debugger**, which you can use to trace execution in your program. To use the debugger for your program, follow the instructions in the section titled "Using the debugger" in the file "\readme.txt" on the CD in the back of the book.

Exercises

```
Problem
Algorithms
Java
Interpreter
Hardware
```

1. Write a program that asks the user to type in the number of people that are expected for dinner, not counting the user. Assuming that the number typed in is n, display a message that says "A table for (n+1) is ready.". For example, if the user types 3, display "A table for 4 is ready.".

2. Modify the program from exercise 1 to display an error message if the number of guests is more than 20.

3. Write a program that asks the user to type in his or her name and age. If the age is less than 47, then indicate that the user is a youngster; otherwise, that he or she is getting on in years.

4. Write a program that asks the user whether Susan is the world's most tenacious novice. If the answer is "yes", then acknowledge the user's correct answer; if the answer is "no", then indicate that the answer is erroneous. If neither "yes" nor "no" is typed in, chastise the user for not following directions.

5. Write a program that calculates how much extra allowance a teenager can earn by doing extra chores. Her allowance is calculated as $10 if she does no extra chores; she gets $1 additional for each extra chore she does.

6. Modify the program in Figure 3.17 to ask for the grade and display it correctly whether it is an A, B, C, D, or F.

Answers to exercises can be found at the end of the chapter.

Just up the Block

Our most recent programming example has contributed another item to our arsenal of programming weapons; namely, the ability to group several statements into one logical section of a program. That's the function of the **curly braces**, { and }. The first one of these starts such a section, called a **block**, and the second one ends the block. Because the two statements after the while are part of the same block, they are treated as a unit; both are executed if the condition in the while is true, and neither is executed if it is false. A block can be used anywhere that a statement can be used, and is treated in exactly the same way as if it were one statement.[25]

At the Fair

Now we're ready to write a program that vaguely resembles a solution to a real problem. We'll start with a simple, rural type of programming problem.

Imagine that you are at a county fair. The contest for the heaviest pumpkin is about to get underway, and the judges have asked for your help in operating the "pumpkin scoreboard". This device has one slot for the current pumpkin weight (the CurrentWeight slot), and another slot for the highest weight so far (the HighestWeight slot); each slot can hold three digits from 0 to 9 and therefore can indicate any weight from 0 to 999. The judges want you to maintain an up-to-date display of the current weight and of the highest weight seen so far. The weights are expressed to the nearest pound. How would you go about this task?

Probably the best way to start is by setting the number in both slots to the first pumpkin weight called out. Then, as each new weight is called out, you change the number in the CurrentWeight slot to match the current weight; if it's higher than the number in the HighestWeight slot, you change that one to match as well. Of course, you don't have to do anything to the HighestWeight slot when a weight less than the previous maximum is called out, because that pumpkin can't be the winner. How do we know when we are done? Since a pumpkin

Problem
Algorithms
Java
Interpreter
Hardware

---

25. If you look at someone else's Java program, you're likely to see a different style for lining up the {} to indicate where a block begins and ends. As you'll notice, my style puts the { and } on separate lines rather than running them together with the code they enclose, to make them stand out, and indents them further than the conditional statement. I find this the clearest, but this is a matter where there is no consensus. The compiler doesn't care how you indent your code or whether you do so at all; it's a stylistic issue.

entered in this contest has to have a weight of at least 1 pound, you enter 0 as the weight when the contest is over. At that point, the number in the HighestWeight slot is the weight of the winner.

The procedure you have just imagined performing can be expressed a bit more precisely by the following algorithm:

1. Ask for the first weight.
2. Set the number in the CurrentWeight slot to this value.
3. Copy the number in the CurrentWeight slot to the HighestWeight slot.
4. Display both the current weight and the highest weight so far (which are the same, at this point).
5. While the CurrentWeight value is greater than 0 (that is, there are more pumpkins to be weighed), do steps 5a to 5d.
   a. Ask for the next weight.
   b. Set the number in the CurrentWeight slot to this weight.
   c. If the number in the CurrentWeight slot is greater than the number in the HighestWeight slot, copy the number in the CurrentWeight slot to the HighestWeight slot.
   d. Display the current weight and the highest weight so far.
6. Stop. The number in the HighestWeight slot is the weight of the winner.

Problem
Algorithms
Java
Interpreter
Hardware

Figure 3.22 is the translation of our little problem into Java. Susan had a question about the formatting of the output statement System.out.println("Highest weight " + HighestWeight);.

Susan: Why do we need both "Highest weight" and HighestWeight in this line?

Steve: Because "Highest weight" is displayed on the screen to tell the user that the following number is supposed to represent the highest weight seen so far. On the other hand, HighestWeight is the name of the variable that holds that information, so including HighestWeight in the output statement will result in displaying the highest weight we've seen so far on the screen. Of course, the same analysis applies to the next line, which displays the label "Current weight" and the value of the variable CurrentWeight.

English	Java
First, we have to tell the compiler what we're up to in this program.	

Tell the compiler where to find the RWVar input and output code

```
import WAJ.*;
```

We're defining a class named Pump1

```
public class Pump1
```

This is the main part of the program

```
{
    public static void main( String args[ ] )
```

Start of program

```
{
```

Define variables

```
int CurrentWeight;
int HighestWeight;
```

Here's the start of the "working" code:

Ask for the first weight

```
System.out.print("Please enter the first weight: ");
```

Set the number in the CurrentWeight slot to the value entered by the user

```
CurrentWeight = RWVar.readInt(System.in);
```

Copy the number in the CurrentWeight slot to the HighestWeight slot

```
HighestWeight = CurrentWeight;
```

Display the current and highest weights

```
System.out.println("Current weight " + CurrentWeight);
System.out.println("Highest weight " + HighestWeight);
```

Problem
Algorithms
Java
Interpreter
Hardware

Figure 3.22: A Java Program (code\pump1\pump1.java)

While the number in the CurrentWeight slot is greater than 0 (i.e., there are more pumpkins to be weighed)	while (CurrentWeight > 0)
Start repeated steps	{
Ask for the next weight	System.out.print("Please enter the next weight: ");
Set the number in the CurrentWeight slot to this value	CurrentWeight = RWVar.readInt(System.in);
If the number in the CurrentWeight slot is more than the number in the HighestWeight slot,	if (CurrentWeight > HighestWeight)
then copy the number in the CurrentWeight slot to the HighestWeight slot	HighestWeight = CurrentWeight;
Display the current and highest weights	System.out.println("Current weight "+CurrentWeight); System.out.println("Highest weight "+HighestWeight);
End repeated steps in while loop	}

Problem
Algorithms
Java
Interpreter
Hardware

We've finished the job; now to clean up

End of main part of program	}
End of class	}

Figure 3.22 continued

Susan had some questions about variable names.

Susan: Tell me again what the different ints mean in this figure. I am confused; I just thought an int held a variable like i. What is going on when you declare HighestWeight an int? So do the "words" HighestWeight work in the same way as i?

Steve: An int is a variable. The name of an int is made up of one or more characters; the first character must be a letter or an underscore (_), whereas any character after the first must be either a letter, an underscore, a dollar sign, or a digit from 0 to 9. To define an int, you write a line that gives the name of the int. This is an example: int HighestWeight;.

Susan: OK, but then how does i take 4 bytes of memory and how does HighestWeight take up 4 bytes of memory? They look so different, how do you know that HighestWeight will fit into an int?

Steve: The length of the names that you give variables has nothing to do with the amount of storage that the variables take up. After the compiler gets through with your program, there aren't any variable names; each variable that you define in your source program is represented by the address of some area of storage. If the variable is an int, that area of storage is 4 bytes long; if it's a char (or a short), the area of storage is 2 bytes long.

Susan: Then where do the names go? They don't go "into" the int?

Steve: A variable name doesn't "go" anywhere; it tells the compiler to set aside an area of memory of a particular length that you will refer to by a given name. If you write int xyz; you're telling the compiler that you are going to use an int (that is, 4 bytes of memory) called xyz.

Susan: If that is the case, then why bother defining the int at all?

Steve: So that you (the programmer) can use a name that makes sense to you. If the compiler had to assign names itself, it wouldn't be very likely to give variables names that you would like!

Problem
Algorithms
Java
Interpreter
Hardware

The topic of the **import** statement was the cause of some discussion with Susan. Here's the play by play:

Susan: Is import a command?

Steve: Right; it's a command to the compiler.

Susan: Then what are the words we have been using for the most part called? Are those just called *code* or just *statements*? Can you make a list of commands to review?

Steve: The words that are defined in the language, such as if, while, for, and the like, are called *keywords*. User-defined names such as variable names are called *identifiers*.

Susan: So import WAJ.* is a code to tell the compiler that it is using info from the WAJ library?

Steve: Essentially correct; to be more precise, when we import WAJ.*, we're telling the compiler to look into the WAJ directory for definitions that we're going to use.

Susan: Then that WAJ file contains the secondary code of byte codes to transform RWVar.readInt and RWVar.readString into something workable?

Steve: Actually, it's in the WAJ directory, not the WAJ file, but you're on the right track.

Susan: So the import statement file directs the compiler to that section in the library where that byte code is stored? In other words, it is like telling the compiler to look in section XXX to find the byte code?

Steve: Right.

Problem
Algorithms
Java
Interpreter
Hardware

Finally, the closing curly brace, }, tells the compiler that it can stop compiling the current block, which in this case is the one called main. Without this marker, the compiler would tell us that we have a missing }, which of course would be true.

Novice Alert

Susan decided a little later in our collaboration that she wanted to try to reproduce this program just by considering the English description, without looking at my solution. She didn't quite make it without peeking, but the results are illuminating nevertheless.

Susan: What I did was to cover your code with a sheet of paper and just tried to get the next line without looking, and then if I was totally stumped, I would look. Anyway, when I saw that if statement, then I knew what the next statement would be but I am still having problems with writing backwards. For example:

```
if (CurrentWeight > HighestWeight)
    HighestWeight = CurrentWeight;
```

That is so confusing because we just want to say that if the current weight is higher than the highest weight, then the current weight will be the new highest weight, so I want to write CurrentWeight = HighestWeight. Anyway, when I really think about it, I know it makes sense to do it the right way; I'm just having a hard time thinking like that. Any suggestions on how to think backward?

Steve: What that statement means is "*set* HighestWeight *to the current value of* CurrentWeight". The point here is that = does *not* mean "is equal to"; it means "set the variable to the left of the = to the value of the expression to the right of the =". It's a lousy way of saying that, but that's what it means.

Susan: Anyway, then maybe I am doing something wrong, and I am tired, but after I compiled the program and ran it, I saw that the HighestWeight label was run in together with the highest number and the next sentence, which said "Please enter the next weight". All those things were on the same line and I thought that looked weird; I tried to fix it but the best I had the stamina for at the moment was to put a space between the " and the P, to at least make a separation.

Steve: It sounds as though you need some printlns in there to separate the lines.

Now it's time for some review on what we've covered in this chapter.

Problem
Algorithms
Java
Interpreter
Hardware

Review

We started out by discussing the tremendous reliability of computers; whenever you hear "it's the computer's fault", the overwhelming likelihood is that the software is to blame rather than the hardware. Then we took a look at the fact that, although computers are calculating engines, many of the functions for which we use them don't have much to do with numeric calculations; for example, the most common use of computers is probably word processing, which doesn't use much in the way of addition or subtraction. Nevertheless, we started out our investigation of programming with numeric variables, which are easier to understand than non-numeric ones. To use variables, we need to write a Java program, which consists primarily of a list of operations to be performed by the computer, along with directions that influence how these operations are to be translated into byte codes.

That led us into a discussion of why and how our Java program is translated into byte codes by a *compiler*. We examined an example program that contained simple *source code statement*s, including some that define variables and others that use those variables and constants to calculate results. We covered the symbols that are used to represent the operations of addition, subtraction, multiplication, division, and *assignment*, which are +, –, *, /, and =, respectively. Whereas the first four of these should be familiar to you, the last one is a programming notion rather than a mathematical one. This may be confusing because the operation of assignment is expressed by the = sign, but is *not* the same as mathematical equality. For example, the statement x = 3; does *not* mean "x is equal to 3", but rather "set the variable x to the value 3".

Then we spent some time pretending to be a compiler, to see how a simple Java program looks from that point of view, in order to improve our understanding of what the compiler does with our programs. This exercise involved keeping track of the locations of variables and instructions, and watching the effect of the instructions on the stack and variables. During this exploration of the machine, we got acquainted with the *byte-code* representation of instructions, which is the actual form of a program that the *Java interpreter* can understand. After a detailed examination of what the compiler does with our source code at *compile time*, we followed what would happen at *run time* (that is, if the sample program were actually executed by the Java interpreter).

Problem
Algorithms
Java
Interpreter
Hardware

Then we began to look at two data types that can hold non-numeric data, namely, the char and the String. The char occupies to 2 bytes of storage, corresponding to one character of data. Examples of appropriate values for a char variable include letters (a–z, A–Z), digits (0–9), and special characters (e.g., ! @ # $ %), as well as "nonprintable" characters such as the "space", which causes output to move to the next character position on the screen.

One char isn't much information, so we often want to deal with groups of them as a single unit; an example would be a person's name. This is the province of the String variable type: Variables of this type can handle an indefinitely long group of chars.

At the beginning of our sample program for Strings and chars, we encountered the line public static void main(String args[ ]), which indicates where we want to start executing our program. A Java program always starts execution at the place indicated by such a line.

As we continued looking at the sample program for Strings and chars, we saw how to assign literal values to both of these types, and noticed that two different types of quotes are used to mark off the literal values: the single quote ('), which is used in pairs to surround a literal char value consisting of exactly one char, such as 'a'; and the double quote ("), which is used in pairs to surround a literal String value such as "This is a test".

This led us to the discussion of the way in which the compiler regulates our access to variables by their type, which is defined at compile time. This is called the *type system*; Java uses this *static type checking* to help make Java programs more robust than programs written in languages that use *dynamic type checking*, where these errors are not detected until run time.

After a short discussion of some of the special characters that have a predefined meaning to the compiler, we took an initial glance at the mechanisms that allow us to get information into and out of the computer, known as *I/O*. We looked at the println function, which provides display on the screen when coupled with the built-in destination called System.out. Immediately afterwards, we encountered the input function RWVar.inputString and its partner System.in, which team up to give us input from the keyboard.

Next, we went over some program organization concepts, including the if statement, which allows the program to choose between two alternatives; the while statement, which causes another statement to be executed while some condition is true; and the *block*, which allows several statements to be grouped together into one logical statement. Blocks are commonly used to enable several statements to be controlled by an if or while statement.

Problem
Algorithms
Java
Interpreter
Hardware

At last we were ready to write a simple program that does something resembling useful work, and we did just that. The starting point for this program, as with all programs, was to define exactly what the program should do; in this case, the task was to keep track of the pumpkin with the highest weight at a county fair. The next step was to define a solution to this problem in precise terms. Then we broke the solution down into steps small enough to be translated directly into Java. Of course, the next step after that was to do that translation. Finally, we went over the Java code, line by line, to see what each line of the program did.

Now that the review is out of the way, we're about ready to continue with some more Java in Chapter 4. First, though, let's step back a bit and see where we are right now.

Conclusion

We've come a long way from the beginning of this chapter. Starting from basic information on how the hardware works, we've made it through our first actual, runnable program. By now, you should have a much better idea whether you're going to enjoy programming (and this book). Assuming you aren't discouraged on either of these points, let's proceed to gather some more tools, so we can undertake a bigger project.

Answers to Exercises

1. Susan's answer to this problem follows, after a short discussion about formatting the output of this program to make it look better. While we're on the topic of formatting, the reason that this program uses two lines to produce the sentence "Please type in the number of guests of your dinner party." is so that the program listing will fit on the page properly. If you prefer, you can combine those into one line that says System.out.print("Please type in the number of guests of your dinner party. ");. Of course, this also applies to the next exercise.

    Here's that conversation about formatting the output of this program to make it look better:

    Steve: By the way, you might want to add a " " in front of the is in is ready, so that the number doesn't run up against the is. That would make the line look like this: System.out.println("A table for " + n + " is ready. ");

    Susan: Okay.

And Figure 3.23, as promised, is Susan's answer to the first dinner party exercise.

```
Problem
Algorithms
Java
Interpreter
Hardware
```

```
import WAJ.*;

public class Basic05
{
    public static void main( String args[ ] )
    {
        int n;

        System.out.print("Please type in the number of guests ");
        System.out.print("of your dinner party. ");
        n = RWVar.readInt(System.in);
        n = n + 1;

        System.out.println("A table for " + n + "is ready. ");
    }
}
```

Figure 3.23: First dinner party program (code\basic05\basic05.java)

To use the debugger for this program, follow the instructions in the section titled "Using the debugger" in the file "\readme.txt" on the CD in the back of the book. These instructions assume that you've installed the examples on drive C:, so that the location of this program is "c:\whosj\code\basic05".

2.   Susan didn't have too much trouble with this one, but did have some questions on how to use else. First, here's our discussion.

Problem
Algorithms
Java
Interpreter
Hardware

> **Steve**: Congratulations on getting your program to work!

> **Susan**: Now, let me ask you this: Can you ever modify else? That is, could I have written else (n>20), or does else always stand alone?

> **Steve**: You can make the controlled block of an if statement or an else statement another if or else. In fact, you can have as many "nested" if or else statements as you wish; however, it's best to avoid very deep nesting because it tends to confuse the next programmer who has to read the program.
>   Figure 3.24 is an example of an else whose controlled block is an if statement.

```
if (x < y)
  {
  System.out.println("x is less than y");
  else
    {
    if (x > y)
       System.out.println("x is greater than y");
    else
       System.out.println("x must be equal to y!");
    }
  }
```

Figure 3.24: else if example

As promised, Figure 3.25 is Susan's answer to exercise 2.

```
import WAJ.*;

public class Basic06
{
  public static void main( String args[ ] )
  {
    int n;

    System.out.print("Excluding yourself, please type the ");
    System.out.print("number of guests in your dinner party.\n");

    n = RWVar.readInt(System.in);

    it (n>20)
        System.out.println("Sorry, your party is too large. ");
    else
      {
      n = n + 1;
      System.out.println("A table for " + n + " is ready. ");
      }
  }
}
```

Problem
Algorithms
Java
Interpreter
Hardware

Figure 3.25: Second dinner party program (code\basic06\basic06.java)

To use the debugger for this program, follow the instructions in the section titled "Using the debugger" in the file "\readme.txt" on the CD in the back of the book. These instructions assume that you've installed the examples on drive C:, so that the location of this program is "c:\whosj\code\basic06".

3.   The program should look like Figure 3.26.

```
import WAJ.*;

public class Basic07
{
    public static void main( String args[ ] )
    {
        String name;
        int age;

        System.out.print("What is your name? ");
        name = RWVar.readString(System.in);

        System.out.println("Thank you, " + name);

        System.out.print("What is your age? ");
        age = RWVar.readInt(System.in);

        if (age < 47)
            System.out.println("My, what a youngster!");
        else
            System.out.println("Hi, Granny!");
    }
}
```

```
Problem
Algorithms
Java
Interpreter
Hardware
```

Figure 3.26: Name and age program (code\basic07\basic07.java)

One point that might be a bit puzzling in this program is why it's not necessary to use println in the lines that send data to System.out before we ask the user for input. For example, in the sequence

```
System.out.print("What is your age? ");
age = RWVar.readInt(System.in);
```

how do we know that the literal String "What is your name? " has been displayed on the terminal before the user has to type in the answer? Obviously, it would be hard for the user to answer our request for information without a clue as to what we're asking for.

As it happens, this is handled by the RWVar.readInt facility. When we use that facility to do output to the screen and input from the keyboard, we can be sure that any screen output we have already requested will be displayed before any input is requested from the user via the keyboard.

4.   Figure 3.27 shows Susan's program, which is followed by our discussion.

```
import WAJ.*;

public class Basic08
{
    public static void main( String args[ ] )
    {
        String answer;

        System.out.print("Please respond to the following statement ");
        System.out.print("with either yes or no\n");

        System.out.print("Susan is the world's most tenacious novice.\n");
        answer = RWVar.readString(System.in);

        if (answer.equals("yes") == false)
            if (answer.equals("no") == false)
                System.out.println("Please answer with either yes or no.");

        if (answer.equals("yes"))
            System.out.print("Your answer is correct\n");

        if (answer.equals("no"))
            System.out.print("Your answer is erroneous\n");
    }
}
```

Problem
Algorithms
Java
Interpreter
Hardware

Figure 3.27: Novice program (code\basic08\basic08.java)

Susan: Steve, look at this. It even runs!

Also, I wanted to ask you one more question about this program. I wanted to put double quotes around the words *yes* and *no* in the third output statement because I wanted to emphasize those words, but I didn't know if the compiler could deal with that so I left it out. Would that have worked if I had?

Steve: Not if you just added quotes, because " is a special character that means "beginning or end of literal String". Here's what you would have to do to make it work:

```
System.out.println("Please answer with either \"yes\" or \"no\".");
```

The \ is a way of telling the compiler to treat the next character differently from its normal usage. In this case, we are telling the compiler to treat the special character " as "not special"; that is, \" means "just the character double quote, please, and no nonsense". This is called an *escape*, because it allows you to get out of the trap of having a " mean something special. We also use the \ to tell the compiler to treat a "non-special" character as "special"; for example, we use it to make up special characters that don't have any visual representation. An example is '\n', the "newline" character, which means "start a new line on the screen".

Susan: So if we want to write some character that means something "special", then we have to use a \ in front of it to tell the compiler to treat it like a "regular" character?

Steve: Right.

Susan: And if we want to write some character that is "regular" and make it do something "special", then we have to use a \ in front of it to tell the compiler that it means something "special"? That's weird.

Steve: It may be weird, but that's the way it works.

Susan: I just now got it. I was going to say, why would you put the first quotation mark before the slash, but now I see. Since you are doing a newline character, you have to have quotes on both sides to surround it which you don't usually have to do because the first quotes are usually started at the beginning of the sentence, and in this case the quote was already ended. OK, thanks for clearing that up.

Steve: You've got it.

Susan: Another thing I forgot is how you refer to the statements in () next to the if keywords; what do you call the info that is in there?

Steve: The condition.

```
Problem
Algorithms
Java
Interpreter
Hardware
```

To use the debugger for this program, follow the instructions in the section titled "Using the debugger" in the file "\readme.txt" on the CD in the back of the book. These instructions assume that you've installed the examples on drive C:, so that the location of this program is "c:\whosj\code\basic08".

5.   Figure 3.28 is Susan's version of this program.

```java
import WAJ.*;

public class Basic09
{
   public static void main( String args[ ] )
   {

      int x;

      System.out.print("Elena can increase her $10 allowance each week ");
      System.out.println("by adding new chores.");

      System.out.print("For every extra chore Elena does, she gets ");
      System.out.println("another dollar.");

      System.out.println("How many extra chores were done? ");
      x = RWVar.readInt(System.in);

      if (x==0)
         {
         System.out.print("There is no extra allowance for Elena ");
         System.out.println("this week. ");
         }
      else
         {
         x = x + 10;
         System.out.print("Elena will now earn " + x);
         System.out.println(" dollars this week.");
         }
   }
}
```

Problem
Algorithms
Java
Interpreter
Hardware

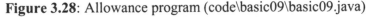

Figure 3.28: Allowance program (code\basic09\basic09.java)

To use the debugger for this program, follow the instructions in the section titled "Using the debugger" in the file "\readme.txt" on the CD in the back of the book. These instructions assume that you've installed the examples on drive C:, so that the location of this program is "c:\whosj\code\basic09".

6.   Figure 3.29 is an answer to this problem.

```java
import WAJ.*;

public class Basic10
{
    public static void main( String args[ ] )
    {
        char c1;
        String grade;
        String s1;
        String s2;
        String s3;

        System.out.print("What grade did you get? ");
        grade = RWVar.readString(System.in);

        if (grade.equals("A"))
            s1 = "Congratulations! ";
        else if (grade.equals("B"))
            s1 = "Congratulations. ";
        else
            s1 = "";

        if (grade.equals("A"))
            s2 = "You got an ";
        else
            s2 = "You got a ";

        s3 = " on the test.";

        System.out.println( s1 + s2 + grade + s3);
    }
}
```

```
Problem
Algorithms
Java
Interpreter
Hardware
```

Figure 3.29: Grading program (code\basic10\basic10.java)

To use the debugger for this program, follow the instructions in the section titled "Using the debugger" in the file "\readme.txt" on the CD in the back of the book. These instructions assume that you've installed the examples on drive C:, so that the location of this program is "c:\whosj\code\basic10".

Chapter 4

More Basics

A Modest Proposal

Now that we have seen how to write a simple program in Java, it's time to acquire some more tools. We'll extend our example program from Chapter 3 for finding the heaviest pumpkin. Eventually, we want to provide the weights of the three heaviest pumpkins, so that first, second, and third prizes can be awarded. It might seem that this would require just a minor modification of the previous program, in which we would keep track of the heaviest so far, second heaviest so far, and third heaviest so far, rather than merely the heaviest so far. However, this modification turns out to be a bit more complicated than it seems. Since this book is intended to teach you how to program using Java, rather than just how to use the Java language, it's worth investigating why this is so. First, though, here are some definitions and objectives for this chapter.

Definitions

An **array** is a group of *elements* of the same type; for example, we can create an array of chars. The array name corresponds to the address of the first of these elements; the other elements follow the first one immediately in memory. We can refer to the individual elements by their indexes; so, if we have an array of chars called m_Data, m_Data[i] refers to the ith char in the array.

An **element** is one of the *variables* that makes up an array.

A **for statement** is a *loop control statement* that causes its *controlled block* to be executed while a specified logical expression (the *continuation expression*) is true. It also provides for a *starting expression* to be executed before the first execution of the controlled statement, and a *modification expression* to be executed after every execution of the controlled statement. For example, in the for statement for (i = 0; i < 10; i ++), the initialization expression is i = 0, the continuation expression is i < 10, and the modification expression is i ++.

Objectives for This Chapter

By the end of this chapter, you should:

```
Problem
Algorithms
Java
Interpreter
Hardware
```

1. Understand the likelihood of error in even a small change to a program.
2. Be aware that even seemingly small changes in a problem can result in large changes in the program that solves the problem.
3. Have some understanding of the type of thinking needed to solve problems with programming.
4. Understand the selection sorting algorithm for arranging values in order.
5. Understand how to use an array to maintain a number of values under one name.
6. Be able to use the for statement to execute program statements a (possibly varying) number of times.
7. Be familiar with the arithmetic operators ++ and +=, which are used to modify the value of variables.

Algorithmic Thinking

Let's take our program modification one step at a time, starting with just the top two weights. Figure 4.1 is one possible way to handle this version of the problem.

```
import WAJ.*;

public class Pump1a
{
  public static void main( String args[ ] )
  {
      int CurrentWeight;
      int HighestWeight;
      int SecondHighestWeight;                              //1

      System.out.print("Please enter the first weight: ");
      CurrentWeight = RWVar.readInt(System.in);
      HighestWeight = CurrentWeight;
      SecondHighestWeight = 0;                              //2
      System.out.println("Current weight "  + CurrentWeight);
      System.out.println("Highest weight "  + HighestWeight);

      while (CurrentWeight > 0)
         {
          System.out.print("Please enter the next weight: ");
          CurrentWeight = RWVar.readInt(System.in);
          if (CurrentWeight > HighestWeight)
             {
              SecondHighestWeight = HighestWeight;          //3
              HighestWeight = CurrentWeight;
             }
          System.out.println("Current weight "  + CurrentWeight);
          System.out.println("Highest weight "  + HighestWeight);
          System.out.print("Second highest weight ");       //4
          System.out.println(SecondHighestWeight);          //5
         }
  }
}
```

Problem
Algorithms
Java
Interpreter
Hardware

Figure 4.1: Finding the top two weights, first try
(code\pump1a\pump1a.java)

The reasons behind some of the new code should be fairly obvious, but we'll go over them anyway. The new lines have numbered comments //1 through //5 so you can find them easily. First, of course, we need a new variable, SecondHighestWeight, to hold the current value of the second-highest weight we've seen so far (line //1). Then, when the first weight is entered, the statement SecondHighestWeight = 0; sets the SecondHighestWeight to 0 (line //2). After all, there isn't any second-highest weight when we've only seen one weight. The first nonobvious change is the addition of the statement

SecondHighestWeight = HighestWeight;, which copies the old HighestWeight to SecondHighestWeight, whenever there's a new highest weight (line //3). On reflection, however, this should make sense; when a new high is detected, the old high must be the second-highest value (so far). Also, we have to copy the old HighestWeight to SecondHighestWeight before we change HighestWeight. After we have set HighestWeight to a new value, it's too late to copy its old value into SecondHighestWeight. Finally, of course, we have to display the last value of the second highest weight (lines //4 and //5).

First, let's see how Susan viewed this solution:

Susan: I noticed that you separate out the main program {} from the other {} by indenting. Is that how the compiler knows which set of {} goes to which statements and doesn't confuse them with the main ones that are the body of the program?

Steve: The compiler doesn't care about indentation at all; that's just for the people reading the program. All the compiler cares about is the number of { it has seen so far without matching }. There aren't any hard rules about this; it's a "religious" issue in Java, where different programmers can't agree on the best way.

Problem
Algorithms
Java
Interpreter
Hardware

Susan: Now on this thing with setting SecondHighestWeight to 0. Is that initializing it? See, I know what you are doing, and yet I can't see the purpose of doing this clearly, unless it is initializing, and then it makes sense.

Steve: That's correct.

Susan: How do you know how to order your statements? For example, why did you put the SecondHighestWeight = HighestWeight; above the other statement? What would happen if you reversed that order?

Steve: Think about it. Let's suppose that

    CurrentWeight is 40
    HighestWeight is 30
    SecondHighestWeight is 15

and the statements were executed in the following order:

1. HighestWeight = CurrentWeight
2. SecondHighestWeight = HighestWeight

What would happen to the values? Well, statement 1 would set HighestWeight to CurrentWeight, so the values would be like this:

> CurrentWeight is 40
> HighestWeight is 40
> SecondHighestWeight is 15

Then statement 2 would set SecondHighestWeight to HighestWeight, leaving the situation as follows:

> CurrentWeight is 40
> HighestWeight is 40
> SecondHighestWeight is 40

This is clearly wrong. The problem is that we need the value of HighestWeight *before* it is set to the value of CurrentWeight, not afterward. After that occurs, the previous value is lost.

Susan: Yes, that is apparent; I was just wondering if the computer had to read it in the order that you wrote it, being that it was grouped together in the {}. For example, you said that the compiler doesn't read the {} as we write them, so I was wondering if it read those statements as we write them. Obviously it has to. So then everything descends in a progression downward and outward, as you get more detailed in the instructions.

To use the debugger for this program, follow the instructions in the section titled "Using the debugger" in the file "\readme.txt" on the CD in the back of the book. These instructions assume that you've installed the examples on drive C:, so that the location of this program is "c:\whosj\code\pump1a".

```
Problem
Algorithms
Java
Interpreter
Hardware
```

A Prize Catch

This program may seem to keep track of the highest and second-highest weights correctly, but in fact there's a hole in the logic. To be exact, it doesn't work correctly when the user enters a new value that's less than the previous high value but more than the previous second-high value. In that case, the new value should be the second-high value, even though there's no new high value. For example, suppose that you enter the following weights: 5, 2, 11, 3, 7. If we were to update SecondHighestWeight only when we see a new high, our program would indicate that 11 was the high, and 5 the second highest; since neither 3 nor 7 is a new high, SecondHighestWeight would remain as it was when the 11 was entered.

Here's what ensued when Susan tried out the program and discovered this problem:

Susan: Steve, the program! I have been playing with it. Hey, this is fun, but look, it took me a while. I had to go over it and over it, and then I was having trouble getting it to put current weights that were higher than second weights into the second-highest weight slot. For example, if I had a highest weight of 40 and the the second-highest weight of 30 and then selected 35 for a current weight, it wouldn't accept 35 as the second-highest weight. It increased the highest weights just fine and it didn't change anything if I selected a lower number of the two for a current weight. Or did you mean to do that to make a point? I am supposed to find the problem? I bet that is what you are doing.

Steve: Yep, and I'm not sorry, either.<G>

Susan: You just had to do this to me, didn't you? OK, what you need to do is to put in a statement that says if the current weight is greater than the second-highest weight, then set the second-highest weight to the current weight, as illustrated in Figure 4.2.

```
else
    {
    if (CurrentWeight > Second HighestWeight)
        Second HighestWeight = CurrentWeight;
    }
```

Problem
Algorithms
Java
Interpreter
Hardware

Figure 4.2: Susan's version of an if statement with an else clause

I hope you are satisfied.

Steve: Satisfied? Well, no, I wouldn't use that word. How about ecstatic? You have just figured out a bug in a program, and determined what the solution is. Don't tell me you don't understand how a program works.

Now I have to point out something about your code. I understood what you wrote perfectly. Unfortunately, compilers aren't very smart, and therefore have to be extremely picky. So you have to make sure to spell the variable names correctly. This would make your answer like the if clause shown in Figure 4.3.

Congratulations again.

As Susan figured out, we have to add an else clause to our if statement, so that the corrected version of the statement looks like Figure 4.3.

```
if (CurrentWeight > HighestWeight)
    {
    SecondHighestWeight = HighestWeight;
    HighestWeight = CurrentWeight;
    }
else
    {
    if (CurrentWeight > SecondHighestWeight)
        SecondHighestWeight = CurrentWeight;
    }
```

Figure 4.3: Using an if statement with an else clause

In this case, the condition in the first if is checking whether CurrentWeight is greater than the previous HighestWeight; when this is true, we have a new HighestWeight and need to update both HighestWeight and SecondHighestWeight. However, if CurrentWeight is not greater than HighestWeight, the else clause is executed. This else contains another if that checks whether CurrentWeight is greater than the current value of SecondHighestWeight. If so, SecondHighestWeight is set to the value of CurrentWeight.

What happens if two (or more) pumpkins are tied for the highest weight? In that case, the first one of them to be encountered is going to set HighestWeight, as it will be the highest yet encountered. When the second pumpkin of the same weight is seen, it won't trigger a change to HighestWeight, since it's not higher than the current occupant of that variable. It will pass the test in the else clause, if (CurrentWeight > SecondHighestWeight), however, which will cause SecondHighestWeight to be set to the same value as HighestWeight. This is reasonable behavior, unlikely to startle the (hypothetical) user of the program, and therefore is good enough for our purposes. In a real application program, we'd have to try to determine what the user of this program would want us to do.

Figure 4.4 shows the corrected program. To use the debugger for this program, follow the instructions in the section titled "Using the debugger" in the file "\readme.txt" on the CD in the back of the book. Assuming that you've installed the examples on drive C:, the location of this program is "c:\whosj\code\pump2".

```
Problem
Algorithms
Java
Interpreter
Hardware
```

```
import WAJ.*;

public class Pump2
{
    public static void main( String args[ ] )
    {
        int CurrentWeight;
        int HighestWeight;
        int SecondHighestWeight;

        System.out.print("Please enter the first weight: ");
        CurrentWeight = RWVar.readInt(System.in);
        HighestWeight = CurrentWeight;
        SecondHighestWeight = 0;
        System.out.println("Current weight " + CurrentWeight);
        System.out.println("Highest weight " + HighestWeight);

        while (CurrentWeight > 0)
            {
            System.out.print("Please enter the next weight: ");
            CurrentWeight = RWVar.readInt(System.in);
            if (CurrentWeight > HighestWeight)
                {
                SecondHighestWeight = HighestWeight;
                HighestWeight = CurrentWeight;
                }
            else
                {
                if (CurrentWeight > SecondHighestWeight)
                    SecondHighestWeight = CurrentWeight;
                }
            System.out.println("Current weight " + CurrentWeight);
            System.out.println("Highest weight " + HighestWeight);
            System.out.println("Second highest weight " + SecondHighestWeight);
            }
    }
}
```

Problem
Algorithms
Java
Interpreter
Hardware

Figure 4.4: Finding the top two weights (code\pump2\pump2.java)

By the way, since we've just been using the if statement pretty heavily, this would be a good time to list all of the conditions that it can test. We've already seen some of them, but it can't hurt to have them all in one place. Figure 4.5 lists these conditions with translations.

Condition Symbol	Controlled block will be executed if:
>	First item is larger than second item.
<	First item is smaller than second item.
>=	First item is larger than or equal to second item.
<=	First item is smaller than or equal to second itcm.
!=	First item differs from second item.
==	First item has the same value as the second item.

Figure 4.5: What if?

You may wonder why we have to use == to test for equality rather than just =. That's because = means "assign right-hand value to variable on left", rather than "compare two items for equality".

Susan had some questions about these comparison operators.

Susan: Are these always conditions of if statements? Aren't they used for anything else?

Steve: Yes. They're used in while and for loops.

Susan: I knew that.

Steve: Sometimes they're also used to do a comparison and save the result for later use.

Susan: I didn't know that.

Steve: You learn something every day (if you're lucky).

Problem
Algorithms
Java
Interpreter
Hardware

What a Tangled Web We Weave

I hope this excursion has given you some appreciation of the subtleties that await in even the simplest change to a working program; many experienced programmers still underestimate such difficulties and the amount of time that may be needed to ensure that the changes are correct. I don't think it's necessary to continue along the same path with a program that can award three prizes. The principle is the same, although the complexity of the code grows with the number of special cases we have to handle. Obviously, a solution that could handle any number of prizes without special cases would be a big improvement, but it will require some major changes in the organization of the program. That's what we'll take up next.

You May Already Have Won

One of the primary advantages of the method we've used so far to find the heaviest pumpkin(s) is that we didn't have to save the weights of all the pumpkins as we went along. If we don't mind saving all the weights, then we can solve the "three prize" problem in a different way. Let's assume for the purpose of simplicity that there are only five weights to be saved, in which case the solution looks like this:

1.   Read in all of the weights.
2.   Make a list consisting of the three highest weights in descending order.
3.   Award the first, second, and third prizes, in that order, to the three entries in the list of highest weights.

```
Problem
Algorithms
Java
Interpreter
Hardware
```

Now let's break those down into substeps which can be more easily translated into Java.

1.   Rcad in all of the weights.
     a.   Read first number.
     b.   Read next number.
     c.   If we haven't read five weights yet, go back to 1b.

Now we have all the numbers; proceed to calculation phase.

2.   Make a list consisting of the three highest weights in descending order.
     a.   Find the largest number in the original list of weights.
     b.   Copy it to the sorted list.
     c.   If we haven't found the three highest numbers, go back to 2a.

Oops. That's not going to work, since we'll get the same number each time.[1]

To prevent that from happening, we have to mark off each number as we select it. Here's the revised version of step 2:

2.   Make a list consisting of the three highest weights in descending order.
     a.   Find the largest number in the original list of weights.
     b.   Copy it to the sorted list.
     c.   Mark it off in the original list of weights, so we don't select it again.
     d.   If we haven't found the three highest numbers, go back to 2a.

Now we're ready for output.

3.   Award the first, second, and third prizes, in that order, to the three entries in the list of highest weights.
     a.   Write first number.
     b.   Write another number.
     c.   If we haven't done them all, go back to 3b.

Unlike our previous approach, this obviously can be generalized to handle any number of prizes. However, we have to address two problems before we can use this approach: First, how do we keep track of the weights? And second, how do we select out the highest three weights? Both of these problems are much easier to solve if we don't have a separate variable for each weight.

```
Problem
Algorithms
Java
Interpreter
Hardware
```

Variables, by the Numbers

The solution to our first question is to use an **array**. This is a variable containing a number of "sub-variables" that can be addressed by position in the array; each of these sub-variables is called an **element**. An array has a name, just like a regular variable, but the elements do not. Instead, each element has a number, corresponding to its position in the array. For example, we might want to create an

---

1. I realize I'm breaking a cardinal rule of textbooks: Never admit that the solution to a problem is anything but obvious, so the student who doesn't see it immediately feels like an idiot. In reality, even a simple program is difficult to get right, and indicating the sort of thought processes that go into analyzing a programming problem might help demystify this difficult task.

array of int values called Weight, with five elements. To do this, we would write this line: int[ ] Weight = new int[5];.[2]

We haven't heard from Susan for a while, but the following exchange should make up for that.

> **Susan**: So then using an array is just another way of writing this same program, only making it a little more efficient?
>
> **Steve**: In this case, the new program can do more than the old program could: The new program can easily be changed to handle virtually any number of prizes, whereas the old program couldn't.
>
> **Susan**: So there is more than one way to write a program that does basically the same thing?
>
> **Steve**: As many ways as there are to write a book about the same topic.
>
> **Susan**: I find this to be very odd. I mean, on the one hand the code seems to be so unrelentingly exact; on the other, it can be done in as many ways as there are artists to paint the same flower. That must be where the creativity comes in. Then I would expect that the programs should behave in different manners, yet accomplish the same goal.
>
> **Steve**: It's possible for two programs to produce similar (or even exactly the same) results from the user's perspective and yet work very differently internally. For example, the array version of the weighing program could produce exactly the same final results as the original version, even though the method of finding the top two weights was quite different.

```
Problem
Algorithms
Java
Interpreter
Hardware
```

Now we can refer to the individual elements of the array called Weight by using their numbers, enclosed in **square brackets** ([ ]); the number in the brackets is called the **index**.[3] Here are some examples:

```
Weight[1] = 123;
Weight[2] = 456;
Weight[3] = Weight[1] + Weight[2];
Weight[i+1] = Weight[i] + 5;
```

---

2. We'll see how arrays work in more detail in Chapters 6 and 8.

3. By the way, if you're wondering how to pronounce Weight[i], it's "weight sub i". "Sub" is short for **subscript**, which is an old term for "index".

As these examples indicate, an element of an array can be used anywhere a "regular" variable can be used.[4] But the most valuable difference between a regular variable and an element of an array is that we can vary which element we are referring to in a given statement, by varying its index. Take a look at the last sample line, in which two elements of the array Weight are used; the first one is element i+1 and the other is element i. As this indicates, we don't have to use a constant value for the element number but can calculate it while the program is executing; in this case, if i is 1, the two elements referred to are element 2 and element 1, while if i is 5, the two elements are elements 6 and 5, respectively.

The ability to refer to an element of an array by number rather than by name allows us to write statements that can refer to any element in an array, depending on the value of the index variable in the statements. Figure 4.6, which solves our three-prize problem, shows how this works in practice.

To use the debugger for this program, follow the instructions in the section titled "Using the debugger" in the file "\readme.txt" on the CD in the back of the book. These instructions assume that you've installed the examples on drive C:, so that the location of this program is "c:\whosj\code\vect1".

This program uses several new features of Java which need some explanation. First, of course, there is the line that defines the array Weight:

```
int[ ] Weight = new int[5];
```

As you might have guessed, this means that we want an array of five elements, each of which is an int. As we have already seen, this means that there are five distinct index values, each of which refers to one element. However, what isn't so obvious is what those five distinct index values actually are. You might expect them to be 1, 2, 3, 4, and 5; actually, they are 0, 1, 2, 3, and 4.

This method of referring to elements in an array is called **zero-based indexing**. Although it might seem arbitrary to start counting at 0 rather than at 1, assembly language programmers find it perfectly natural, because the calculation of the address of an element is simpler with such indexing; the formula is "(address of first element) + (element number) * (size of element)".

Problem
Algorithms
Java
Interpreter
Hardware

---

4. What I'm calling a *regular variable* here is technically known as a **scalar variable**; that is, one with only one value at any given time.

```
import WAJ.*;

public class Vect1
{
  public static void main( String args[ ] )
  {
    int[ ] Weight = new int[5];
    int[ ] SortedWeight = new int[3];
    int HighestWeight;
    int HighestIndex;
    int i;
    int k;

    System.out.println("I'm going to ask you to type in five weights, in pounds.");

    for (i = 0; i < 5; i ++)
      {
      k = i + 1;
      System.out.print("Please type in weight #" + k  + ": ");
      Weight[i] = RWVar.readInt(System.in);
      }

    for (i = 0; i < 3; i ++)
        {
        HighestWeight = 0;
        HighestIndex = 0;
        for (k = 0; k < 5; k ++)
            {
            if (Weight[k] > HighestWeight)
                {
                HighestWeight = Weight[k];
                HighestIndex = k;
                }
            }
        SortedWeight[i] = HighestWeight;
        Weight[HighestIndex] = 0;
        }

    System.out.println("The highest weight was: "  + SortedWeight[0]);
    System.out.println("The second highest weight was: "  + SortedWeight[1]);
    System.out.println("The third highest weight was: "  + SortedWeight[2]);
  }
}
```

Problem
Algorithms
Java
Interpreter
Hardware

Figure 4.6: Using an array (code\vect1\vect1.java)

Why does it matter what assembly language programmers find natural? This bit of history is relevant because C, a predecessor of Java, was originally intended to replace assembly language so that programs could be moved from one machine architecture to another with as little difficulty as possible. One reason for some of the eccentricities of Java is that it takes a lot of its syntax from C++ and its predecessor, C.[5]

The last two lines in the variable definition phase define two variables, called i and k, which have been traditional names for **index variables** (i.e., variables used to hold indexes) since at least the

---

5. Here's an interesting side note on a case where the inventors of a commonly used facility should have used zero-based indexing, but didn't. We're still suffering from the annoyances of this one.

Long ago, there was no standard calendar, with year numbers progressing from one to the next, when January 1st came around. Instead, years were numbered relative to the reign of the current monarch; for example, the Bible might refer to "the third year of Herod's reign". This was fine in antiquity, when most people really didn't care what year it was. There were few retirement plans or fiftieth wedding anniversaries to celebrate anyway. However, it was quite annoying to historians to try to calculate the age of someone who was born in the fourth year of someone's reign and died in the tenth year of someone else's. According to Grolier's Multimedia Encyclopedia:

"About AD 525, a monk named Dionysius Exiguus suggested that years be counted from the birth of Christ, which was designated AD (anno Domini, "the year of the Lord") 1. This proposal came to be adopted throughout Christendom during the next 500 years. The year before AD 1 is designated 1 BC (before Christ)."

The encyclopedia doesn't state when the use of the term BC started, but the fact that its translation is English is a suspicious sign indicating that this was considerably later. In any event, this number system made matters quite a bit easier. Now you could tell that someone who was born in AD 1200 and died in AD 1250 was approximately 50 years old at death.

Unfortunately, however, there was still a small problem. Zero hadn't yet made it to Europe from Asia when the new plan was adopted, so the new calendar numbered the years starting with 1, rather than 0; that is, the year after 1 BC was 1 AD. Although this may seem reasonable, it accounts for a number of oddities of our current calendar.

1.   Date ranges spanning AD and BC are hard to calculate, since you can't just treat BC as negative. For example, if someone were born in 1 BC and died in 1 AD, how old was that person? You might think that this could be calculated as $1 - (-1)$, or 2; however, the last day of 1 BC immediately preceded the first day of 1 AD, so the person might have been only a few days old.

2.   The twentieth century consists of the years 1901 to 2000; the year numbers of all but the last year of that century actually start with the digits *19* rather than *20*.

3.   Similarly, the third millennium starts on January 1, 2001, not 2000.

The reason for the second and third of these oddities is that since the first century started in 1 AD, the second century had to start in 101 AD; if it started in 100 AD, the first century would have consisted of only 99 years (1–99), rather than 100.

If only they had known about the zero! Then the zeroth century would have started at the beginning of 0 AD and ended on the last day of 99 AD. The first century would have started at 100 AD, and so on; coming up to current time, we would be living through the last years of the nineteenth century, which would be defined as all of those years whose year numbers started with *19*. The second millennium would start on January 1, 2000, as everyone would expect.

Problem
Algorithms
Java
Interpreter
Hardware

invention of FORTRAN in the 1950s.[6] The inventors of FORTRAN used a fairly simple method of determining the type of a variable: If it began with one of the letters I through N, it was an integer. Otherwise, it was a **floating-point variable** (i.e., one that can hold values that contain a fractional part, such as 3.876). This rule was later changed so that the user could specify what type the variable was, as we do in Java, but the default rules were the same as in the earlier versions of FORTRAN, to allow programs using the old rules to continue to compile and run correctly.

Needless to say, Susan had some questions about the names of index variables.

> **Susan**: So whenever you see i or k you know you are dealing with an array?

> **Steve**: Not necessarily. Variables named i and k are commonly used as indexes, but they are also used for other purposes sometimes.

> **Susan**: Anyway, if i and k are sometimes used for other purposes, then the compiler doesn't care what you use as indexes? Again, no rules, just customs?

> **Steve**: Right. It's just for the benefit of other programmers, who will see i and say "oh, this is probably an index variable".

```
Problem
Algorithms
Java
Interpreter
Hardware
```

I suspect one reason for the durability of these short names is that they're easy to type, and many programmers aren't very good typists.[7] In Java, the letters i, j, k, m, and n are commonly used as

---

6. Actually, the second most common index variable, after i, is probably j. However, I don't use j as an index variable in this book because in the font I use for program listings, the bottom curve of the j runs into the opening [and thus makes the listings hard to read.

7. I strongly recommend learning how to type (i.e., touch-type). I was a professional programmer without typing skills for over 10 years before agreeing to type (someone else's) book manuscript. At that point, I decided to teach myself to touch-type, so I wrote a *Dvorak keyboard* driver for my Radio Shack Model III computer and started typing. In about a month I could type faster than with my previous two finger method and eventually got up to 80+ words per minute on English text. If you've never heard of the Dvorak keyboard, it's the one that has the letters laid out in an efficient manner; the "home row" keys are AOEUIDHTNS rather than the absurd set ASDFGHJKL;. This "new" (1930s) keyboard layout reduces effort and increases speed and accuracy compared to the old QWERTY keyboard, which was invented in the 1880s to prevent people from typing two keys in rapid succession and jamming the type bars together. This problem has been nonexistent since the invention of the Selectric typewriter (which uses a ball rather than type bars) in the 1960s, but inertia keeps the old layout in use even though it is very inefficient.

In any event, since I learned to type, writing documentation has required much less effort. This applies especially to writing articles or books, which would be a painful process otherwise.

indexes; however, I (the letter "ell") generally isn't, because it looks too much like a 1 (the numeral one). The compiler doesn't get confused by this resemblance, but programmers very well might.

After the variable definitions are out of the way, we can proceed to the executable portion of our program. First, we type out a note to the user, stating what to expect, with the line:

System.out.println("I'm going to ask you to type in five weights, in pounds.");.

Then we get to the code in Figure 4.7.

```
for (i = 0; i < 5; i ++)
  {
  k = i + 1;
  System.out.print("Please type in weight #" + k + ": ");
  Weight[i] = RWVar.readInt(System.in);
  }
```

Figure 4.7: Using a for statement (from code\vect1\vect1.java)

The first line here is called a for **statement**, which is used to control a for **loop**; this is a loop control facility similar to the while loop we encountered in Chapter 3. The difference between these two statements is that a for loop allows us to specify more than just the condition under which the **controlled block** will be repetitively executed.[8]

A for statement specifies three expressions (separated by ";") that control the execution of the for loop: a starting expression, a continuation expression, and a modification expression. In our case, these are i = 0, i < 5, and i ++, respectively. Let's look at the function and meaning of each of these components.

First, the **starting expression**, i = 0. This is executed once, before the block controlled by the for statement is executed. In this case, we use it to set our index variable, i, to 0, which will refer to the first element of our Weight array.

Next, the **continuation expression**, i < 5. This specifies under what conditions the statement controlled by the for will be executed; in this case, we will continue executing the controlled statement as long as the value of i is less than 5. Be warned that the continuation

```
Problem
Algorithms
Java
Interpreter
Hardware
```

---

8. You may sometimes see the term *controlled statement* used in place of *controlled block*; since, as we have already seen, a block can be used anywhere that a single statement can be used, *controlled statement* and *controlled block* are actually just two ways of saying the same thing.

expression is actually executed *before* every execution of the controlled block; thus, if the continuation expression is false when the loop is entered, the controlled block will not be executed at all.

The notion of the continuation expression is apparently confusing to some novices. Susan fell into that group.

> **Susan**: In your definition of for, how come there is no ending expression? Why is it only a modification expression? Is there never a case for a conclusion?

> **Steve**: The "continuation expression" tells the compiler when you want to continue the loop; if the continuation expression comes out false, then the loop terminates. That serves the same purpose as an "ending expression" might, but in reverse.

Finally, let's consider the **modification expression**, i ++.[9] This is exactly equivalent to i = i + 1, which means "set i to one more than its current value", an operation technically referred to as **incrementing a variable**. You may wonder why we need two ways to say the same thing; actually, there are a few reasons. One is that ++ requires less typing, which as we know isn't a strong point of many programmers; also, the ++ (pronounced "plus plus") operator doesn't allow the possibility of mis-typing the statement as, for example, i = j + 1;, when you really meant to increment i. Another reason why this feature was added to the C language is that, in the early days of C, compiler technology wasn't very advanced, and the ++ operator allowed the production of more efficient programs. You see, many machines can add one to a memory location by a single machine language instruction, usually called something like *increment memory*. Even a simple compiler can generate an "increment memory" instruction as a translation of i ++, whereas it takes a bit more sophistication for the compiler to recognize i = i + 1 as an increment operation. Since incrementing a variable is a very common operation in C this was worth handling specially, and this special handling has been carried over into C++ and subsequently to Java.

Now that we have examined all the parts of the for statement, we can see that its translation into English would be something like this:

Problem
Algorithms
Java
Interpreter
Hardware

1.   Set the index variable i to 0.
2.   If the value of i is less than 5, execute the following block (in this case, the block with the System.out.print and RWVar.readInt

---

9. You don't need a space between the variable name and the ++ operator; however, I think it's easier to read this way.

statements). Otherwise, skip to the next statement after the end of the controlled block; that is, the one following the closing }.
3.   Add one to the value of i and go back to step 2.

Susan didn't think these steps were very clear. Let's listen in on the conversation that ensued.

Susan: Where in the for statement does it say to skip to the next statement after the end of the controlled block when i is 5 or more?

Steve: It doesn't have to. Remember, the point of {} is to make a group of statements act like one. A for statement always controls exactly one "statement", which can be a block contained in {}. Therefore, when the continuation expression is no longer true, the next "statement" to be executed is whatever follows the } at the end of the block.

Susan: Okay, now I get it. The {} work together with the < 5 to determine that the program should go on to the next statement.

Steve: Right.

Susan: Now, on the "controlled block" — so other statements can be considered controlled blocks too? I mean is a controlled block basically just the same thing as a block? I reviewed your definition of *block*, and it seems to me that they are. I guess it is just a statement that in this case is being controlled by for.

Problem
Algorithms
Java
Interpreter
Hardware

Steve: Correct. It's called a *controlled block* because it's under the control of another statement.

Susan: So if we used while before the {} then that would be a while controlled block?

Steve: Right.

Susan: Then where in step 3 or in i++ does it say to go back to step 2?

Steve: Again, the for statement executes one block (the *controlled block*) repeatedly until the continuation expression is false. Since a block is equivalent to one statement, the controlled block can also be referred to as the *controlled statement*. In the current example, the block that is controlled by the for loop consists of the following lines:

```
{
k = i + 1;
System.out.print("Please type in weight #"  + k  + ": ");
Weight[i] = RWVar.readInt(System.in);
}
```

Susan: Okay. But now I am a little confused about something else here. I thought that System.out statements were just things that you would type in to be seen on the screen.

Steve: That's correct, except that System.out is a variable used for I/O, not a statement.

Susan: So then why do we need that k thing? Can't we just say "Please type in weight #" + i + 1 +": "?

Steve: No, that won't work. If we wrote the line that way, it would start out by displaying "Please type in weight #01". This is another of the "features" of Java that I'm a little dubious about.[10] The problem is that the + sign doesn't mean "add" when one of the things being "added" is a String; instead, it means "add a String to the end of another String". Even if the second item being "added" isn't a String, that doesn't matter; it will be made into a String and then stuck onto the end of the first item. This is useful when we want to run a bunch of Strings and numbers together on a line, but it is a pain when we want to do arithmetic in that same line. Therefore, we have to create another variable called k that is set to i + 1 and use k in our System.out line. That way, the first time, it will say
    Please enter weight #1:
The second time, it will say
    Please enter weight #2:
and so on. The number of the weight we're asking for is one more than i; therefore, we set k to i + 1 before we get to the output statement so that it will stick the correct number into the output line at that point.

Susan: How does k end up as #1?

Steve: The first time, i is 0; therefore, when we set k to i + 1, the value of k is 1. The # comes from the end of the preceding part of the output statement. Let's assume that i is 0, as it will be the first time through the loop. In that case, if we were to write

System.out.print("Please type in weight #" + i + 1 +": ");

the compiler would think we wanted to do the following:

Problem
Algorithms
Java
Interpreter
Hardware

---

10. Okay, I'm *very* dubious.

1. Start with the String "Please type in weight #".
2. Convert the value of i to a String, producing the String value "0", and add this value to the end of the previous String, producing "Please type in weight #0".
3. Convert the value 1 to a String, producing the String value "1", and add this value to the end of the previous String, producing "Please type in weight #01".
4. Add the String value ": " to the end of the previous String, producing "Please type in weight #01: ".

This happens because + has two meanings, one for Strings and one for numbers. If *either* of the two expressions being "added" is a String, the compiler assumes you want the String +, which means to append the expression after the + to the expression before the +. If this means converting one or the other of these expressions to a String from whatever type it might be, that's what the compiler will do. Isn't Java a nice simple language?

Susan: That is dumb.

Steve: I can't say I'm terribly impressed by that design decision either, but if they didn't have some way to chain output items together the language would be even clumsier than it is now. That's why they broke their own rule against operator overloading in the case of Strings.

Problem
Algorithms
Java
Interpreter
Hardware

Now let's continue with the next step in the description of our for loop, the modification expression i ++. In our example, this will be executed five times. The first time, i will be 0, then 1, 2, 3, and finally 4. When the loop is executed for the fifth time, i will be incremented to 5; therefore, step 2 will end the loop by skipping to the next statement after the controlled block.[11] A bit of terminology is useful here: Each time through the loop is called an *iteration*.
Let's hear Susan's thoughts on this matter.

Susan: When you say that "step 2 will end the loop by skipping to the next statement after the controlled block", does that mean it is now going on to the next for statement? So when i is no longer less than 5, the completion of the loop signals the next controlled block?

Steve: In general, after all the iterations in a loop have been performed, execution proceeds to whatever statement follows the controlled block.

---

11. In case you're wondering why the value of i at the end of this loop will be 5, the reason is that at the end of each pass through the loop, the modification expression (i ++) is executed before the continuation expression that determines whether the next execution will take place (i < 5). Thus, at the end of the fifth pass through the loop, i is incremented to 5 and then tested to see if it is still less than 5. Since it isn't, the loop terminates at that point.

In this case, the next statement is indeed a for statement, so that's the next statement that is performed after the end of the current loop.

The discussion of the for statement led to some more questions about loop control facilities and the use of parentheses.

Susan: How do you know when to use ()? Is it only with if and for and while and else and stuff like that, whatever these statements are called? I mean they appear to be modifiers of some sort; is there a special name for them?

Steve: The term **loop control** applies to statements that control loops that can execute controlled blocks a (possibly varying) number of times; these include for and while. The if and else statements are somewhat different, since their controlled blocks are executed either once or not at all. The () are needed in those cases to indicate where the controlling expression(s) end and the controlled block begins. You can also use () to control the order of evaluation of an arithmetic expression: The part of the expression inside parentheses is executed first, regardless of normal ordering rules. For example, 2*5+3 is 13, while 2*(5+3) is 16.[12]

Susan: So if you just wrote while CurrentWeight > 0 with no (), then the compiler couldn't read it?

Problem
Algorithms
Java
Interpreter
Hardware

Steve: Correct.

Susan: Actually it is beginning to look to me as I scan over a few figures that almost everything has a caption of some sort surrounding it. Everything either has a " " or () or {} or [ ] or <> around it. Is that how it is going to be? I am still not clear on the different uses of () and {}; does it depend on the control loop?

Steve: The {} are used to mark the controlled block, while the () are used to mark the conditional expression(s) for the if, while, for, and the like. However, (and) also have other meanings in Java, which we'll get to eventually.

Susan: OK, I think I have it: {} define blocks and () define expressions. How am I to know when a new block starts? I mean if I were doing the writing, it would be like a new paragraph in English, right? So are there any rules for knowing when to stop one block and start another?

---

12. If you recall the problem that we had with printing an expression that had an arithmetic calculation in it (Figure 4.7), we could also have used () to cause the expression i + 1 to be executed before the String + operation, so that the line in question would have read System.out.print("Please type in weight #" + (i + 1) + ": ");. That would have eliminated the need for the extra variable k.

> **Steve**: It depends entirely on what you're trying to accomplish. The main purpose of a block is to make a group of statements act like one statement; therefore, for example, when you want to control a group of statements by one if or for, you group those statements into a block.

Now that we've examined the for statement in excruciating detail, what about the block it controls? We've already discussed the first and second statements in the block, k = i + 1; and System.out.print("Please type in weight #" + k + ": ");. As we've already seen, these two statements combine to generate a message to the user of the program indicating what value we're waiting for. When the second of these statements is executed during the first iteration of the loop, it will generate the output:

Please type in weight #1:

The same request, with a different value for the weight number, will show up each time the user hits ENTER, until five values have been accepted.

The third and final statement in the controlled block,

Weight[i] = RWVar.readInt(System.in);

Problem
Algorithms
Java
Interpreter
Hardware

is a little different. Here, we're waiting for the user to type a number in at the keyboard and storing it in a variable. Unlike our previous input statements, in this case the variable we're using is different each time through the loop: To be exact, it's the ith element of the Weight array. So, on the first iteration, the value the user types in will go into Weight[0]; the value accepted on the second iteration will go into Weight[1]; and so on, until on the fifth and last iteration, the typed-in value will be stored in Weight[4].

Here's Susan's take on this:

> **Susan**: Now I understand why you used the example of i = i + 1; in Chapter 3; before, it didn't make sense why you would do that silly thing. Anyway, now let me get this straight. To say that, in the context of this exercise, means you can keep adding 1 to the value of i? I am finding it hard to see where this works for the number 7, say, or anything above 5 for that matter. So, it just means you can have 4 +1 or + another 1, and so on? See where I am having trouble?

> **Steve**: Remember, an int variable such as i is just a name for a 4-byte area of RAM, which can hold any value between −2147483648 and 2147483647. Therefore, the statement i ++; means that we want to

recalculate the contents of that area of RAM by adding 1 to its former contents.

Susan: No, that is not the answer to my question. Yes, I know all that<G>. What I am saying is this: I assume that i ++; is the expression that handles any value over 4, right? Then let's say that you have pumpkins that weigh 1, 2, 3, 4, and 5 pounds, consecutively. No problem, but what if the next pumpkin was not 6 but say 7 pounds? If at that point, the highest value for i was only 5 and you could only add 1 to it, how does that work? It just doesn't yet have the base of 6 to add 1 to. Now do you understand what I am saying?

Steve: I see the problem. We're using the variable i to indicate which weight we're talking about, not the weight itself. In other words, the first weight is Weight[0], the second is Weight[1], the third is Weight[2], the fourth is Weight[3], and the fifth is Weight[4]. The actual values of the weights are whatever the user of the program types in. For example, if the user types in 3 for the first weight, 9 for the second one, 6 for the third, 12 for the fourth, and 1 for the fifth, then the array will look like this:

Element	Value
Weight[0]	3
Weight[1]	9
Weight[2]	6
Weight[3]	12
Weight[4]	1

Problem
Algorithms
Java
Interpreter
Hardware

The value of i has to increase by only one each time because it indicates which element of the array Weight is to store the current value being typed in by the user. Does this clear up your confusion?

Susan: I think so. Then it can have any whole number value 0 or higher (well, up to the size of an int); adding the 1 means you are permitting the addition of at least 1 to any existing value, thereby allowing it to increase. Is that it?

Steve: No, I'm not permitting an addition; I'm performing it. Let's suppose i is 0. In that case, Weight[i] means Weight[0], or the first element of the Weight array. When I add 1 to i, i becomes 1. Therefore, Weight[i] now means Weight[1]. The next execution of i ++; sets i to 2; therefore, Weight[i] now means Weight[2]. Any time an i is used in an expression, for example, Weight[i], i + j, or i + 1, you can replace the i by whatever the current value of i is. The only place where you can't replace a variable such as i by its current value is when it is being modified, as in i ++ or the i in i = j + 1. In those cases, i means the address where the value of the variable i is stored.

Susan: OK, then i is not the number of the value typed in by the user; it is the location of an element in the Weight array, and that is why it can increase by 1, because of the i ++?

Steve: Correct, except that I would say "that is why it *does* increase by 1". This may just be terminology.

Susan: But in this case it can increase no more than 4 because of the i < 5 thing?

Steve: Correct.

Susan: But it has to start with a 0 because of the i = 0 thing?

Steve: Correct.

Susan: When you say Weight[i] = RWVar.readInt(System.in); does that mean you are telling the computer to place that variable in the index? So this serves two functions, displaying the weight the user types in and associating it to the index?

Steve: No, that statement tells the computer to place the value read in from the keyboard into element i of array Weight.

Susan: Okay, but what do you mean by the ith element? So does Weight[i] mean you are directing the number that the user types in to a certain location in memory?

Steve: Yes, to the element whose index is the current value of i.

Susan: What I am confusing is what is being seen on the screen at the time that the user types in the input. So the user sees the number on the screen but then it isn't displayed anywhere after that number is entered? Then the statement Weight[i] = RWVar.readInt(System.in); directs it to a location somewhere in memory with a group of other numbers that the user types in?

Steve: Correct.

Susan: So then Weight[i] = RWVar.readInt(System.in); means that the number the user is typing has to go into one of those locations but the only word that says what that location could be is Weight; it puts no limitations on the location in that Weight array other than when you defined the index variable as int i;. This means the index cannot be more than will fit into an int.

Problem
Algorithms
Java
Interpreter
Hardware

Steve: Correct. The current value of i is what determines which element of Weight the user's input goes into.

Susan: I think I was not understanding this because I kept thinking that i was what the user typed in and we were defining its limitations. Instead we are telling it where to go.

Steve: That's right.

Now that we have stored all of the weights, we want to find the three highest of the weights. We'll use a sorting algorithm called a **selection sort**, which can be expressed in English as follows:

1. Repeat the following steps three times, once through for each weight that we want to select.
2. Search through the list (i.e., the Weight array), keeping track of the highest weight seen so far in the list and the index of that highest weight.
3. When we get to the end of the list, copy the highest weight we've found to the next element of another list (the "output list", which in this case is the array SortedWeight).
4. Finally, set the highest weight we've found in the original list to 0, so we won't select it as the highest value again on the next pass through the list.

Problem
Algorithms
Java
Interpreter
Hardware

Let's take a look at the portion of our Java program that implements this sort, in Figure 4.8.

```
for (i = 0; i < 3; i ++)
    {
    HighestWeight = 0;
    HighestIndex = 0;
    for (k = 0; k < 5; k ++)
        {
        if (Weight[k] > HighestWeight)
            {
            HighestWeight = Weight[k];
            HighestIndex = k;
            }

        }
    SortedWeight[i] = HighestWeight;
    Weight[HighestIndex] = 0;
    }
```

Figure 4.8: Sorting the weights (from code\vect1\vect1.java)

Now let's look at the correspondence between the English description of the algorithm and the code.

1. Repeat the following steps once through for each prize:

    ```
    for (i = 0; i < 3; i ++)
    ```

    (During this process the variable i is the index into the SortedWeight array where we're going to store the weight for the current prize we're working on. While we're looking for the highest weight, i is 0; for the second-highest weight, i is 1; finally, when we're getting ready to award a third prize, i is 2.)
2. Search through the input list. For each element of the list Weight, we check whether that element (Weight[k]) is greater than the highest weight seen so far in the list (HighestWeight). If that is the case, then we reset HighestWeight to the value of the current element (Weight[k]), and the index of the highest weight so far (HighestIndex) to the index of the current element (k).
3. When we get to the end of the input list, HighestWeight is the highest weight in the list, and HighestIndex is the index of that element of the list that had the highest weight. Therefore, we can copy the highest weight to the current element of another list (the "output list"). As mentioned earlier, i is the index of the current element in the output list. Its value is the number of times we have been through the outer loop before; that is, the highest weight, which we will identify first, goes in position 0 of the output list, the next highest in position 1, and so on.

    ```
    SortedWeight[i] = HighestWeight;
    ```

4. Finally, set the highest weight in the input list to 0, so we won't select it as the highest value again on the next pass through the list.

    ```
    Weight[HighestIndex] = 0;
    ```

    This statement is the reason that we have to keep track of the "highest index"; that is, the index of the highest weight. Otherwise, we wouldn't know which element of the original Weight array we've used, and therefore wouldn't be able to set it to 0 to prevent its being used again.

Here's Susan's rendition of this algorithm:

Problem
Algorithms
Java
Interpreter
Hardware

Susan: OK, let me repeat this back to you in English. The result of this program is that after scanning the list of user input weights, the weights are put in another list, which is an ordering list, named k. The program starts by finding the highest weight in the input list. It then takes it out, puts it in k, and replaces that value it took out with a 0, so it won't be picked up again. Then it comes back to find the next highest weight and does the same thing all over again until nothing is left to order. Actually this is more than that one statement. But is this what you mean? That one statement is responsible for finding the highest weight in the user input list and placing it in k. Is this right?

Steve: It's almost exactly right. The only error is that the list that the weights are moved to is the SortedWeight array, rather than k. The variable k is used to keep track of which is the next entry to be put into the SortedWeight array.

Susan: OK. There was also something else I didn't understand when tracing through the program. I did see at one point that i=3. Well, first I didn't know how that could be because i is supposed to be < 3, but then I remembered that i ++ expression in the for loop, so I wondered if that is how this happened. I forgot where I was at that point, but I think it was after I had just completed entering 5 values and i was incrementing with each value. But see, it really should not have been more than 4 because if you start at 0 then that is where it should have ended up.

Problem
Algorithms
Java
Interpreter
Hardware

Steve: The reason that i gets to be 3 after the end of the loop is that at the end of each pass through the loop, the modification expression (i ++) is executed before the continuation expression (i < 3). So at the end of the fifth pass through the loop, i is incremented to 3 and then tested to see if it is still less than 3. Since it isn't, the loop terminates at that point.

Susan: I get that. But I still have a question about the statement if Weight[k] > HighestWeight. Well, the first time through, this will definitely be true because we've initialized HighestWeight to 0, since any weight would be greater than 0. Is that right?

Steve: Yes. Every time through the outer (i) loop, as we get to the top of the inner loop, the 0 that we've just put in HighestWeight should be replaced by the first element of Weight; that is, Weight[0], except of course if we've already replaced Weight[0] by 0 during a previous pass. It would also be possible to initialize HighestWeight to Weight[0] and then start the loop by setting k to 1 rather than 0. That would cause the inner (k) loop to be executed only four times per outer loop execution, rather than five, and therefore would be more efficient.

Susan: Then HighestIndex=k; is the statement that sets the placement of the highest number to its rank?

Steve: Right.

Susan: Then I thought about this. It seems that the highest weight is set first, then the sorting takes place so it makes four passes (actually five) to stop the loop.

Steve: The sorting is the whole process. Each pass through the outer loop locates one more element to be put into the SortedWeight array. Is that what you're saying here?

Susan: Then the statement Weight[HighestIndex] = 0; comes into play, replacing the highest number selected on that pass to 0.

Steve: Correct.

Susan: Oh, when k is going through the sorting process, why does i increment through each pass? It seems that k should be incrementing.

Steve: Actually, k increments on each pass through the inner loop, or 15 times in all. It's reset to 0 on each pass through the outer loop, so that we look at all of the elements again when we're trying to find the highest remaining weight. On the other hand, i is incremented on each pass through the outer loop or three times in all, once for each "highest" weight that gets put into the SortedWeight array.

Susan: OK, I get the idea with i, but what is the deal with k? I mean I see it was defined as an int, but what is it supposed to represent, and how did you know in advance that you were going to need it?

Steve: It represents the position in the original list, as indicated in the description of the algorithm. Since that position is a number, we can use an int to represent it.

Susan: I still don't understand where k fits into this picture. What does it do?

Steve: It's the index in the "inner loop", which steps through the elements looking for the highest one that's still there. We get one "highest" value every time through the "outer loop", so we have to execute that outer loop three times. Each time through the outer loop, we execute the inner loop five times, once for each entry in the input list.

Susan: Too many terms again. Which is the "outer loop" and which is the "inner loop"?

Problem
Algorithms
Java
Interpreter
Hardware

Steve: The outer loop executes once for each "highest" weight we're locating. Each time we find one, we set it to 0 (at the end of the loop) so that it won't be found again the next time through.

Susan: OK, now I am confused with the statement if (Weight[k] > HighestWeight). This is what gets me: If I understand this right (and obviously I don't) how could Weight[k] ever be greater than HighestWeight, since every possible value of k represents one of the elements in the Weight array, and HighestWeight is the highest weight in that array? For this reason I am having a hard time understanding the code for step 2, but not the concept.

Steve: The value of HighestWeight at any time is equal to the highest weight that has been seen *so far*. At the beginning of each execution of the outer loop, HighestWeight is set to 0. Then, every time that the current weight (Weight[k]) is higher than the current value of HighestWeight, we reset HighestWeight to the value of the current weight.

Susan: I still don't understand this statement. Help.

Problem
Algorithms
Java
Interpreter
Hardware

Steve: Remember that HighestWeight is reset to 0 on each pass through the outer loop. Thus, this if statement checks whether the kth element of the Weight array exceeds the highest weight we've seen before in this pass. If that is true, obviously our "highest" weight isn't really the highest, so we have to reset the highest weight to the value of the kth element; if the kth element isn't the true highest weight, at least it's higher than what we had before. Since we replace the "highest" weight value with the kth value any time that the kth value is higher than the current "highest" weight, at the end of the inner loop, the number remaining in HighestWeight will be the true highest weight left in Weight. This is essentially the same algorithm as we used to find the highest weight in the original version of this program, but now we apply it several times to find successively lower "highest" weights.

Susan: OK, I understand now; i increments to show how many times it has looped through to find the highest number. You are doing a loop within a loop, really; it is not side by side, is it?

Steve: Correct.

Susan: So when you first enter your numbers, they are placed in an index called i, then they are going to be cycled through again, placing them in a corresponding index named k, looking for the top three numbers. To start out through each pass, you first set the highest weight to the first weight since you have preset the highest weight to 0. But to find the top three numbers, you have to look at each place or element in the index. At the end of each loop you sort out the highest number and then set that removed element to 0 so it won't be selected again. You do this whole thing three times.

Steve: That's right, except for some terminology: Where you say "an index called i", you should say "an array called Weight", and where you say "an index called k", you should say "an array called SortedWeight". The variables i and k are used to step through the arrays, but they are not the arrays themselves.

Susan: OK, then the index variables are just the working representation of what is going on in those arrays. But aren't the numbers "assigned" an index? Let's see; if you lined up your five numbers, you could refer to each number as to its placement in an array. Could you then have the column of weights in the middle of the two indexes of i and k to each side?

Steve: If I understand your suggestion, it wouldn't work, because k and i vary at different speeds. During the first pass of the outer loop, i is 0, whereas k varies from 0 to 5; on the second pass of the outer loop, i is 1, whereas k varies from 0 to 5 again, and the same for the third pass of the outer loop. The value of i is used to refer to an individual element of the SortedWeight array, the one that will receive the next "highest" weight we locate. The value of k is used to refer to an individual element of the Weight array, the one we're examining to see if it's higher than the current HighestWeight.

Problem
Algorithms
Java
Interpreter
Hardware

Susan: This is what gets me; how do you know in advance that you are going to have to set HighestIndex to k? I see it in the program as it happens and I understand it then, but how would you know that the program wouldn't run without doing that? Trial and error? Experience? Rule books? <G>

Steve: Logic. Let's look at the problem again. The sorting algorithm that we're using here is called *selection sort*, because each time through the outer loop it selects one element out of the input array and moves it to the output array. To prevent our selecting the same weight (i.e., the highest one in the original input) every time through the outer loop, we have to clear each weight to 0 as we select it. But to do that, we have to keep track of which one we selected; that's why we need to save HighestIndex.

Being a glutton for punishment, Susan brought up the general problem of how to create an algorithm in the first place.

Susan: Do they make instruction sheets with directions of paths to follow? How do you identify problems? I mean, don't you encounter pretty much the same types of problems frequently in programming, and can't they be identified some way so that if you knew a certain problem could be categorized as a Type C problem, let's say, you would approach it with a Type C methodology to the solution? Does that make sense? Probably not.

Steve: It does make sense, but for some reason such "handbooks" are rare. Actually, my earlier book *Efficient C/C++ Programming*, was designed to provide something like you're suggesting, with solutions to common problems at the algorithmic level, although the examples were mostly in C and C++ (as the title indicates). There's also a book called *Design Patterns*, by Gamma, Helm, Johnson, and Vlissides, that tries to provide tested solutions to common design problems at a much higher level.

Details, Details

Let's work through the steps of the algorithm in more detail.[13] The algorithm for reading in all of the weights (step 1) should be fairly self-explanatory, once you're familiar with the syntax of the for statement; it causes the statements in its controlled block to be executed three times, with the index variable i varying from 0 to 2 in the process.

Problem
Algorithms
Java
Interpreter
Hardware

The algorithm for making a list consisting of the three highest weights in descending order (step 2) is quite similar to the process we went through to find the highest weight in our previous two programs; however, the reason for the HighestIndex variable may not be obvious. We need to keep track of which element of the original array (i.e., Weight) we have decided is the highest so far, so that this element won't be selected as the highest weight on *every* pass through the Weight array. To prevent this error, step 4 sets each "highest" weight to a value that won't be selected on a succeeding pass. Since we know there should be no 0 weights in the Weight array, we can set each selected element to 0 after it has been selected, to prevent its re-selection. Figure 4.9 shows a picture of the situation before the first pass through the data, with 0 in SortedWeight to indicate that those locations have been initialized to 0, as the Java language guarantees.

---

13. They're in the section titled "You May Already Have Won".

Index	Contents of Weight	Contents of SortedWeight
0	5	0
1	2	0
2	11	0
3	3	
4	7	

Figure 4.9: Initial situation

In Figure 4.9, the highest value is 11 in Weight[2]. After we've located it and copied its value to SortedWeight[0], we set Weight[2] to 0, yielding the situation in Figure 4.10.

Index	Contents of Weight	Contents of SortedWeight
0	5	11
1	2	0
2	0	0
3	3	
4	7	

Figure 4.10: After the first pass

Now we're ready for the second pass. This time, the highest value is the 7 in Weight[4]. After we copy the 7 to SortedWeight[1], we set Weight[4] to 0, leaving the situation in Figure 4.11.

Index	Contents of Weight	Contents of SortedWeight
0	5	11
1	2	7
2	0	0
3	3	
4	0	

Figure 4.11: After the second pass

On the third and final pass, we locate the 5 in Weight[0], copy it to SortedWeight[2], and set Weight[0] to 0. As you can see in Figure 4.12, SortedWeight now has the results we were looking for: the top three weights in descending order.

Problem
Algorithms
Java
Interpreter
Hardware

Index	Contents of Weight	Contents of SortedWeight
0	0	11
1	2	7
2	0	5
3	3	
4	0	

Figure 4.12: Final situation

By the way, it's also possible to initialize a variable to a value other than the default one at the same time as you define it. For example, the statement int i = 12; defines an int variable called i and sets it to the value 12 at the same time. This is generally a good practice to follow when possible; if you initialize the variable when you define it, you don't have to remember to write a separate statement to do the initialization. Of course, we can't do this with variables that have to be reinitialized on every time through a loop, as is the case with HighestWeight and HighestIndex.

Problem
Algorithms
Java
Interpreter
Hardware

To Really Foul Things Up Requires a Computer

This program will work all right as long as the user types in reasonable values. But what if all the values were typed in as negative values? In that case, the program wouldn't work, because the initial value of HighestWeight, which is supposed to be lower than any of the typed-in values, would actually be *higher* than any of those values. The result would be that all of the highest weights would come out as 0. This erroneous result is an example of *program failure*.

We should take some time here to discuss the idea of program failure, because its consequences can be quite serious. The first question, of course, is what it means to say that a program "fails". The simplest answer is that it doesn't work correctly, but that isn't very specific.

As you can imagine, this notion was the topic of some discussion with Susan.

Susan: What do you mean by a program failing? I know it means it won't work, but what happens? Do you just get error messages, and it won't do anything?

Steve: In general, a program "failing" means that it does something unexpected and erroneous. Exactly what happens depends on the particular situation; for example, because of some safety features in Java arrays, you'll get an error message if you attempt to misuse an array by referring to a nonexistent element.

In general, a program failure may or may not produce an error message. In the specific case that we've just seen, we'll get erroneous output indicating that the top three weights are all 0. However, it's entirely possible for a program to just "hang" (run endlessly), "crash" your system, produce an obviously ridiculous answer, or worst of all, provide a seemingly correct but actually erroneous result.

The causes of program failure are legion. A few of the possibilities are these:

1. Problems isolated to our code.
    a. The original problem could have been stated incorrectly.
    b. We could have been using inappropriate algorithm(s).
    c. The algorithm(s) might have been implemented incorrectly.
    d. The input to the program might be outside the expected range.

Problem
Algorithms
Java
Interpreter
Hardware

And so on. . .

2. Problems interacting with other programs.
    a. We might be misusing a function supplied by the system, like the System.out.println facility.
    b. The documentation for a system function might be incorrect or incomplete. This is especially common in "guru"-oriented operating systems, where the users are supposed to know everything.
    c. A system function might be unreliable. This is more common than it should be.
    d. The compiler might be generating the wrong instructions. I've seen this on a few rare occasions.
    e. Another program in the system might be interfering with our program. This is quite common in some popular

operating environments that allow several programs to be executing concurrently.[14]

And so on. . .

With a simple program such as the ones we're writing here, errors like the ones listed under problems with our code are more likely, as we have relatively little interaction with the rest of the system. As we start to use more sophisticated mechanisms in Java, we're more likely to run into instances of interaction problems.

To make the idea of program failure more concrete, let's spend a little time discussing a horrible example of "input outside the expected range". This example is especially relevant as I write these words in April 1997, because we're all going to be intimately familiar with its results any day now.

Terror in the Year Zero

Problem
Algorithms
Java
Interpreter
Hardware

As I've mentioned in Chapter 2, RAM and disk storage were much more expensive in the past than they are today. For this reason, a very large number of programs written before the 1980s, and even some written since then, have employed a space-saving "shortcut" when dealing with dates. To be precise, these programs use a 2-digit number to represent the year portion of a date in the form "YYMMDD" (that is, two digits for the year, two for the month, and two for the day), which saves storage compared to storing the entire year as in the form "YYYYMMDD". I'm sure this seemed like (and may have even been) a good idea at the time, but it has turned out to be a very expensive way to save money; many of these programs are still in use, and none of them will work much longer, if indeed they haven't already started to fail.

How will these programs fail? There are many possible ways, but I can think of a few that are certain to occur.

1. Interest calculations such as for credit card debt, which depend on the number of days since the last payment.
2. Automated inventory systems that calculate the number of items to order based on criteria such as the average of the last 6 months' orders.

---

14. Especially those whose names begin with "W".

3. Programmed maintenance schedules for automobiles, commercial building control systems, and the like, that control the availability of the device based on how long it has been since the last maintenance was done. For example, many elevators are programmed to stop working as a safety measure if an excessive amount of time has elapsed since they were last maintained.

To see how these calculations might be incorrect when the year 2000 rolls around, let's take the first one of these as a more detailed example. Suppose that we have a program that calculates the interest due on a credit card in the following (somewhat oversimplified) way:

1. Calculate the "day number" of the previous payment by the following procedure:[15]
   a. Multiply the year number by 365.
   b. Add the day of the month.
   c. Add the day number of the beginning of this month. This is the number of days in the year before the first of the month. This number is 0 for January, 31 for February, 59 for March, and so on.
2. Calculate the day number of the current payment by the same procedure as above, substituting the correct values for the year number, day of the month, and day number of the beginning of the month.
3. Subtract the day number of the previous payment from the day number of the current payment. The result is the number of days between the previous payment and the current payment.

```
Problem
Algorithms
Java
Interpreter
Hardware
```

For example, if the last payment was on 991103 (that is, November 3rd, 1999), and the current payment was on 991202 (that is, December 2nd, 1999), we calculate the day number of the last payment as 99 * 365 (for the year part) + 3 (for the day of the month) + 304 (for the number of days in the year before the first of November), which gives us a day number of 36442. Then we calculate the day number of the current payment as 99 * 365 (for the year part) + 2 (for the day of the month) + 334 (for the number of days in the year before the first of December), or a day number of 36471. Subtracting the first of these numbers from the second, we

---

15. I know I'm disregarding leap year, but that would just be another complication that isn't needed to explain the Year 2000 problem.

determine that the number of days between these two payments is 29, which is correct.

Now let's look at the next billing cycle, where the previous payment date will be 991202. Let's suppose that the next payment is on January 2, 2000, which will be represented as 000102. In that case, we calculate the day number of the last payment as 99 * 365 (for the year part) + 2 (for the day of the month) + 334 (for the number of days in the year before the first of December), which gives us a day number of 36471. Then we calculate the day number of the current payment as 0 * 365 (for the year part) + 2 (for the day of the month) + 0 (for the number of days in the year before the first of January), or a day number of 2. Subtracting the first of these numbers from the second, we determine that the number of days between these two payments is... -36469. Somehow that doesn't seem right!

If the credit card company (and their customers) are lucky, the bills this program generates will be obviously idiotic. If they're not so lucky, they may appear to be correct but in fact will be wrong in some unpredictable way. Similar horrors will occur in the inventory control, automobile, and elevator maintenance examples.

Problem
Algorithms
Java
Interpreter
Hardware

The people responsible for these defective programs can't really claim that these problems are beyond their control; after all, the fact that the year 2000 was coming has been known for quite some time. Given this, surely the companies that are affected by this problem will have everything fixed by January 1st, 2000. Won't they?

I'll Think about It Tomorrow

I'm afraid that's not going to happen. The first reason is that, as I write this in 1997, many companies haven't even started working on the problem! How did such a vital task get put off until it's too late?

That's easy to explain. Pretend you are a reasonably competent manager[16] working for Amalgamated Conglomerate. Here are some of the major characteristics of the project we need to do:

1. Its success is absolutely essential to the survival of the company.
2. It is mind-numbingly boring, tedious work, which implies even higher turnover than usual in software projects.
3. It is completely invisible to the customer, who has undoubtedly requested a number of new features that will have to be postponed to work on this project.

---

16. If that's not an oxymoron.

4.   The skills learned are completely worthless when the project is over.[17]
5.   The deadline cannot be postponed by even one day.

Now I want a show of hands: Who would like to lead this project? As I suspected, I'm not likely to get very many volunteers.

But why should fixing these problems be so difficult? All we have to do is to change the date fields to use four digits rather than two for the year portion of the date, and change all of the code that refers to those date fields. How hard could that be?

Much harder than it would be if modern software design rules had been applied. The problem here is that everyone wrote their own date calculation routines, and used these date fields throughout their programs, often without documenting how they worked or where they were used. Some of these programs are thirty years old, and the people who worked on them are long gone, if they're even still alive. The only way to fix these date problems is to go over the code, line by line, searching for any reference to dates.[18] Once each such reference is found, it has to be fixed. Unfortunately, the chance of introducing a new error when fixing an old one is not negligible; in fact, it can be quite high. This means that extremely thorough and careful testing is needed to try to ensure that new errors haven't been introduced in this process.

Okay, so it's a lot of work. But these companies have had plenty of time to fix it, so why haven't they done it by now?

Problem
Algorithms
Java
Interpreter
Hardware

In the Long Run, We Are All Dead

There are a number of excuses, but the truth of the matter is this: Although the company desperately needs these programs to be fixed, it's not in any individual manager's interest to be in charge of the project. And since there isn't any "company" to do it if the individual managers don't want to, it doesn't get done.

In my opinion, this situation has exposed a serious flaw in the structure of corporations: Within a corporation, there is no market. This means that while the benefits of fixing this problem would have

---

17. At least until the year 9999, when we'll have to convert to five-digit dates.

18. This is actually too optimistic, as it assumes that you have the source code to examine. Believe it or not, many companies are using programs whose source code has been lost; they have an even worse time trying to figure out what has to be fixed, or even what the program is doing right now.

accrued to the entire company, the difficulties would have fallen on the individual managers who were running the projects. Therefore, the most sensible course of action from the point of view of the individual manager was to duck responsibility; with any luck, he or she would have retired or at least moved to another company before the day of reckoning arrived.

Was there any way of preventing this outcome? Yes, but it would have required managers to act as entrepreneurs rather than employees. That is, if companies were organized as a number of autonomous groups who bought and sold one another's products, then anyone who could fix bugs like the Year 2000 problem would have been able to make a good living doing so. Because of the laws of supply and demand, the fewer people who wanted to work on such projects, the more money each one would make. As a result, the rewards for fixing the problem would be commensurate with the difficulty and risk of taking on the project, so we wouldn't be in the mess that we're in today.

Are there any benefits to be gained from this mess? I can think of some. Of course, one attractive prospect is the possible collapse of certain large universally hated bureaucratic organizations under the weight of massive program failure. If that occurs, it will be worth the estimated $600 billion price tag for fixing the problem in companies around the world. It's also within the realm of possibility that this fiasco will encourage a serious reconsideration of the reward and penalty structure of whatever corporations are still in business after January 1st, 2000.

As interesting and even vital as the Year 2000 problem may be, hasn't it taken us a bit afield from our task of learning how to program? I don't think so. If you're going to write programs that anyone is going to depend on, you should have a good understanding of how serious program failure can be as well as some of the more common causes of such failure, even if they are outside the technical aspects of programming.[19]

Problem
Algorithms
Java
Interpreter
Hardware

Garbage in, Garbage Out

In the meantime, there's something else we should do if we want our example program to work as it should. As the old saying "Garbage in, garbage out" suggests, by far the best solution to handling

---

19. For a number of other perspectives on this Year 2000 problem, see the February '96 issue of *American Programmer* magazine.

spurious input values (such as the negative weight values I mentioned previously) is to prevent them from being entered in the first place. What we want to do is to check each input value and warn the user if it's invalid. Figure 4.13 illustrates a new input routine that looks like it should do the trick.

```
for (i = 0; i < 5; i ++)
  {
  k = i + 1;
  System.out.print("Please type in weight #" + k + ": ");
  Weight[i] = RWVar.readInt(System.in);
  if (Weight[i] <= 0)
    {
    System.out.println("I'm sorry, " + Weight[i] +
      " is not a valid weight.");
    }
  }
```

Figure 4.13: Garbage prevention, first attempt (from code\vect2a\vect2a.java)

Most of this should be familiar; the only line that has a new construct in it is the if statement. The condition <= means "less than or equal to", which is reasonably intuitive.

To use the debugger for this program, follow the instructions in the section titled "Using the debugger" in the file "\readme.txt" on the CD in the back of the book. These instructions assume that you've installed the examples on drive C:, so that the location of this program is "c:\whosj\code\vect2a".

Unfortunately, this program won't work as we intended. The problem is what happens after the error message is displayed; namely, the loop continues at the top with the next weight, and we never correct the erroneous input. Susan didn't have much trouble figuring out exactly what that last statement meant.

Problem
Algorithms
Java
Interpreter
Hardware

Susan: When you say that "we never correct the erroneous input", does that mean that it is added to the list and not ignored?

Steve: Right.

To fix this problem completely, we need to use the approach shown in the final version of this program (Figure 4.14).

```
import WAJ.*;

public class Vect3
{
   public static void main( String args[ ] )
   {
      int[ ] Weight = new int[5];
      int[ ] SortedWeight = new int[3];
      int HighestWeight;
      int HighestIndex;
      int i;
      int k;

      System.out.println("I'm going to ask you to type in five weights, in pounds.");

      for (i = 0; i < 5; )
      {
         k = i + 1;
         System.out.print("Please type in weight #"  + k  + ": ");
         Weight[i] = RWVar.readInt(System.in);
         if (Weight[i] <= 0)
         {
            System.out.println("I'm sorry, " + Weight[i]  + " is not a valid weight.");
         }
         else
            i ++;
      }

      for (i = 0; i < 3; i ++)
      {
         HighestIndex = 0;
         HighestWeight = 0;
         for (k = 0; k < 5; k ++)
         {
            if (Weight[k] > HighestWeight)
            {
               HighestWeight = Weight[k];
               HighestIndex = k;
            }
         }
         SortedWeight[i] = HighestWeight;
         Weight[HighestIndex] = 0;
      }

      System.out.println("The highest weight was: " + SortedWeight[0]);
      System.out.println("The second highest weight was: " + SortedWeight[1]);
      System.out.println("The third highest weight was: " + SortedWeight[2]);
   }
}
```

Problem
Algorithms
Java
Interpreter
Hardware

Figure 4.14: Finding the top three weights using arrays
(code\vect3\vect3.java)

To use the debugger for this program, follow the instructions in the section titled "Using the debugger" in the file "\readme.txt" on the CD in the back of the book. These instructions assume that you've installed the examples on drive C:, so that the location of this program is "c:\whosj\code\vect3".

Now let's look at the changes that we've made to the program from the last revision. The first change is that the first for loop has only two sections rather than three in its control definition (inside the ()). As you may recall, the first section specifies the initial condition of the index variable; in this case, we're starting i out at 0, as is usual in C++ and Java. The second section indicates when we should continue executing the loop; here, it's as long as i is less than 5. But the third section, which usually indicates what to do to the index variable, is missing. The reason for this is that we're going to adjust the index variable manually in the loop, depending on what the user enters.

In this case, if the user enters an invalid value (i.e., less than or equal to 0), we display an error message and leave i as it was, so that the next time through the loop, the value will go into the same element in the Weight array. When the user enters a valid value, the else clause increments i so that the next value will go into the next element in the array. This fixes the error in our previous version that left incorrect entries in the array.

Now that we have beaten the pumpkin-weighing example to a pulp,[20] let's review the mass of information to which I've subjected you so far in this chapter.

Problem
Algorithms
Java
Interpreter
Hardware

Review

We started out by extending our pumpkin-weighing program to tell us the highest two weights rather than just the highest one. During this exercise, we learned the use of the else clause of an if statement. We also saw that making even an apparently simple change to a working program can introduce an error; in this case, we were copying the highest weight to the next-highest weight only when a new high weight was detected. This would produce an incorrect result if a value higher than the previous second highest but lower than the current highest weight were entered.

Next we extended the program again, this time to handle any number of prizes to be given to the highest weight, second-highest

---

20. Pumpkin pie, anyone?

weight, third-highest weight, and so on. This required a complete reorganization of the program; the new version used the *selection sort* algorithm to produce a list of as many of the highest weights as we need, in descending order. To do this, we had to use an *array*, or set of values with a common name, to store all of the weights as they were read in. When they had all been entered, we searched through them three times, once to find each of the top three elements. An array, just like a regular variable, has a name. However, unlike a regular variable, an array does not have a single value, but rather consists of a number of *elements*, each of which has a separate value. An element is referred to by a number, called an *index*, rather than by a unique name; each element has a different index. The lowest index is 0, and the highest index is 1 less than the number of elements in the array; for example, with a 10-element array, the legal indexes are 0 through 9. The ability to refer to an element by its index allows us to vary the element we are referring to in a statement by varying the index; we put this facility to good use in our implementation of the selection sort, which we'll review shortly.

We then added the for statement to our repertoire of loop control facilities. This statement provides more precise control than the while

Problem
Algorithms
Java
Interpreter
Hardware

statement. Using for, we can specify a *starting expression*, a *continuation expression*, and a *modification expression*. The starting expression sets up the initial conditions for the loop. Before each possible execution of the controlled block, the continuation expression is checked, and if it is true, the controlled block will be executed; otherwise, the for loop will terminate. Finally, the modification expression is executed after each execution of the controlled block. Most commonly, the starting expression sets the initial value of a variable, the continuation expression tests whether that variable is still in the range we are interested in, and the modification expression changes the value of the variable. For example, in the for statement

    for (i = 0; i < 5; i ++)

the starting expression is i = 0, the continuation expression is i < 5, and the modification expression is i ++. Therefore, the block controlled by the for statement will be executed first with the variable i set to 0; at the end of the block, the variable i will be incremented by 1, and the loop will continue if i is still less than 5.

Then we used the for statement and a couple of arrays to implement a *selection sort*. This algorithm goes through an "input list" of n elements once for each desired "result element". In our case, we want the top three elements of the sorted list, so the input list has to be scanned three times. On each time through, the algorithm picks the highest value remaining in the list and adds that to the end of a new "output list". Then it removes the found value from the input list. At the end of this process, the output list has all of the desired values from the input list, in descending order of size.

While it's important to insure that our programs work correctly when given correct input, it's also important to make sure that they work correctly even when given improper input. So the next improvement we made to our pumpkin-weighing program was to tell the user when an invalid value had been entered and ask for a valid value in its place. This involved a for loop without a modification expression, since we wanted to increment the index variable i to point to the next element of the array only when the user typed in a valid entry; if an illegal value was typed in, we requested a legal value for the same element of the array.

Exercises

1.   If the program in Figure 4.15 is run, what will be displayed?

Problem
Algorithms
Java
Interpreter
Hardware

```
import WAJ.*;

public class Morbas01
{
   public static void main( String args[ ] )
   {
      int[ ] x = new int[4];
      int Result;
      int i;

      x[0] = 3;
      for (i = 1; i < 4; i ++)
           x[i] = x[i-1] * 2;

      Result = 0;
      for (i = 0; i < 4; i ++)
           Result = Result + x[i];

      System.out.println(Result);
   }
}
```

Figure 4.15: Exercise 1 (code\morbas01\morbas01.java)

2. Write a program that asks the user to type in a weight, and display the weight on the screen.

3. Modify the program from exercise 2 to ask the user to type as many weights as desired, stopping as soon as a 0 is entered. Add up all of the weights entered, and display the total on the screen at the end of the program.

Answers to exercises can be found at the end of the chapter.

Conclusion

We've covered a lot of material in this chapter in our quest for better pumpkin weighing, ranging from sorting data into order based on numeric value through the anatomy of arrays. Next, we'll take up some more of the language features you will need to write any significant Java programs.

```
Problem
Algorithms
Java
Interpreter
Hardware
```

Answers to Exercises

1. The correct answer is 45. In case this isn't obvious, consider the following:
   a. The value of x[0] is set to 3.
   b. In the first for loop, the value of i starts out at 1.
   c. Therefore, the first execution of the assignment statement x[i] = x[i–1] * 2; is equivalent to x[1] = x[0] * 2;. This clearly sets x[1] to 6.
   d. The next time through the loop i is 2, so that same assignment statement x[i] = x[i–1] * 2; is equivalent to x[2] = x[1] * 2;. This sets x[2] to 12.
   e. Finally, on the last pass through the loop, the value of i is 3, so that assignment statement x[i] = x[i–1] * 2; is equivalent to x[3] = x[2] * 2; This sets x[3] to 24.
   f. The second for loop just adds up the values of all the entries in the x array; this time, we remembered to initialize the total, Result, to 0, so the total is calculated and displayed correctly.

To use the debugger for this program, follow the instructions in the section titled "Using the debugger" in the file "\readme.txt" on the CD in the back of the book. These instructions assume that you've installed the examples on drive C:, so that the location of this program is "c:\whosj\code\morbas01".

2.   Here's Susan's solution to this problem, in Figure 4.16:

```
import WAJ.*;

public class Morbas03
{
  public static void main( String args[ ] )
  {
    int weight;

    System.out.println("Please write your weight here: ");

    weight = RWVar.readInt(System.in);

    System.out.println("I wish I only weighed " + weight + " pounds.");
  }
}
```

Figure 4.16: A weight program (code\morbas03\morbas03.java)

Here are the questions that she came up with during the process:

> **Susan**: Would this work? Right now by just doing this it brought up several things that I have not thought about before.
> First, is the println really necessary here, or would the program work with just a print?

> **Steve**: You can use whichever you want; however, with print the user would type the answer to the question on the same line as the question; with println, the answer would be typed on the next line, as the println would cause the active screen position to move to the next line at the end of the question.

> **Susan**: OK, that is good, since I intended for the weight to be typed on a different line. Now I understand this much better.
> But I have another question: How does the program handle the ENTER? I don't see where it comes into the programs you have written. It just seems that at the end of any pause an ENTER would be appropriate. So is the ENTER something that is part of the compiler that it just knows that by the way the code is written an ENTER will necessarily come next?

Problem
Algorithms
Java
Interpreter
Hardware

Steve: The RWVar.readInt input mechanism lets you type until you hit an ENTER, then takes the result up to that point.

To use the debugger for this program, follow the instructions in the section titled "Using the debugger" in the file "\readme.txt" on the CD in the back of the book. These instructions assume that you've installed the examples on drive C:, so that the location of this program is "c:\whosj\code\morbas03".

3. This was an offshoot of the previous question, which occurred when Susan wondered whether the program in Figure 4.16 would terminate. Let's start from that point in the conversation.

    Susan: Would this only run once? If so, how would you get it to repeat?

    Steve: We could use a while loop. Let's suppose that we wanted to add up all the weights that were entered. Then the program might look like Figure 4.17.

```
import WAJ.*;

public class Morbas04
{
    public static void main( String args[ ] )
    {
        int weight;
        int total;

        System.out.print("Please type in your weight, typing 0 to end:");
        weight = RWVar.readInt(System.in);

        total = weight;

        while (weight > 0)
            {
            System.out.print("Please type in your weight, typing 0 to end:");
            weight = RWVar.readInt(System.in);
            total = total + weight;
            }

        System.out.println("The total is: " + total);
    }
}
```

Problem
Algorithms
Java
Interpreter
Hardware

Figure 4.17: The weight-totalling program (code\morbas04\morbas04.java)

In case you were wondering, the reason we have to duplicate the statements to read in the weight is that we need an initial value for the variable weight before we start the while loop so that the condition in the while will be calculated correctly.

By the way, there's another way to write the statement total = total + weight; that uses an operator analogous to ++, the increment operator: total += weight;. This new operator, +=, means "add what's on the *right* to what's on the *left*". The motivation for this shortcut, as you might imagine, is the same as that for ++: It requires less typing, is more likely to be correct, and is easier to compile to efficient code.

Let's see what Susan has to say about this program and the += notation.

Susan: Darling, here we go again. Now why are you doing total = total + weight? What is that doing?

Steve: It's calculating the total by adding each weight to the previous total.

Susan: Here's something else that was very confusing. You say that += means "add what's on the right to what's on the left", but your example shows that it is the other way around. Unless this is supposed to be mirror imaged or something, I don't get it.

Steve: No, the example is correct. total += weight; is the same as total = total + weight;, so we're adding the value on the right of the += (i.e., weight) to the variable on the left (i.e., total). Is that clearer now?

Susan: OK, I think I've got it now. I guess if it were more like an equation, you would have to subtract total from the other side when you moved it. Why is it that the math recollection that I have, instead of helping me, just confuses me?

Steve: Because, unfortunately, the = is the same symbol used to mean "is equal to" in mathematics. The = in Java means something completely different: "set the thing on the left to the value on the right".

Susan: Ugh, this still seems backwards to me.

Steve: .yhw wonk t'nod I erus m'I

Susan: DARLING!! I am serious, I don't like this a bit. Okay, this is the deal, say this:

Add the old value of total and the value of weight on the right side, and put the result back into the total on the left side thereby modifying the total on the left side to a new value.

Problem
Algorithms
Java
Interpreter
Hardware

THIS IS MY DECREE. DO NOT CHANGE.

Steve: Yes, ma'am. Can I humbly restate your decree as follows: "Add the value on the right of the += (weight) to the old value of the variable on the left of the +=, (total) replacing the old value of total with the newly calculated value."?

Susan: Okay, as long as you keep my decree as it is.

To use the debugger for this program, follow the instructions in the section titled "Using the debugger" in the file "\readme.txt" on the CD in the back of the book. These instructions assume that you've installed the examples on drive C:, so that the location of this program is "c:\whosj\code\morbas04".

```
Problem
Algorithms
Java
Interpreter
Hardware
```

Chapter 5

"You Know My Methods"

Large Problems, Small Files?

Java was intended to be suitable for writing large programs.[1] Such programs are usually composed of many classes defined in a similar number of *source-code files*, as I mentioned in Chapter 3.[2]

In such a case, we must have some way for code in one source-code file to refer to code in another one. Similarly, we have to be able to specify where execution of our program should start; this latter requirement is taken care of by the Java rule that execution always starts at main.

We'll get back to this discussion as soon as we look at the definitions and objectives for this chapter.

Definitions

A **source-code file** is a file that contains source code for a program. Almost every part of every Java program starts out as a source-code file.

A **package** is an organizing unit that combines a number of *source-code* and *byte-code* files of a generally useful nature.

---

1. Note that this does not mean that it is in fact suitable for this purpose.

2. I know I still haven't told you exactly what a class is. For the moment, you can think of it as part of a larger program. If you're patient, I suspect that you'll learn more about classes than you may actually want to!

A class **file**, which contains *byte-code* instructions, is the result of compiling a *source-code file*.

A **method** is a section of code somewhat like a *block*, but its characteristics are different from those of a block. For one thing, you can't substitute a method for a statement; also, a method has a name, whereas blocks are anonymous. This name enables one method to start execution of another one.

A **method call** (or just "call" for short) causes execution to be transferred temporarily from the current method to the one named in the call.

A **called method** is a method that starts execution as a result of a method call.

A **calling method** is a method that suspends execution as a result of a method call.

`Problem`
`Algorithms`
`Java`
`Interpreter`
`Hardware`

A return **statement** is the mechanism used by a called method to return a value to the calling method, which picks up just where it left off. A method that doesn't return a value doesn't need a return statement; in that case, its execution will end after its last statement has been executed.

Objectives for This Chapter

By the end of this chapter, you should:

1. Understand how source code is organized.
2. Understand how and when to use methods to reduce the amount of code you have to write.
3. Understand how your source code is turned into a usable program.
4. Understand how storage is assigned to different types of variables.
5. Understand how methods can call one another.

Good Things Come in Small Packages

As we've already seen, the computer can't execute source code. Therefore, any source code we write has to be translated into byte-code instructions; the result of such translation is one or more class files. If we have a number of classes that work together, we can use a package to organize the source code for (and the use of) these classes.

The idea of these different types of files led to the following discussion with Susan:

Susan: So a class file is like some kind of interface between your code and the binary numbers of the machine? I am confused.

Steve: The source code for each class is translated by the compiler into a class file. These class files can then be referred to as needed when the classes they define are actually used in a program. As I've mentioned before, a number of classes can be grouped into a logical unit called a package. We've been using some of the classes that are defined in packages that come with the Java language; for example, System.in and System.out are defined in a class called java.lang.System, which is part of a package called java.lang.

Susan: So java.lang is a package? Is that a set of already written programs that you can refer to?

Steve: Yes.

Susan: The packages contain code segments that are generalized, and the other types of files contain code segments that are program specific?

Steve: Right.

Susan: Where are these packages? I am serious.

Steve: They are in various places in the directory structure of your computer (or a computer on the Internet), based on their names. As this indicates, there are a number of packages, including ones written for more specialized purposes by different companies.

Susan: So what is a "source file"? Is it a set of code written by the programmer?

Steve: It's a file containing part of a program in source code. Most significant programs consist of a number of files, rather than one big one, partly because it's easier to find and edit one logical segment of a

```
Problem
Algorithms
Java
Interpreter
Hardware
```

program in its own file than to locate it mixed in with a lot of other code, all in one big file.

Susan: Okay then, so a source-code file is just a big logical segment? How is it delineated from the rest of the program? Is it named? How do you find it?

Steve: Yes, it has a name, just like any other file.

Susan: So a source file is like a package, only, as we have discussed, it is more specific than a package; it is for the program that you are working on?

Steve: Right.

Susan: Where are these files and how do they get there?

Steve: In the case of files you write, they go wherever you tell the J++ compiler to put them. For example, in the case of your "weight-writing" program, the code you wrote is in a source file in a directory called code\morbas03. That source file is compiled to make a class file, which you can run by using the Java interpreter. Whenever your program refers to classes from the standard Java packages or to classes I've written, those classes will be made available to your program by the interpreter.

Problem
Algorithms
Java
Interpreter
Hardware

Susan: So then the source file is a "mini-program" within a program that holds the source code to be later compiled?

Steve: It contains part of the source code of a program, which needs to be compiled and combined with other previously compiled code before it can be used. I think that's the same as what you're saying.

So far, a *method* sounds a lot like a *block*, but there are significant differences between these two concepts. Let's take a look at those differences.

Functioning Normally

There are basically two differences between a block and a method. First, a block can be used anywhere a statement can be used, but this is not true of a method. Second, a method has a name, which can be used to refer to it from another method. These differences are the result of the way in which we use a method: by mentioning its name from another method. This is known as a *method call*, or just a *call*, for short.

When we call a method, we usually have to provide it with input (for example, some values to be averaged) and it usually produces output which we use in further processing (for example, the average of the input values). Some methods, though, have only one or the other. For example, some pairs of methods consist of one **storage method** and one **retrieval method**; the first stores data for the second to retrieve later. In that case, the storage method may not give us anything back when we call it, and the retrieving method may not need any input from us.

To see how and why we might use a method, we'll take a look at a program having some duplicated code (Figure 5.1). I'd like you to look particularly at this line,

    AverageWeight = (FirstWeight + SecondWeight) / 2;

and this one,

    AverageAge = (FirstAge + SecondAge) / 2;

These two lines are awfully similar; the only difference between them is that one of them averages two weights and the other averages two ages. Although this particular example doesn't take too much code to duplicate, it may not be too difficult for you to imagine the inefficiency and nuisance of having to copy and edit many lines of code every time we want to do exactly the same thing with different data. Instead of copying the code and editing it to change the name of the variables, we can write a method that averages whatever data we give it.

To use the debugger for this program, follow the instructions in the section titled "Using the debugger" in the file "\readme.txt" on the CD in the back of the book. These instructions assume that you've installed the examples on drive C:, so that the location of this program is "c:\whosj\code\nofunc".

```
Problem
Algorithms
Java
Interpreter
Hardware
```

```
import WAJ.*;

public class Nofunc
{
    public static void main( String args[ ] )
    {
        int FirstWeight;
        int SecondWeight;
        int FirstAge;
        int SecondAge;
        int AverageWeight;
        int AverageAge;

        System.out.print("Please type in the first weight: ");
        FirstWeight = RWVar.readInt(System.in);

        System.out.print("Please type in the second weight: ");
        SecondWeight = RWVar.readInt(System.in);

        AverageWeight = (FirstWeight + SecondWeight) / 2;

        System.out.print("Please type in the first age: ");
        FirstAge = RWVar.readInt(System.in);

        System.out.print("Please type in the second age: ");
        SecondAge = RWVar.readInt(System.in);

        AverageAge = (FirstAge + SecondAge) / 2;

        System.out.println("The average weight was: " + AverageWeight);
        System.out.println("The average age was: " + AverageAge);
    }
}
```

```
Problem
Algorithms
Java
Interpreter
Hardware
```

Figure 5.1: A sample program with duplicated code
(code\nofunc\nofunc.java)

Figure 5.2 is a picture of a method call.

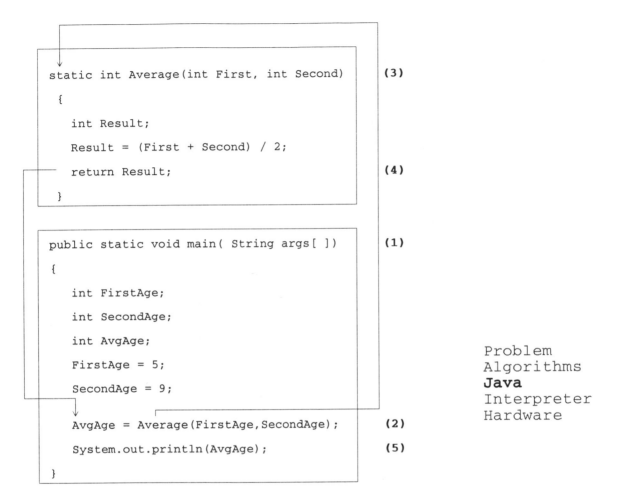

```
static int Average(int First, int Second)          (3)

 {

    int Result;

    Result = (First + Second) / 2;

    return Result;                                  (4)

 }


public static void main( String args[ ])           (1)

 {

    int FirstAge;

    int SecondAge;

    int AvgAge;

    FirstAge = 5;

    SecondAge = 9;

    AvgAge = Average(FirstAge,SecondAge);           (2)

    System.out.println(AvgAge);                     (5)

 }
```

Problem
Algorithms
Java
Interpreter
Hardware

Figure 5.2: A method call

The calling method **(1)** is main; the method call is at position **(2)**. The called method is Average **(3)**, and the return is at position **(4)**; the returned value is stored in the variable AvgAge, as indicated by the = in the statement AvgAge = Average(FirstAge,SecondAge); and the calling method, main, resumes execution at line **(5)**.[3]

---

3. If you don't provide a return statement, then the called method will just return to the calling method when it gets to its closing }. However, this is not legal for a method that is defined to return a value. This of course leads to the question of why we'd call a method that *doesn't* return a value. One possibility is that the method exists only to produce output on the screen, rather than to return any results. The actions that a method performs other than returning a value are called **side effects**.

By the way, it's important to distinguish between returning a value from a method, which is optional, and returning control from a called method to the calling method, which always happens at the end of the called method (unless the program has terminated due to an error in the called method).

In case this distinction isn't clear, you may be interested to know that Susan had the same reaction.

Susan: The sentence that reads, "By the way..." isn't very clear to me, what exactly is it that you are saying?

Steve: I'm saying that when a method is finished executing, it always returns to the calling method so that the calling method can continue executing. That is, when the called method terminates, the interpreter continues execution at the next instruction in the calling method. However, this doesn't mean that a called method always has to return a *value* to the calling method when it finishes.

Susan: Okay, I understand this now.

Problem
Algorithms
Java
Interpreter
Hardware

While we're on the subject of the calling method, in case you're wondering why we started the example at the beginning of main, it's because every Java program starts executing at that point. When the main method calls another method, such as Average, then main is suspended until Average is finished. When Average finishes, main resumes where it left off.

This isn't limited to one "level" of calls. The same thing can happen if Average, for example, calls another method, let's say Funca; Average will wait until Funca returns before continuing. Then when Average finishes, it will return to main, which will take up where it left off.

This idea of calling and returning from methods led to the following discussion with Susan:

Susan: So if you wanted to be really mean, you could get into someone's work in progress and stick a return somewhere in the middle of it and it would end the program right there? Now that I am thinking about it, I am sure you could do a whole lot worse than that. Of course, I would never do such a thing, but what I am saying is that whatever you are doing when the program gets to the return statement, then it is *the end*? Next stop, C:\?

Steve: If you're in the main program, then a return statement means "back to the C:\ prompt". If you're in a method other than main, it means "back to the method that called this method". In the case of a method that returns a value, the expression in the return statement tells the compiler what value to use in place of the method call. For example, the statement AvgAge = Average(i,j); sets AvgAge to the result in the return statement of the method Average. As you can see by looking at that method, the returned value is the average of the two input values, so that is the value that AvgAge is set to by this statement.

Susan: Let's see if I have this right: The return statement has to match the type of the method statement. This is so confusing.

Steve: Right, the return value has to match the int. That's because a method has a return type, just like the type of a variable. In this case, int is the type of the Average method, and the value is filled in by the return statement.

Susan: OK, then all this is saying is that the value that is produced is the same type as that declared at the beginning of a program. Since we declared the type of Average as an int, if the value produced were a letter or a picture of a cow, then you would get an error message?

Steve: Well, actually a letter (i.e., a char) would be acceptable as an int, due to rules left over from C. Otherwise, you're exactly correct.

Susan: The picture helps with the calling confusion. But I don't understand why int main is the calling method if the calling method suspends execution. How can you initiate a method if it starts out suspended? I am serious.

Problem
Algorithms
Java
Interpreter
Hardware

Steve: The main method starts execution as the first method in your program. Therefore, it isn't suspended unless and until it calls another method.

Above Average

I think it's time for a more detailed example of how we would use a method. Suppose we want to average sets of two numbers and we don't want to write the averaging code more than once. The Average method just illustrated provides this service; its input is the two numbers we want to average, and its output is the average. Figure 5.3 shows the code for the method Average without all the lines and arrows.

```
static int Average(int First, int Second)
{
        int Result;

        Result = (First + Second) / 2;

        return Result;
}
```

Figure 5.3: A method to average two values

As had become routine, I couldn't sneak this idea (of writing a method) past Susan without a discussion.

> **Susan:** When you say, "and we don't want to write the averaging code more than once", are you just saying if you didn't do the Average method thing then you would have to write this program twice? I mean, for example, would you have to write a program separately for weights and then another one from the beginning for ages?
>
> **Steve:** We wouldn't have to write an entirely separate program; however, we would have to write the averaging code twice. One of the main purposes for writing a method is so that we don't have to repeat code.

Problem
Algorithms
Java
Interpreter
Hardware

To analyze this piece of code, let's start at the beginning. Every method starts with a **method declaration**, which tells the compiler some vital statistics of the method. The method declaration consists of three required parts:

1.   a return type
2.   the method's name
3.   an argument list

There are also several optional parts, called *qualifiers*, which provide the compiler with more details about the method being declared. In the current case, we have one qualifier, the static declaration. We'll take up the meaning of this qualifier in Chapter 7. For now, it's enough to know that this qualifier is necessary whenever we want to write a simple function like Average, where we supply all the data necessary for the function to work.

In the case of our Average method, the rest of the method declaration is int Average(int First, int Second). The return type is int, the name of the method is Average, and the argument list is (int First, int Second). Let's take these one at a time.

Return to Sender

The first part of the method declaration that we'll discuss here is the **return type**, in this case int. This indicates that the method Average will provide a value of type int to the calling method when the Average method returns. Looking at the end of the method, you will see a statement that says return Result;. Checking back to the variable definition part of the method, we see that Result is indeed an int, so the value we're returning is of the correct type. If that were not the case, the compiler would tell us that we had a discrepancy between the declared return type of our method and the type actually returned in the code. This is another example where the compiler helps us out with *static type checking*, as mentioned in Chapter 3; if we say we want to return an int and then return some other incompatible type such as a String, we've made a mistake.[4] It's much easier for the compiler to catch this and warn us than it is for us to locate the error ourselves when the program doesn't work correctly.

Susan wanted to know more about the return type. Here's the conversation that ensued:

> **Susan**: This return type thing — it will have to be the same type of value as the output is?
>
> **Steve**: For our purposes here, the answer is yes. As I've already mentioned, there are exceptions to this rule, but we won't need to worry about them.
>
> **Susan**: Do you always use the word return when you write a method?
>
> **Steve**: Yes, if you're writing a method that has a return value. Methods that don't have return values (like main) don't have to have an explicit return statement. When execution gets to the end of the method, it will return to the calling method, as though the statement return; had been executed.

The method name (in this case, Average) follows the same rules as a variable name. This is not a coincidence, because both method names and variable names are **identifiers**, which is a fancy word for "user-

Problem
Algorithms
Java
Interpreter
Hardware

---

4. What do I mean by an *incompatible type*? Java has rules that, for example, allow us to return a char variable where an int is expected; the compiler will convert the char into either of those types for us automatically. This is convenient sometimes, but it reduces the chances of catching an error of this kind, and therefore is less safe than it could be. This practice is a legacy from C, which means that it probably won't be changed for practical reasons, even though it is less than desirable theoretically.

defined names". The rules for constructing an identifier are pretty simple, as specified in the *Java Language Specification*:

> An identifier is an unlimited-length sequence of Java letters and Java digits, the first of which must be a Java letter. An identifier cannot have the same spelling (Unicode character sequence) as a keyword, ... Two identifiers are the same only if they are identical, that is, have the same Unicode character for each letter or digit.

In other words:

1. Your identifiers can be as long as you wish; the compiler is required to distinguish between two identifiers, no matter how many identical characters they contain, as long as at least one character is different in the two names.[5]
2. They can be made of any combination of Java letters and Java digits, as long as the first character is a letter.[6] For historical reasons, the underscore character _ and the dollar sign $ count as letters.[7]
3. The upper and lower case versions of the same character aren't considered equal as far as names are concerned; that is, the variable xyz is a different variable from Xyz, whereas XYZ is yet another variable. Of course, *you* may get confused by having three variables with those names, but the compiler considers them all distinct.

Problem
Algorithms
Java
Interpreter
Hardware

By the way, the reason that the first character of an identifier can't be a digit is to make it easier for the compiler to figure out what's a number and what isn't. Another rule is that user-defined names cannot conflict with names defined by the Java language (keywords); some examples of keywords that we've already seen are if and int.

Finally, we have the **argument list**. In this case, it contains two arguments, an int called First, which holds the first number that our

---

5. You don't have to worry about wasting space in your program by using long identifiers. They go away when your program is compiled and are replaced by addresses of the variables or methods to which they refer.

6. What is a "Java letter"? This category includes all the English letters in both upper and lowercase (that is, a-z and A-Z). However, because Java is intended to be internationally useful, a Java letter is pretty much any character in any language that is used to make up words in that language. This means that you can use Greek letters, for example, in your identifiers, although that is much more convenient if you have a keyboard and display that can handle them.

7. You should avoid using the $ in your identifiers, as names using that character are sometimes generated by compiler writers and other language implementers.

Average method uses to calculate its result; the second argument (also an int) is called Second, which of course is the other number needed to calculate the average. In other cases, there might be several entries in the argument list, each of which provides some information to the called method. But what exactly *is* an argument?

For the Sake of Argument

The question of what is an argument is more subtle than it may appear. An argument is a value that is supplied by a method (the *calling method*) that wishes to use the services of another method (the *called method*). For example, the calling method might be our main method, and the called method might be our Average method, whereas the arguments are two int values to be averaged. Arguments are actually copies of values from the calling method; that is, the compiler will set the variable named in the argument list of the called method to the value supplied by the calling method. This process of making a copy of the calling method's argument is referred to as *call by value*, and the resulting copy is called a **value argument**.

Figure 5.4 is an example of this argument passing mechanism at work with only one argument. In this program, main sets x to 46 and then calls Birthday with x as the argument. When Birthday starts, a new variable called age is created, and set to 46, because that's the value of x, the argument with which main called Birthday. Birthday adds 1 to its variable age, and then returns the new value of that variable to main. What value will be printed for the variable age by the line System.out.println("Your age was: " + x);? Answer: 46, because the variable age in Birthday was a *copy* of the argument from main, not the actual variable x named in the call to Birthday. On the other hand, the value of y in the main program will be 47, because that is the return value from Birthday.

To use the debugger for this program, follow the instructions in the section titled "Using the debugger" in the file "\readme.txt" on the CD in the back of the book. These instructions assume that you've installed the examples on drive C:, so that the location of this program is "c:\whosj\code\BirthdayTest".

```
Problem
Algorithms
Java
Interpreter
Hardware
```

```
import WAJ.*;

public class BirthdayTest
{
    public static void main( String args[ ] )
    {
    int x;
    int y;

    x = 46;
    y = Birthday(x);

    System.out.println("Your age was: " + x);
    System.out.println("Happy Birthday: your age is now " + y);
    }

    static int Birthday(int age)
    {
    age ++;
    return age;
    }

}
```

Problem
Algorithms
Java
Interpreter
Hardware

Figure 5.4: Argument passing with one argument
(code\BirthdayTest\BirthdayTest.java)

As you might have guessed, the notion of copying the argument when a method is called occasioned an intense conversation with Susan.

Susan: This is tough. I don't get it at all. Does this mean the value of the int named x will then be copied to another location in the method named Birthday?

Steve: Yes, the value in the int named x will be copied to another int called age before the execution of the first line in the method Birthday. This means that the original value of x in main won't be affected by anything that Birthday does.

Susan: Now for the really confusing part. I don't understand when you say, "An argument like the one here (int age) is actually a copy of a value in the calling method". Now I have read this over and over and nothing helped. I thought I understood it for a second or two and then I would lose it; finally, I have decided that there is very little in this section that I do understand. Help.

Steve: When you write a method, the compiler inserts code at the beginning of the method to make a copy of the data that the calling method supplies. This copy of the data is what the called method actually refers to, not the original. Therefore, if you change the value of an argument, it doesn't do anything to the original data in the calling method.[8]

Susan: I don't understand why it is a copy of the calling method and not the called method.

Steve: It's not a copy of the calling method; it's a copy of the value from the calling method, for the use of the called method. In the sample program, main sets x to 46 and then calls Birthday with x as the argument. When Birthday starts, a new variable called age is created, and set to 46, because that's the value of x, the argument with which main called Birthday. Birthday adds 1 to its variable age, and returns the new value of age to main. What value will be printed for the variable age by the line System.out.println("Your age was: " + x);? Answer: 46, because the variable age in Birthday was a *copy* of the value of the argument from main, not the actual variable (x) specified in the call to Birthday. Does this explanation clarify this point?

Susan: I still don't understand the program. It doesn't make any sense. If x = 46, then it will always be 46, no matter what is going on in the called method. So why call a method? You know what, I think my biggest problem is that I don't understand the argument list. I think that is where I am hung up on this.

Problem
Algorithms
Java
Interpreter
Hardware

Steve: The arguments to the method call (x, in the case of the method call Birthday(x)) are transferred to the value of the argument in the method itself (the int variable age, in the case of the method Birthday(int age)).

Susan: In that case, why bother putting an x there, why not just put 46? Would it not do the same thing in the called method, since it is already set to 46?

Steve: Yes, but what if you wanted to call this method from another place where the value was 97 rather than 46? The reason that the argument is a variable is so you can use whatever value you want.

Susan: If we called Birthday with the value 46, then the 46 would be 46++, right?

---

8. This is the behavior when the variables being provided are ints, shorts, chars, or any of the other "primitive" types that are part of the Java language itself. As we'll see later, things can get considerably more complicated when we use variables of other types.

Steve: 46++ is a syntax error, because you can't change the value of a literal constant. Only a variable can be modified.

Susan: So if you want to state a literal value, do you always have to declare a variable first and then set a variable to that literal value?

Steve: No, sometimes you can use a literal value directly without storing it in a variable. For example,

System.out.print(15);

   or

System.out.print("Hello, my name is Steve Heller");

What I was trying to say is that you can't *change* a literal value. Thus, 15++; is not legal, because a literal value such as 15 represents itself, that is, the value 15. If you could write 15++;, what should it do? Change all occurrences of 15 to 16 in the program?

Susan: I get that. Now how does age get initialized to the value of x?

Problem
Algorithms
Java
Interpreter
Hardware

Steve: The compiler does that when it starts the method, because you have stated in the method declaration that the argument to the method is called age, and you have called the method with an argument called x. So the compiler copies the value from x into age right before it starts executing the method.

Susan: Oh, OK. That makes sense, because maybe later on you want to call the same method again and change only a little part of it, but you still need the original to be the same, so you can just change the copy instead of the original. Is that the purpose?

Steve: The reason that the called method gets a copy of data rather than the original is so that the person writing the calling method knows that the original variable hasn't been changed by calling a method. This makes it easier to create programs by combining your own methods with methods that have already been written. Is that what you meant?

Susan: So is everything copied? I am getting confused again; are you going to talk a little more about copying in the book? Have I just not gotten there? Anyway, if you haven't mentioned this more, I think you should; it explains hidden stuff.

Steve: Don't worry, we're going to go into *much* more detail about how this works.

General Delivery

The same analysis that we have just applied to the Birthday method applies also to the Average method that we started out with; the arguments First and Second are copies of the values specified in the call to Average.

Now that we have accounted for the Average method's input and output, we can examine how it does its work. First, we have a variable definition for Result, which will hold the value we will return to the calling method; namely, the average of the two input values.

Then we calculate that average with the statement Result = (First + Second) / 2;. Once the average has been calculated, we're ready to return it to the calling program, which is accomplished by the line return Result;. Finally, we reach the closing }, which tells the compiler that the method is done.

Using a Method

Now that we have seen how to write the Average method, let's see how to use it to solve our original problem. The program in Figure 5.5 uses our Average method twice, once to average two weights, and once to average two ages.

As before, calling a method requires specifying its name and its argument(s) and doing something with the return value, if any. In this case, we call Average with the arguments FirstWeight and SecondWeight, and store the result in AverageWeight. This is accomplished via the line AverageWeight = Average(FirstWeight, SecondWeight);. Later, we call Average with the arguments FirstAge and SecondAge, and store the result in AverageAge. We do this via the line AverageAge = Average(FirstAge, SecondAge);.

To use the debugger for this program, follow the instructions in the section titled "Using the debugger" in the file "\readme.txt" on the CD in the back of the book. These instructions assume that you've installed the examples on drive C:, so that the location of this program is "c:\whosj\code\func1".

Problem
Algorithms
Java
Interpreter
Hardware

```
import WAJ.*;

public class Func1
{
    public static void main( String args[ ] )
    {
        int FirstWeight;
        int SecondWeight;
        int FirstAge;
        int SecondAge;
        int AverageWeight;
        int AverageAge;

        System.out.print("Please type in the first weight: ");
        FirstWeight = RWVar.readInt(System.in);

        System.out.print("Please type in the second weight: ");
        SecondWeight = RWVar.readInt(System.in);

        AverageWeight = Average(FirstWeight, SecondWeight);

        System.out.print("Please type in the first age: ");
        FirstAge = RWVar.readInt(System.in);

        System.out.print("Please type in the second age: ");
        SecondAge = RWVar.readInt(System.in);

        AverageAge = Average(FirstAge, SecondAge);

        System.out.println("The average weight was: " + AverageWeight);
        System.out.println("The average age was: " + AverageAge);
    }

    static int Average(int First, int Second)
    {
        int Result;

        Result = (First + Second) / 2;

        return Result;
    }

}
```

Problem
Algorithms
Java
Interpreter
Hardware

Figure 5.5: Using the Average method (code\func1\func1.java)

Why we would want a method to average two numbers wasn't obvious to Susan at first. After some discussion, however, she agreed that it was valuable. Here's the conversation that convinced her:

Susan: In general, I just don't understand why you even need to call the Average method in the first place; it looks like extra steps to me. It seems to me that all you need are your two input values, which end up just giving you the results right there for weight and age. I think that this is what bothers me the most. For example, when you get done with the set of weights, you should just have your results right then and there instead of calling the method of Average.

Steve: But what is the result you want? You want the average of the weights. Where is that calculated?

Susan: After you are done with that, then you already have written a set of ages so you can just use the result of that. It just seems like you are going in circles unnecessarily with this program. That is why I don't understand it.

Steve: Again, just because you have a set of ages doesn't mean that you have the average age; some code somewhere has to calculate that average.

Then our discussion returned to the topic of how the main program works.

Problem
Algorithms
Java
Interpreter
Hardware

Susan: Oh, OK, so AverageWeight = Average(FirstWeight, SecondWeight); is the part that starts the Average method running?

Steve: Right.

The next topic we discussed was how to create a new program and get it to run.

Susan: Now when you start out a new program, are all the new source files named with a java extension?

Steve: Yes.

Susan: So this code in Average is where the real averaging takes place, right? Is this the "Average command"? I thought Average meant to average, so what is the deal?

Steve: The deal is that something has to do the averaging; rather than writing the same code every time we need to average another set of two numbers, we put that code in one place (the Average method) and call it whenever we need its assistance. I've updated the text to explain this motivation for using methods.

Susan: So does that mean you could put the Average method anywhere you want? Then could it or any "submethod" be put anywhere you want because the main method would always be executed first? Or could you mess up the code if you put it in a really ridiculous place like inside an output or input statement, or could the compiler ignore something like that and go about business as usual? I guess because of the brackets it should ignore such a thing, but I am not sure. See, these are the things that we novices are obliged to ponder.

Steve: You can't start a method definition in the middle of another method. That's called a *nested method* and it's not allowed in Java. The rule can be stated approximately as, "You can start a method definition anywhere except in the middle of another definition."

Susan: So then the "cue" for the Average method to begin is the word Average(weight) or Average(age), when the compiler sees that word it just begins that separate method to start its little calculation.

Problem
Algorithms
Java
Interpreter
Hardware

Steve: That's right, except that it needs two arguments, not just one.

Susan: And that method, since it was named Average, causes the averaging method to work. Is that how it goes?

Steve: If I understand your question, it's not the name that makes the Average method do the averaging; it's the code that adds up the two values and divides by 2. We could replace all the references to Average with the word Glorp and the compiler wouldn't care; however, a future programmer trying to read the program probably wouldn't be amused by that name.

Susan: Oh, so there is nothing magical about the word Average; I thought it might trigger a method of averaging. Well, that sounds reasonable; it's more for us humans than the computer. And then that brings up another question, along the same line of thinking. After the Average method has done its thing, how does the program go from return Result; to the next output statement that asks for the ages? What triggers that change? I am not seeing this in the code.

Steve: The return keyword tells the compiler to hand back control to the method that called the one where the return is, as indicated in Figure 5.2.

This discussion didn't slake her thirst for knowledge about how to write a program. Here is how we continued:

Susan: Can I mix ints with Strings?

Steve: Mixing ints with Strings is a dubious proposition, sort of like asking a desk to make you lunch; could you be more specific about what you're trying to do?

Susan: What if you wanted to add a numerical value to your program: You have to put in an int, right? So if you added an int, what else would you have to do to make it work? Or would you have to start over with another main method after the first part and then declare new variables? I tried that too, and the compiler did not like that either. Very inflexible it is. I will tell you after one more try what I am doing. This will keep you in suspense.

Steve: It depends on what you're trying to do with the int. It's usually best to have a specific problem in mind that you're trying to solve by writing a program. Then you can see how to use these facilities (ints, Strings, arrays, etc.) to solve your problem; if not, you can ask me how they would fit into the solution.

As for your second suggestion, you are allowed to have more than one main method in a particular program, but only one can be the "active" main at any given time. The interpreter determines which one is active based on the name of the program you're running and where it is in the directory structure.

Problem
Algorithms
Java
Interpreter
Hardware

Susan: I am not really trying to solve anything, I just want to have the user type in more info and that info is a number — wait!! That is it; in that case it will be like a character and it doesn't need an int, right? That's right. I can still use a String. We are not crunching any numbers with this.

Steve: As long as you don't try to do any calculations, you can read the data into a String, even data that looks like a number; of course, that data entry method is pretty loose, since if the user types "abc" as an age, the program will accept it.

Susan: Can you define a String without a word but with just a wildcard type of variable like when we use i in ints? In other words, does it matter what we call a variable?

Steve: A variable is always a "wildcard", whether it's an int or a String. For example, an int variable always has a name, such as i, or index, or whatever makes sense to you, and a value, which is a number such as 14 or 99. A String variable also has a name, such as FirstName, or street, or whatever makes sense to you, and a value, which consists of characters rather than a number, such as "Susan" or "Wesley".

A Convincing Argument

As you can see, using a method isn't very difficult. We have to provide it with the material to work on (its input arguments) and can store its return value in a variable for further processing (or use it directly, if we wish).

But there's a little more at work with arguments than meets the eye. How does the variable FirstWeight, for example, get transformed into the variable First that we used when writing the method?

This explanation requires us to to look at some more underlying software technology: To be precise, we're going to spend some time examining the infrastructure that makes computers usable for programmers.

A First-class Solution

```
Problem
Algorithms
Java
Interpreter
Hardware
```

We've already seen that the function of a compiler is to convert our human-readable Java program into byte codes that can be interpreted by the Java interpreter. In addition, the compiler doesn't actually turn a whole program into one byte-code file; instead, it translates each source file into one or more class files. These files contain the instructions that correspond to the source-code statements you've written, but not the "infrastructure" needed to allow them to be interpreted. We'll see what that infrastructure does for us shortly.

Why does the Java compiler produce all these different class files rather than one file that contains the byte-codes for the whole program? Because, as I've mentioned before, Java was intended to be useful in writing large programs. Such programs can consist of hundreds or even thousands of source-code files, each containing hundreds or thousands of lines of code. Once each source file is compiled, the class files resulting from that compilation can be referred to by other programs. When one source file is changed, only those files that have been affected have to be recompiled.[9]

To make such a system work, it's necessary to set up conventions as to which parts will be executed first, where data needed by more

---

9. The alert reader may wonder why I said, "those files that have been affected" rather than, "those files that have been changed". The reason is that even if we don't change a particular file, we may have to recompile it if it uses a class that has been changed.

than one file will be stored, and so on. Also, a lot of operations aren't supplied as part of the language itself but are very handy in writing programs, such as the I/O methods that we've already seen. These make up the infrastructure needed to execute Java programs.

Susan found this explanation to be helpful.

> **Susan**: This is beginning to come into focus. So you write your source code, and it has a middle man called a class file so it can be used by other programs. Close?

> **Steve**: No, exactly right!

Operating Systematically

As is often the case in programming, this infrastructure is divided into several layers, the higher ones depending on the lower ones for more fundamental services. The lowest level of the infrastructure is supplied by the **operating system**, a program that deals with the actual hardware of your computer. By far the most common operating system for Intel CPUs, as this is written, is MS-DOS (which is also the basis for Windows 95), followed by OS/2 and Windows NT. All of these provide some of the same facilities. For example, you are accustomed to dealing with files and directories when using application programs such as word processors and spreadsheets; however, the disk drive in your computer doesn't know anything about files or directories. As we have seen in Chapter 2, all it can do is store and retrieve fixed-size pieces of data called *sectors*, given an absolute address on the disk described by a platter, track number, and sector number. Files are a creation of the operating system, which keeps track of which parts of which files are stored where on the disk.[10]

A modern operating system provides many more facilities than just keeping track of file storage. For example, it arranges for code and data to be stored in separate areas of RAM with different *access rights*, so that code can't be accidentally overwritten by a runaway program; that is, one that writes outside the memory areas it is

```
Problem
Algorithms
Java
Interpreter
Hardware
```

---

10. You might say that files are "virtual"; that is, they're a figment of the operating system's imagination. Nonetheless, they are quite useful. This reminds me of the story about the man who went to a doctor, complaining that his brother had thought he was a hen for many years. The doctor asked why the family hadn't tried to help the brother before, and the man replied, "We needed the eggs".

supposed to use. This is a valuable service, as errors of this kind are quite difficult to find and can cause havoc when they occur.

That's the good news. The bad news is that MS-DOS was created before the widespread availability of reasonably priced CPUs with memory protection facilities and therefore doesn't take advantage of these facilities, although they are present in Windows 3.1 and Windows 95, which run "on top of" MS-DOS. Running under plain MS-DOS, it's entirely possible for a runaway program written in most languages to destroy anything else in memory. Theoretically, we should all be running "real" operating systems by the time you read this; so far, though, the rumors of the demise of MS-DOS have been greatly exaggerated.

This notion intrigued Susan. Here's how that conversation went:

Susan: What is a runaway program?

Steve: One that is writing in areas that it shouldn't, thus destroying data or programs outside its assigned memory areas.

Susan: How would an operating system actually separate code from data areas? Would it be a physical thing?

Problem
Algorithms
Java
Interpreter
Hardware

Steve: What makes this possible are certain hardware mechanisms built into all modern CPUs, so that certain areas of memory can be assigned to specific programs, for use in predefined ways. When these mechanisms are used, a program can't write (or read, in some cases) outside its assigned area. This prevents one program from interfering with another.

One of the advantages of Java, however, is that Java programs are run under control of a *Java interpreter*, which means that they can be prevented from running wild. In fact, such safety is a primary goal of the Java language, and there are quite a few error checks made by the interpreter to ensure that your program doesn't affect anything that it isn't supposed to.

As this suggests, the Java interpreter is another layer of the infrastructure needed to run a Java program. Its basic operation is fairly simple: It uses each of the byte codes that result from compiling a Java program to determine which piece of code to execute on the real CPU. In other words, it is a "virtual CPU" that behaves exactly like a real CPU that uses Java byte codes as its machine language.[11]

---

11. In fact, it's quite possible to build such a CPU; you may see them on the market in the relatively near future if they aren't already available by the time you read this.

The next level of the infrastructure is supplied by the aforementioned packages, which contain standardized segments of code that can perform I/O, mathematical functions, and other commonly used operations. So far, we have used the java.io and java.lang packages to do screen output in our example programs and when using Strings.[12]

Don't Call Me, I'll Call You

Now let's get back to our averaging example. In Figure 5.5, there are two calls to the method Average: The first one is used to average two weights and the other to average two ages. One point I didn't stress was exactly how the Average method "knew" which call was which; that is, how did Average return to the right place after each time it was called? The answer is fairly simple: The interpreter notifies the called method of the address of the next byte-code instruction that should be executed after the called method is finished (the **return address**), and the called method stores that return address in its piece of the stack.

As you might have guessed, Susan and I went over this in gory detail. Here's the play by play:

> **Susan**: Yes, I think this is what has confused me in the past about methods. I never fully understood the mechanism by which one method calls another. I still don't. But I guess it is by the position of the next address in a stack?

> **Steve**: The stack is used to pass arguments and get return values from methods, but its most important use is to keep track of the return address where the calling method is supposed to continue after the called method is done.

> **Susan**: This is how I am visualizing the use of the stack pointer. In one of my other books, it showed how the clock worked in the CPU and it seemed to cycle by pointing in different directions as to what was to happen next in a program. So it was sort of a pointer. Is this how this pointer works? So let me get this straight. All CPUs have some kind of stack pointer, but they are used only for calling methods? Exactly where is the instruction call? It sounds to me like it is in the hardware, and I am having a very difficult time understanding how a piece of hardware can have an instruction.

```
Problem
Algorithms
Java
Interpreter
Hardware
```

---

12. Another package that we've used is the WAJ package, which supplies the ReadInt and ReadString methods.

Steve: All of the instructions executed in a Java program are executed by the interpreter. When a method call is performed, in particular, the interpreter does a number of things, of which two are relevant here.

1.   It saves the address of the next instruction (the contents of the **Java program counter**) on the stack.[13]

2.   It changes the Java program counter to point to the first byte-code instruction of the called method.

The return byte-code instruction (or a variant of this instruction) is used to return to the calling method. It does this by the following steps:

1.   It retrieves the saved value of the program counter from the stack.

2.   It sets the Java program counter back to that value.

The result of this is that execution of the program continues with the next byte-code instruction in the calling method.

Susan: Are you saying that, rather than the pointer of a stack actually pointing to the top of the physical stack, wherever it points to by definition will be the top of the stack, even if it really doesn't look like it?

Steve: Absolutely correct.

```
Problem
Algorithms
Java
Interpreter
Hardware
```

It's time to go over the material we've covered in this chapter.

Review

First, we added the fundamental programming concept of the *method*. A method is a piece of code that can "stand alone"; it can be compiled separately from other methods, and provides some service that we can use via a mechanism known as a *method call*. The method that makes the call is known as the *calling method*, and the one it calls is known as the *called method*. Before we can call a method, we need to know what input values it needs and what it returns. This information is provided by a *method declaration* at the beginning of each method. This includes an *argument list*, which

---

13. The Java program counter is a variable in the Java interpreter that keeps track of the address of the next instruction to be executed, just as the dedicated program counter register does in a real CPU.

specifies input values that the called method uses (if any), and a *return type*, which specifies the type of the value that it produces when it's finished (if any). When we call a method, it executes until it reaches the end of its code or reaches a return statement, whichever comes first. When either of these events happens, the program continues execution in the calling method immediately after the place where the method call occurred. Ordinarily, as in our example, an argument to a method is actually a copy of the variable in the calling program, so that the called method can't modify the "real" value in the caller. This way of passing an argument is known as *call by value*.[14]

We also saw that method and variable names can be of any length, consisting of upper or lower case Java letters (or both), Java digits, and the special characters underscore (_) and dollar sign ($). To make it easier for the compiler to distinguish numbers from variable names, the first character can't be a digit. Also, a variable name can't be the same as a *keyword*, or name defined by the language; examples of keywords we've seen so far include if, for, and int.

After finishing the construction of our Average method, we saw how to use it by making a method call.

Conclusion

We've covered a lot of material in this chapter, ranging from the anatomy of methods through a lot more information on what's going on "underneath the covers" of even a fairly simple Java program. Next we'll see how to write a realistic, although simplified, application program using some more advanced concepts in Java.

```
Problem
Algorithms
Java
Interpreter
Hardware
```

---

14. As we'll see in Chapter 6, argument passing is considerably more complicated when we're dealing with variables other than the primitive types that are built into the Java language.

Chapter 6

Taking Inventory

A class **Act**

Now we have enough of the fundamentals of programming under our belts to look at one of the more powerful features of Java: the ability to create user-defined data types. What are these, and why do we care?

In Java, the available data types are mostly divided into two groups: **primitive** (i.e., defined in the language itself) and **user defined** (i.e., defined by the programmer).[1] The primitive types that we've been using are char, short, and int, all of which have been inherited from C.[2]

In this chapter, we'll see how to give the compiler enough information to create our own data types. Let's start out with some definitions and objectives.

Definitions

A **primitive type** (sometimes called a **native type**) is a data type that is built into the Java language and cannot be replaced or modified by the Java programmer.

---

1. There are a couple of exceptions to this division: Strings act partially like a primitive type and partially like a user-defined type, and *arrays* can be used with both primitive and user-defined types, but can't themselves be redefined by the user.

2. There are actually several other primitive Java types that we haven't used: byte, long, float, double, and boolean. We'll use float to keep track of numbers that have fractional parts in some examples in this and later chapters. The boolean type is useful for keeping track of a true/false condition, as we'll see later in this chapter. The others are covered to some extent in Appendix A.

A class is a user-defined type.

A class **definition** tells the compiler what facilities the class supplies and how to implement those facilities. A class definition is found in a source-code file, which has the extension .java.

An **object** is a programming construct that represents a specific item of user-defined data that we wish to keep track of in a program. Note that an object is similar to a variable in that it represents an item of data. However, unlike a variable, we cannot use an object directly but must refer to it via a **reference**.

A **reference** is a variable that refers to an object and thus allows us to use that object.

A **field** is a variable that is part of the definition of a class.

Object-oriented programming is the organization of programs as collections of objects, rather than as collections of methods operating on variables of primitive data types.

```
Problem
Algorithms
Java
Interpreter
Hardware
```

A **class interface** is the set of operations that objects of that class can perform, as contrasted with the implementation of those operations.

Encapsulation is the concept of hiding the details of a class inside the implementation of that class rather than exposing them in the interface. This is one of the primary organizing principles that characterize object-oriented programming.

Objectives for This Chapter

By the end of this chapter, you should:

1.   Understand what a user-defined type (a class) is, and how it is defined.
2.   Understand how variables of some simple classes are created, destroyed, and copied.
3.   Understand how and why access to the internals of a class is controlled.

Pay Some Attention to the Man behind the Curtain

Susan had a revealing question here.

> **Susan**: I think I need to find out something here. I am getting the impression that what is "primitive" is C and what is "user-defined" is Java. Is that right? And if so, why?

> **Steve**: Close, but not exactly right. Java inherited much of its syntax from C++ (the successor to C), but user-defined types aren't supported as well in Java as in C++. As to why, the answer is pretty simple: The reason that Java was invented in the first place was to create a simpler language by keeping only the necessary features from C++ and adding new features that the designers thought would be useful but didn't exist in C++. As to whether they picked the right features in the first category, I'm not convinced. In any event, Java is the way it is (for now, anyway), and we'll have to make the best of it.

In Java, it is not possible to create user-defined data types that behave in the same way as primitive types, so it is important to distinguish the characteristics of these two kinds of data types. Native variables in Java can be defined, initialized, assigned values, passed as arguments and return values, and compared to other values of the same type. However, most of these facilities don't work the same way for user-defined data types in Java. To explain this difference, we're going to have to go into detail about how we use **objects** (that is, data items of a user-defined type). We can never use objects directly; instead, we have to refer to them via **references**.

```
Problem
Algorithms
Java
Interpreter
Hardware
```

What is a reference? We can think of it as a "secretary" for an object. Whenever we want to do anything with an object, we ask a reference to pass the message along to it. This may seem a distinction without a difference; after all, why should we care whether we access an object directly or through a reference?

Unfortunately, we do have to be concerned with this apparently arcane topic, because there are some very important differences between the way references are treated by the compiler and the way primitive variables are treated. For example, while the == operator can be applied to references, it doesn't tell you whether the objects that the references refer to have the same value; instead, it tells you whether the references refer to the same object. To compare the values of two objects, you have to write a function (usually called equals) for this purpose.

We'll see soon enough how these differences affect the way that we use references in our programs. First, though, let's start by defining a simple class.

Second-class Citizens

In Java, a user-defined data item is called an **object**. Each object has a type, just as a primitive variable does. For example, if we define a class called StockItem (as we will do in this chapter), then an object can be of type StockItem, just as a primitive variable can be of type int, char, or one of the other primitive types. However, an additional step is required with user-defined types. Since the compiler has no intrinsic knowledge of these types, we have to tell it exactly what they are and how they work. We do this by defining a class, which specifies both the data contained in the user-defined variable and what operations can be performed on these data.

Here's how Susan reacted upon her first encounter with this idea:

> **Susan**: I can tell that there is only one thing that I think that I understand about this. That is, that Java is not a language. You have to *make it up* as you go along.

Problem
Algorithms
Java
Interpreter
Hardware

That may be overdoing it a bit, but there is a grain of truth in her observation: Java is more of a "language kit" than it is a language. What do I mean by this?

I mean that to use Java in the most effective way, it is necessary to make up our own data types. So far in this book, we have been using data types that were previously defined, either by the compiler and language (*primitive* types, e.g., short, int, char) or by packages (class types, e.g., String). Now we're going to actually make up our own types; the difference between using preexisting types and making up new types is analogous to the difference between using a program and writing a program, but carried to the next higher level.

In the event that you find this notion hard to understand, you're not alone; neither did Susan.

> **Susan**: This is an outrage! I didn't understand one other word as I was far beyond anything that could even be described as shock. I think I did faint. I may as well have been in a coma.

Interestingly enough, she did in fact understand this idea of making up our own data types, so perhaps she was overestimating the degree of her shock.

Before we get back to the technical explanation of how we create new data types, I'm sure one more question is burning in your mind: *Why* should we do this? What's wrong with the primitive types like char and int? The answer is simple: We make up types so that we can match the language to the needs of the problem we're trying to solve. For example, suppose we want to write a program to do inventory control for a small business like a grocery store. Such a program needs objects representing items in the store, which have prices, names, and so on. We'd need to define each of these types of objects so that it can display the behavior appropriate to the thing it represents. The availability of objects that have relevance to the problem being solved makes it much easier to write (and *read*) a program to handle inventory than if everything has to be made of ints and chars.

I suspect that the advantages of making up one's own data types may still not be apparent to you, so let me make an analogy with natural languages. Making up new data types in Java is in some ways quite similar to making up new words in English, for example. You might think that if everyone made up new words, the result would be chaos. Actually, this is correct, with the very important exception of technical jargon and other vocabularies that are shared by people who have more in common than simply being speakers of English. For example, physicians have their own "language" in the form of medical terminology. Of course, a cynical observer might conclude that the reason for such specialized vocabulary is to befuddle or impress the naive listener, and of course it can be used for that purpose. However, there is also a much more significant and valid reason: to make it possible for experts in a field to communicate with one another quickly and precisely. The same is true of creating our own data types; they enable us to write programs that are more understandable to those who are conversant with the problems being solved. It's much easier to talk to a store owner about inventory objects than about ints and chars!

Here's the discussion that Susan and I had on this topic:

Problem
Algorithms
Java
Interpreter
Hardware

Susan: Why should we have user-defined data types?

Steve: So that you can match the language to the needs of the problem you're trying to solve. For example, if you were writing a nurse's station program in Java, you would want to have objects that represented nurses, doctors, patients, various sorts of equipment, and so on. Each of these objects would display the behavior appropriate to the thing or person it was representing.

Susan: Why do you need that? What if each individual who spoke English made up a unique version of English (well, it is user defined, right?), how could we communicate? This is garbage.

Steve: We need user-defined types for the same reason that specialists need jargon in their technical fields. For example, why do you health-care professionals need words like tachycardia? Why don't you just say "a fast heartbeat" in simple English?

Hey, that's not a bad way to explain this: adding classes is like adding specialized vocabulary to English. I don't remember ever seeing that explanation before; what do you think of it?

Susan: Huh? Then you are saying that, by defining a class of objects, they can take on more realistic qualities than just abstract notions? That is, if I wanted to define *nurse* in a program, then I would do it with a class named nurse and then I can define in that program the activities and functions that the nurse objects would be doing. Is this how you keep everything straight, and not mix them up with other objects?

Problem
Algorithms
Java
Interpreter
Hardware

Steve: Yes, that's one of the main benefits of object-oriented programming. You might be surprised how hard it can be to teach an old-line C programmer the importance of this point.

Susan: So is this what object-oriented programming is? I have heard of it, but never knew what it meant. Could it also be described as user-defined programming? I guess there are advantages to teaching a novice; you don't have to undo old ideas to make way for newer ones. So anything that is user defined is a class? That is, primitive variables are not classes?

Steve: Every user-defined type is a class; data items of a class type are called *objects*. Variables of primitive types are not objects in the strict sense.

Susan: OK, so if I want to make up something, then what I make up is called a class as opposed to the other type of stuff that isn't made up by the user and is really Java; that is called *primitive*. That is intuitive, thank you. Then the class is made up of data items? And what about primitive variables; are they objects? I guess just the variables of the class are called *objects*, because I just made an effort to move and read your definition for *object*. So primitive variables are not objects, they are just variables. Am I am talking in circles again?

Steve: No, you're not; you're making perfect sense. The only point you have missed is that there are methods in the objects, as well as data items. We'll get into that shortly.

Susan: So Steve, tell me this: What have I been doing up to this point? How does this new stuff compare to the old stuff and which one is it that the programmer really uses? (Let's see, do I want curtain 1 or 3; which one holds the prize?) I just want to get a little sense of direction here; I don't think that is a whole lot to ask, do you?

Steve: What you've been doing up to this point is *using* classes (String, RWVar) as well as primitive types like int and char. This new stuff shows how to *create* classes rather than just using them.[3]

Assuming that I've sold you on the advantages of making up our own data types, let's see how we can actually do it. Each data type is represented by a class, whose definition is contained in a file with the extension .java. This class definition tells the compiler (and the class user) both *what* the class does and *how* the objects of that class actually perform the specified functions. Let's take a look at a step-by-step description of how to create and use a class.

Problem
Algorithms
Java
Interpreter
Hardware

1. Write the class definition, which will be stored in a file with the extension .java; in our example, the first one of these will be stored in the file item1.java. This definition is the code that tells the compiler how to perform the operations that objects of the class support.
2. Write the program that uses objects in the class to do some work; the first such program we'll write will be itemtst1.java.
3. Compile the class implementation definition to produce a class file (item1.class). This makes the class available for use by the user program.
4. Compile the user program to produce a class file (itemtst1.class).
5. Run the user program.

Taking Stock

Now let's start on our first class definition, which is designed to help solve the problem of maintaining inventory in a small grocery store. We need to keep track of all the items that we carry, so we're going to define a class called StockItem. The StockItem class, like other classes,

---

3. In case you were wondering, you can't create new primitive types.

is composed of a number of methods and fields. To make this more concrete, think of something like Lego™ blocks, which you can put together to make parts that can in turn be used to build bigger structures. The smallest Legos are the primitive types, and the bigger, composite ones are class types.

For the compiler to be able to define an object correctly, we'll have to tell it the names and types of the fields that will be used to store the information about each StockItem; this enables the compiler to allocate memory for a StockItem.

So how do we identify these fields? By considering what fields each StockItem object will need to keep track of its corresponding item in the stock of the store. After some thought, I've come up with the following list of fields:

1.   the name of the item (m_Name)
2.   the number in stock (m_InStock)
3.   the distributor that we purchase it from (m_Distributor)
4.   the price we charge (m_Price)
5.   the item number, or UPC (m_UPC)

Problem
Algorithms
Java
Interpreter
Hardware

What I mean by *an item* is actually something like "chunky chicken soup, 16 oz.", rather than a specific physical object like a particular can of soup. In other words, every can of soup with the same item number is considered equivalent to every other can of soup with the same item number. Therefore, any given item can be described by the above data. For the item number, we'll use the Universal Product Code (UPC), which is printed as a bar code on almost every product other than fresh produce; it's a 10-digit number, which we'll represent as a String for convenience.

Susan took me to task about the notion of a StockItem object versus a specific physical object like a particular can of soup. It didn't take too long to clear this one up.

> **Susan**: When you say, "rather than a specific physical object", how much more specific can you get than "chunky chicken soup, 16 oz."?
>
> **Steve**: Each can of chunky chicken soup is at least slightly different from every other one; at the very least, they are in different places.

Let's recap what we know about a StockItem so far. We need a field in the StockItem class definition for each value in the above description: the name of the item (m_Name), its price (m_Price), the number of items in stock (m_InStock), the name of the distributor (m_Distributor), and the UPC (m_UPC) of the item.

Of course, merely storing this data isn't very useful unless we can do something with it. Therefore, objects of the StockItem class also need to be able to perform several operations on their data; we'll start by giving them the ability to display their contents. Figure 6.1 illustrates a very simple way that this class might be used.

```java
import WAJ.*;

public class Itemtst1
{
    public static void main( String args[ ] )
    {
        StockItem item1;
        StockItem item2;

        item1 = new StockItem();
        item2 = new StockItem("Chunky Chicken",32,129,
            "Bob's Distribution","123456789");

        item1.Display();
        item2.Display();
    }
}
```

Problem
Algorithms
Java
Interpreter
Hardware

Figure 6.1: The initial sample program for the StockItem class
(code\itemtst1\itemtst1.java)

This program defines a StockItem named item1, assigns it a value, and displays that value on the screen via a method called Display, and finally terminates normally.

To use the debugger for this program, follow the instructions in the section titled "Using the debugger" in the file "\readme.txt" on the CD in the back of the book. These instructions assume that you've installed the examples on drive C:, so that the location of this program is "c:\whosj\code\itemtst1".

By the time we're done with this chapter, you'll understand exactly how all the operations in this program (and several other example programs) are performed by the StockItem class. First, we'll need some more definitions to clarify the terms that we'll need for the discussion.

More Definitions

A **constructor** is a method that creates new variables of the class type. All constructors have the same name as the class for which they are constructors; therefore, the constructors for StockItem variables also have the name StockItem.

A **default constructor** is a constructor that is used when no initial value is specified for an object. Because it is a constructor, it has the same name as the class; since it is used when no initial value is specified, it has no arguments. Thus, StockItem() is the default constructor for the StockItem class.

Stock in Trade

Before we can implement the methods for our StockItem class, we have to define what a StockItem is in more detail than my previous sketch.[4] Let's start with the simplified version of the definition for that class in Figure 6.2, which includes the specification of the default constructor, the display method, and another constructor that is specific to the StockItem class.

Problem
Algorithms
Java
Interpreter
Hardware

Your first reaction is probably something like, "What a bunch of malarkey!" Let's take it a little at a time, and you'll see that this seeming gibberish actually has its own rhyme and reason. First we have the line public class StockItem. This tells the compiler that what follows is the definition of a class, which as we have already seen is a specification of the operations that can be performed on objects of a given user-defined type; in this case, the type is StockItem. So that the compiler knows where this description begins and ends, it is enclosed in {}, just like any other block of information that is to be treated as one item.

But what about the public part? This is a new type of declaration called an **access specifier**, which tells the compiler the "security classification" of the item following it. This particular access specifier, public, means that any method, whether or not it is defined in this class, can use the item to which it is prefixed; in this case, it means that the StockItem class is accessible to any program that wants to use it.

---

4. By the way, in using a functional class such as StockItem to illustrate these concepts, I'm violating a venerable tradition in programming tutorials. Normally, example classes represent zoo animals, or shapes, or something equally useful in common programming situations.

```
import WAJ.*;

public class StockItem
{
private int m_InStock;
private int m_Price;
private String m_Name;
private String m_Distributor;
private String m_UPC;

StockItem()
{
    m_InStock = 0;
    m_Price = 0;
    m_Name = "";
    m_Distributor = "";
    m_UPC = "";
}

StockItem(String Name, int InStock,int Price, String Distributor, String UPC)
{
    m_InStock = InStock;
    m_Price = Price;
    m_Name = Name;
    m_Distributor = Distributor;
    m_UPC = UPC;
}

void Display()
{
    System.out.print("Name: ");
    System.out.println(m_Name);
    System.out.print("Number in stock: ");
    System.out.println(m_InStock);
    System.out.print("Price: ");
    System.out.println(m_Price);
    System.out.print("Distributor: ");
    System.out.println(m_Distributor);
    System.out.print("UPC: ");
    System.out.println(m_UPC);
    System.out.println();
}

void SetName(String Name)
{
    m_Name = Name;
}
}
```

Problem
Algorithms
Java
Interpreter
Hardware

Figure 6.2: The initial class definition for the StockItem class
(code\itemtst1\StockItem.java)

Since the StockItem class is public, we can use StockItem objects anywhere in our programs.[5] You may be wondering why everything isn't public; why should we prevent ourselves (or users of our classes) from using everything in the classes? It's not just hardheartedness; it's actually a way of improving the reliability and flexibility of our software, as I'll explain later.

As you might imagine, this notion of access specifiers didn't get past Susan without a battle. Here's the blow-by-blow account.

Susan: So is public a word that is used often or is it just something you made up for this example?

Steve: It's a keyword of the Java language, which has intrinsic meaning to the compiler. In this context, it means "any method, inside or outside this class, can access the following item." Because it is a keyword, you can't have a variable named public, just as you can't have one named if.

Susan: These access specifiers: What are they, anyway? Are they always used in classes?

Steve: Yes.

Susan: Why aren't they needed for primitive variables?

Steve: Because you can't define access specifiers for primitive types; their internals are predefined in the compiler and aren't accessible to the programmer.

Susan: What does *internals* mean? Do you mean stuff that is done by the compiler rather than stuff that can be done by the programmer?

Steve: Yes, in the case of primitive data types. In the case of class types, *internals* means the details of implementation of the type rather than what it does for the user.

Susan: You know, I understand what you are saying about *internals*; that is, I know what the words mean, but I just can't picture what you are doing when you say *implementation*. I don't see what is actually happening at this point.

Steve: The implementation of a class is the code that is responsible for actually doing the things that the objects of the class are supposed to do.

Problem
Algorithms
Java
Interpreter
Hardware

---

5. By the way, public is a keyword in Java; that is, it is defined in the language. This means that you cannot have a method or variable called public.

All of the code in the item1.java file is part of the implementation of StockItem.

Susan: So on these fields, that m_ stuff, do you just do that to differentiate them from a primitive variable? If so, why would there be a confusion, since you have already told the compiler you are defining a class? Therefore, all that is in that class should already be understood to be in the class rather than the primitive language. I don't like to look at that m_ stuff; it's too cryptic.

Steve: It's true that the compiler can tell whether a variable is a field or a local variable. However, it can still be useful to give a different name to a field so that the *programmer* can tell which is which. Remember, a field looks like an argument or a local variable in a class implementation, although you don't have to declare it as you would an argument or a local variable.

Now we're up to the line that says StockItem(). This is the declaration for a method called a *constructor*, which tells the compiler how to create an object; as we have already seen, there's no way for it to know this otherwise. This particular constructor is the *default constructor* for the StockItem class. It's called the "default" constructor because it is used when no initial value is specified by the user; the empty parentheses after the name of the method indicate the lack of arguments to the method. The name of the method is the clue that it's a constructor; the name of a constructor is always the same as the name of the class for which it's a constructor, to make it easier for the compiler to identify constructors among all of the possible methods in a class.

This idea of having fields and methods "inside" objects wasn't intuitively obvious to Susan.

Problem
Algorithms
Java
Interpreter
Hardware

Susan: Now where you talk about mixing a String and an int in the same method, can this not be done in the native language?

Steve: It's not in the same method but in the same object. We are creating a user-defined object that can be used more or less the way we use a primitive variable.

Susan: OK, so you have a class StockItem. And it has a method called StockItem. But a StockItem is an object, so in this respect a method can be inside an object?

Steve: Actually, every method is inside a class. In this particular case, a StockItem is an object that is composed of a number of methods and fields (variables).

Susan: OK, I think I am seeing the big picture now. But you know that this seems like such a departure from what I thought was going on before, where we used primitive types in methods rather than the other way around. Like when I wrote my little program, it would have ints in it but they would be in the method main. So this is a complete turnabout from the way I used to think about them. This is hard.

Steve: Yes, that is a difficult transition to make. Interestingly enough, experience isn't necessarily an advantage here; you haven't had as much trouble with it as some professional programmers who have a lot more experience in writing methods as "stand-alone" things with no intrinsic ties to data structures. However, it is one of the essentials in object-oriented programming; in Java, all methods live "inside" classes, and do the bidding of objects of those classes, rather than being wild and free.

Problem
Algorithms
Java
Interpreter
Hardware

Why do we need to write our own default constructor? Well, although we have already specified the fields used by the class, that isn't necessarily enough information for the compiler to know how to initialize the objects of the class correctly. The compiler will make assumptions as to the correct values of the fields of an object. In the case of a StockItem, these assumptions actually will be correct; however, it's generally considered better form for us to initialize the fields of our object ourselves anyway, just so the next programmer knows that we didn't forget. Figure 6.3 shows what the code to our first default constructor looks like.

```
StockItem()
{
    m_InStock - 0;
    m_Price = 0;
    m_Name = "";
    m_Distributor = "";
    m_UPC = "";
}
```

Figure 6.3: The default constructor for the StockItem class (from code\itemtst1\item1.java)

Actually, this method isn't all that different from a "regular" method. The main difference is that it is used to create a new object rather than to do something for, or with, an existing object.

Susan had an objection to my cavalier use of the empty String "" in the default constructor.

Susan: Excuse me, but what kind of value is " "? Do you know how annoying it is to keep working with nothing?

Steve: It's not " ", but "". The former has a space between the quotes, and the latter does not; the former is a one-character String consisting of one space, whereas the latter is a zero-character String.

Susan: OK, so the "" is an empty String, but could you please explain how this works?

Steve: The "" means that we have a String with no data in it.

Susan: OK, so this is only setting the Strings in the default constructor to a value that the compiler can understand so you don't get an error message, although there is no real data. We're trying to fool the compiler, right?

Steve: Close, but not quite. Basically, we want to make sure that we know the state of the Strings in a default StockItem.

Susan: Yes, I remember. So this is just the way to initialize a String when you don't know what real value it will end up having?

Steve: Right.

Scoped Out

Problem
Algorithms
Java
Interpreter
Hardware

Now let's get back to the fields of StockItem. One important characteristic of any variable is its **scope**: The scope of a variable is the part of the program in which it can be accessed. Until now, we've been dealing with **local** variables, which are defined and accessed only inside a particular method. Now we have to deal with another scope called class **scope**, which applies to all fields of a class.[6] Fields have class scope, which means that each object of a given class has its own set of fields. In the case of StockItem, this set of fields consists of m_InStock, m_Price, m_Name, m_Distributor, and m_UPC. Methods of a class can access fields of that class without defining them, as though they were arguments or local variables of those methods.

In addition to scope, each field has another attribute we have already encountered: an access specifier. The access specifier is used to control access by methods of other classes to that field or method.

---

6. Actually, I'm describing "normal" fields here. There is another kind that we won't be covering.

If you look back at Figure 6.2, you'll see that the keyword private precedes the definition of each of the fields in the StockItem class. The keyword private is an access specifier, like public; however, where a public access specifier allows any method to access the item following it, a private access specifier allows only methods of that class to access the item that follows it.

Although scope rules and access specifiers are similar in some ways, in that they affect where a variable can be used, they aren't exactly the same. Scope defines where a variable exists and therefore where it is visible, whereas access specifiers control where a variable (or method) is accessible. That is, if you write a program that tries to read or modify a private variable from outside the class implementation, the compiler knows what you're trying to do but won't let you do it. On the other hand, if you try to access a local variable from a method where it isn't defined, the compiler just tells you it has never heard of that variable, which indeed it hasn't in that context. For example, let's suppose that the local variable x defined in method abc has no existence in any other method; in that case, if you try to access a variable named x in another method, say def, where it hasn't been defined, you'll get an error message from the compiler telling you that there is no variable x in method def. However, if there is a private field called x defined in class ghi, and you try to access that field from a method of another class, the compiler will tell you that you're trying to do something illegal. It knows which x you mean, but it won't let you access it because you don't have permission.

Susan had some more questions about access specifiers, including this new one, private.

Problem
Algorithms
Java
Interpreter
Hardware

> **Susan**: It seems to me that the access specifiers act more like scope than anything. Are they about the same?
>
> **Steve**: Yes, the difference between public and private is somewhat analogous to the difference between local variables and class fields, but an access specifier controls what methods can access the field, whereas the difference between local variables and class fields affects where a variable is stored and when it is initialized. However, because fields are defined inside classes, they can't be exactly like local variables; a field must always live inside a single occurrence of an object of its class.
>
> **Susan**: Are they necessary for every class?
>
> **Steve**: Pretty much. The default access specifier for a class is one commonly referred to as "package access", but for some reason there's

no keyword to specify it. In any event, this default specifier grants access to all classes in the same package. Of course, this also means that if you don't use explicit access specifiers, then everything declared in that class will be accessible to every other class in that package. As you'll see, it's usually better to make fields private, so the private specifier is almost always needed in a class.

Susan: So does the scope of a variable refer to where it is, or where you can see it?

Steve: Both. The scope of a variable is that part of the program in which it exists. It is visible, although perhaps not accessible, depending on its access specifier, in that part of the program. In the case of a class field, its scope is the same as the scope of the object of which it is a part: It comes into existence when that object is created, and becomes inaccessible when that object becomes inaccessible (because the last reference to it has ceased to exist). In the case of a local variable, its scope is from the point of its declaration to the end of the block in which it was declared.

Susan: OK, that makes sense now. Are there any other kinds of access specifiers or are these the only ones?

Steve: Actually, there's another one we'll be using later.

Susan: Wonderful; I can't wait.

Steve: Don't worry, they won't hurt (at least, not very much).

```
Problem
Algorithms
Java
Interpreter
Hardware
```

Susan also wanted some more details about this new class scope.

Susan: How about explaining the difference between a class scope and a public access specifier?

Steve: Fields declared in a class always have class scope; that means that they live as long as the object that contains them. The access specifier determines who can access these variables, but does not affect their lifetimes.

Of course, the constructor StockItem(), by virtue of being a method of the StockItem class, has access to all the fields of that class, so the private access specifier doesn't apply to it. We'll see later how that access specifier comes into play.

Now that we know what kind of variables the StockItem() method deals with, namely, its fields, its behavior isn't very mysterious: It simply initializes the fields to 0 or "", whichever is appropriate to their types.

But why does it need to do this? Because the fields of the StockItem class are the "raw material" the StockItem methods use to implement the behavior that we want a StockItem to display.

Susan wasn't buying all this malarkey about fields without a fight. Here's how it went:

> **Susan**: What do m_InStock and m_Price and the others actually do? It seems we are missing a verb here.

> **Steve**: They don't do anything by themselves. They are the fields used to store the count and price of the goods described by a StockItem object, respectively. In the default constructor, they are both set to 0, indicating a StockItem with no content. Any StockItem object that is created without a value is set to this empty state. That is, we don't have to worry about the initial state of a StockItem that we create without a specified value, because the default constructor ensures that such a StockItem is set to a known value when it is created. And because the fields are private, the user of the class can't access them directly, but has to use methods of StockItem to do anything with or to them.

> **Susan**: Okay, that makes more sense now.

```
Problem
Algorithms
Java
Interpreter
Hardware
```

The fields of a class are set, used, and changed by the methods of that class in the course of implementing the behaviors that the StockItem class definition promises.

So much for the "high-altitude" description of what a class does. Now let's get back to the details that make it work, starting with the line where the StockItem() method is used in the test program in Figure 6.1, StockItem item1 = new StockItem();. Remember that the basic idea of constructing a class is to add data types to the language that aren't available "out of the box". One of the functions that we have to help the compiler with is initialization; a main purpose for the StockItem() constructor is to initialize objects of the StockItem type that have no values explicitly assigned to them. That's why it's called a *default constructor*.

Susan didn't immediately cotton to the idea of calling a default constructor when creating an object.

> **Susan**: Sure, defining an object is simple if you don't lose your mind defining the classes first.

Steve: It *is* simple for the application programmer (the user of the class). We're doing the hard part so he or she can just use the objects without having to worry about any of this stuff.

Susan: Huh? Isn't the "user of the class" always the same as the "writer of the class"?

Steve: Not necessarily. You've been using Strings for some time now without having to be concerned about how they work. This is not unusual.

Susan: Yeah, but if you are a programmer you will be a class writer, not just a user.

Steve: That's usually the case, but certainly not with respect to all the classes. You may very well write your own application-specific classes but use the ones from the standard packages for all of the low-level stuff like Strings, I/O, and so on.

You should generally write a default constructor for every class you define, to guarantee the state of any "default constructed" object. If you define some other constructor but don't define a default constructor, programs using your class won't be able to create objects without specifying their values.

So why did I say "generally", rather than "always"? Because there are some times when you don't want to allow an object to be created unless the "real" data for it is available. In that case, all you have to do is to define some other constructor but avoid defining a default constructor. This will cause a compiler error in any user code that tries to create an object of that class without specifying any initial values.

Susan thought that the idea of having to define a default constructor for each class was a bit off the wall.

Problem
Algorithms
Java
Interpreter
Hardware

Susan: When you say that "you should define one of these (default constructors) for every class you define...", my question is how? What are you talking about? I thought a default meant just that, it was a default; you don't have to do anything with it; it is set to a preassigned value.

Steve: It's true that the class user doesn't have to do anything with the default constructors. However, the class writer (that's us, in this case) often has to define a default constructor so that when the class user defines an object without providing an initial value, the new object has a reasonable state for an "empty" object.

Shop till You Drop

Now let's continue with our analysis of the StockItem class (Figure 6.2). Before we can do anything with an inventory record, we have to enter the inventory data. This means that we need another constructor that actually sets the values into the object. We also need some way to display the data for a StockItem on the screen, which means writing a Display method.

The next method in that figure is the constructor that creates an object with actual data. Figure 6.4 shows the code for that constructor.

```
StockItem(String Name, int InStock, int Price, String Distributor, String UPC)
{
    m_InStock = InStock;
    m_Price = Price;
    m_Name = Name;
    m_Distributor = Distributor;
    m_UPC = UPC;
}
```

Problem
Algorithms
Java
Interpreter
Hardware

Figure 6.4: Another constructor for the StockItem class (from code\itemtst1\item1.java)

Let's start the analysis with the method's header: StockItem(String Name, short InStock, short Price, String Distributor, String UPC). We can tell that this method is a constructor because its name, StockItem, is the same as the name of the class. If you're a C programmer, you may be surprised to see two methods that have the same name, differing only in the types of their arguments. This is not legal in C, but it is in Java; it's called **method overloading**, and as you'll see, it's a very handy facility that isn't limited to constructors. The combination of the method name and argument types is called the **signature** of a method; two methods that have the same name but differ in the type of at least one argument are distinct methods.[7] In the case of the default constructor, there are no arguments, so that constructor is used where no initial data are specified for the object. The statement item1 = StockItem(); fits that description, so the default constructor is used. However, in the next statement of the sample program (Figure 6.1), we have the expression:

---

7. Note that the names of the arguments are not part of the signature, so you can't have two methods that differ only in the names of their arguments.

StockItem("Chunky Chicken",32,129,"Bob's Distribution","123456789");

This is clearly a call to a constructor, because the name of the method is the name of a class, StockItem. Therefore, the compiler looks for a constructor that can handle the set of arguments in this call, and finds:

StockItem(String Name, int InStock, int Price, String Distributor, String UPC)

The first, fourth, and fifth arguments to the constructor are Strings, whereas the second and third are ints. Since these types all match those specified in the expression in the sample program, the compiler can translate that expression into a call to this constructor.

As you can see, nothing about this constructor is terribly complex; it merely sets the fields of the object being constructed to the values of the corresponding arguments to the method.

But why do we need more than one constructor? Susan had that same question, and I had some answers for her.

Susan: How many constructors do you need to say the same thing?

Steve: They don't say exactly the same thing. It's true that every constructor in the StockItem class makes a StockItem; however, each argument list varies. The default constructor makes an empty StockItem and therefore doesn't need any arguments, whereas the constructor StockItem(String Name, int InStock, int Price, String Distributor, String UPC) makes a StockItem with the values specified by the Name, InStock, Price, Distributor, and UPC arguments in the constructor call.

Susan: Are you saying that in defining a class you can have two methods that have the same name, but they are different in only their arguments and that makes them unique?

Steve: Exactly. This is the language feature called *method overloading*.

Susan: So StockItem item1; is the default constructor in case you need something that can create uninitialized objects?

Steve: Not quite; the default constructor for the StockItem class is StockItem(), which doesn't need any arguments, because it constructs an empty StockItem. The line item1 = StockItem(); causes the default constructor to be called to create an empty StockItem.

```
Problem
Algorithms
Java
Interpreter
Hardware
```

Susan: And the line item2 = StockItem("Chunky Chicken",32,129,"Bob's Distribution","123456789"); is a constructor that finally gets around to telling us what we are trying to accomplish here?

Steve: No, that line causes a StockItem with the specified contents to be created, by calling the constructor StockItem(String Name, int InStock, int Price, String Distributor, String UPC);, and assigns that StockItem to the variable named item2.

Susan: So are you saying that for every new StockItem you have to have a new constructor for it?

Steve: No, there's one constructor for each *way* that we can construct a StockItem. One for situations where we don't have any initial data (the default constructor), and one for those where we are supplying the data for a StockItem. There could be other ones too, but those are all we have right now.

Once that expression has been translated, the compiler assigns the result of the expression to the StockItem object called item2, as requested in the whole statement:

Problem
Algorithms

item2 = StockItem("Chunky Chicken",32,129,"Bob's Distribution","123456789");

Java
Interpreter
Hardware

The last two statements is the test program (Figure 6.1) are item1.Display(); and item2.Display(), which display the values of item1 and item2 on the screen, respectively. Figure 6.5 shows the code for the Display method.

```
void Display()
{
        System.out.print("Name: ");
        System.out.println(m_Name);
        System.out.print("Number in stock: ");
        System.out.println(m_InStock);
        System.out.print("Price: ");
        System.out.println(m_Price);
        System.out.print("Distributor: ");
        System.out.println(m_Distributor);
        System.out.print("UPC: ");
        System.out.println(m_UPC);
}
```

Figure 6.5: Display method for the StockItem class (from code\itemtst1\StockItem1.java)

This is also not very complicated; it just uses System.out.print and System.out.println to display each of the parts of the StockItem object on the screen, along with some identifying information that makes it easier to figure out what the values represent.

Susan wanted to know how we could use System.out.print (and System.out.println) without defining a special version of these methods for this class.

> **Susan**: Hey, how come you don't have to define System.out.print and System.out.println as class methods? Does the compiler just use the native System.out.print? And that works OK?

> **Steve**: We're using System.out.print and System.out.println only for types that already have it defined, which includes all of the primitive types, as well as the String class. To display a StockItem, we have to write our own method, which is what we're doing here.

> **Susan**: Then please explain to me why System.out.print is being used in Figure 6.5, which is for the StockItem class.

> **Steve**: It's being used for Strings and ints, not objects of the StockItem class. The fact that the Strings and ints are inside the StockItem class is irrelevant in this context; they're still Strings and ints, and therefore can be displayed by System.out.print.

> **Susan**: So the stuff you get out of the standard packages is only for the use of class types? Not primitive?

> **Steve**: The java.io library is designed to be able to handle both primitive types and class types; however, the latter use requires the class writer to do some extra work, which we won't be tackling.

Problem
Algorithms
Java
Interpreter
Hardware

That should clear up most of the potential problems with the meaning of this Display method. However, it does contain one construct that we've seen before without explanation: void. This is the return type of the Display method, as might be apparent from its position immediately before the class name StockItem. But its meaning might not be as obvious, so let me clear up the mystery: as a return type indicator, void means simply that this method doesn't supply a return value at all.

You won't be surprised to learn that Susan had a few questions about this idea of methods that return no value.

> **Susan**: How can a method not return a value? Then what is the point?

Steve: The point of calling a method that returns no value is that it causes something to happen. The Display method is one example; it causes the value of a StockItem object to be displayed on the screen. Another example is a "storage method"; calling such a method can cause it to modify the value of some piece of data it is maintaining, so when you call the corresponding "retrieval method", you'll get back the value the "storage method" put away. Such lasting effects of a method call (other than returning a value) are called *side effects*.

Susan: But even a side effect is a change, so then it does do something after all, right?

Steve: Sure, it does something; every method should do something, or you wouldn't write (or call) it. However, some methods don't return any value to the calling program, in which case we specify their return type as void.

That takes care of the public entries in the class definition. Now what about the private entries?

As I mentioned before in the discussion of how a class is defined, the access specifier private means that only methods of the class can access the item after that specifier. It's almost always a good idea to mark all the fields in a class as private, for two reasons.

Problem
Algorithms
Java
Interpreter
Hardware

1.   If we know that only methods of a class can change the values of member data, then we know where to look if the values of the data are incorrect. This can be extremely useful when debugging a program.
2.   Marking fields as private simplifies the task of changing or deleting those fields should that become necessary. You see, if the fields are public, then we have no idea what methods in what programs are relying on their values. That means that changing or deleting these fields can cause havoc anywhere in the system. Allowing access only by methods of the class where the fields are defined means that we can make changes freely as long as all of the methods are kept up to date.

Both of these advantages of keeping fields private can be summed up in the term **encapsulation**, which means "hiding the details inside the class rather than exposing them to users of the class". This is one of the primary organizing principles that characterizes object-oriented programming.

Susan wasn't buying this encapsulation idea without a struggle.

Susan: I don't get why you say calling something private is the same as encapsulation. Calling it private is the access specifier.

Steve: Yes, private is the access specifier. However, when we make all the fields private, we are effectively encapsulating the details of how the class is implemented within the class. That is, the user cannot access those fields directly, but must go through our class methods to get at them, as though they were inside a guarded building.

Susan: So then could you say that something is encapsulated every time you are calling something private?

Steve: Not unless all the fields are private.

Susan: What if you wanted to leave one field public and the rest private, then it would not be encapsulated?

Steve: Right. If there's any way for the user to get at the internals of the class, you can't consider the object encapsulated.

There's only one more point about the fields in the StockItem class that needs clarification; surely the price of an object in the store should be in dollars and cents, and yet we have only an int to represent it. As you know by now, an int can hold only a whole number. What's going on here?

Problem
Algorithms
Java
Interpreter
Hardware

Only that I've decided to store the price in cents rather than dollars and cents. That is, when someone types in a price, I'll assume that it's in cents, so "246" would mean 246 cents, or $2.46. This would, of course, not be acceptable in a real program, but for now it's OK.

This allows prices up to about $20,000,000.00 (as well as negative numbers for things like coupons or rebates), which should be acceptable for almost anything except a large corporation or government agency. Later we'll see how to use another kind of variable that can hold numbers with fractional parts. For now, though, let's stick with the int.

There's one more method that we need to cover in this class: SetName(String Name). Figure 6.6 shows the code for this method.

```
void SetName(String Name)
{
    m_Name = Name;
}
```

Figure 6.6: The SetName method of the StockItem class (from code\itemtst1\item1.java)

This is about as simple as a method can get. All it does is change the name of an existing StockItem to whatever the Name argument specifies. However, as simple as it is, it is essential in the discussion of one of the major stumbling blocks in learning (and using) Java: the fact that we can never deal with an object directly but only through a *reference* to that object.

References Required

I alluded to this characteristic of Java briefly near the beginning of this chapter, and now it's time to delve into it in excruciating detail. Let's start with a few pictures. Let's say that Figure 6.7 represents the situation after a StockItem called item1 has been set to its initial value (leaving out some of the fields that don't matter here).

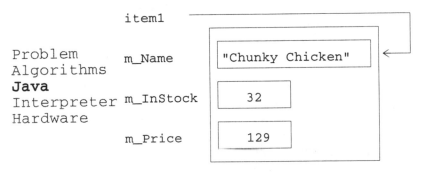

Figure 6.7: item1 and its object

That seems fine. Figure 6.8 shows the situation after the statement item2 = item1; has been executed.

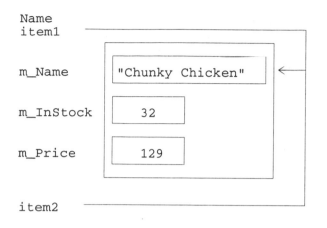

Figure 6.8: item1, item2, and their object

That's certainly a simple way to make those two variables have the same value. But what would happen if we were to execute the statement item1.SetName("Sliced Beef");? Figure 6.9 shows the situation at that point.

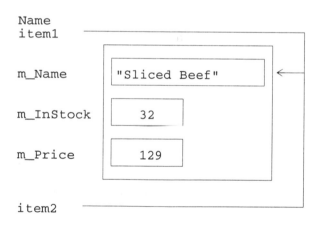

Problem
Algorithms
Java
Interpreter
Hardware

Figure 6.9: item1, item2, and their object

As you can see, since these two variables, item1 and item2, share an m_Name field, changing that field changes the value of both variables.

To understand this characteristic of Java in detail, let's look at a program that illustrates it (Figure 6.10).

```java
import WAJ.*;

public class ReferenceTest1
{
   public static void main( String args[ ] )
   {
      StockItem item1;
      StockItem item2;
      int x;
      int y;

      x = 3;
      y = x;

      System.out.println("The value of x is: ");
      System.out.println(x); System.out.println();
      System.out.println("The value of y is: ");
      System.out.println(y); System.out.println();

      x = 2;

      System.out.println("The value of x has been changed to 2");
      System.out.println();
      System.out.println("The value of x is: ");
      System.out.println(x); System.out.println();
      System.out.println("The value of y is: ");
      System.out.println(y); System.out.println(); System.out.println();

      item1 = new StockItem("Chunky Chicken",32,129,
      "Bob's Distribution","123456789");

      System.out.println("The value of item1 is: ");
      item1.Display();

      item2 = item1;

      System.out.println("The value of item2 is: ");
      item2.Display();

      item1.SetName("Sliced Beef");
      System.out.println("The name of item1 has been changed to Sliced Beef");
      System.out.println();
      System.out.println("The value of item1 is: ");
      item1.Display();
      System.out.println("The value of item2 is: ");
      item2.Display();
   }
}
```

Problem
Algorithms
Java
Interpreter
Hardware

Figure 6.10: A sample program for references
(code\reference1\ReferenceTest1.java)

If you run that program, you'll discover that its output is as shown in Figure 6.11.

The value of x is:
3

The value of y is:
3

The value of x has been changed to 2

The value of x is:
2

The value of y is:
3

The value of item1 is:
Name: Chunky Chicken
Number in stock: 32
Price: 129
Distributor: Bob's Distribution
UPC: 123456789

The value of item2 is:
Name: Chunky Chicken
Number in stock: 32
Price: 129
Distributor: Bob's Distribution
UPC: 123456789

The name of item1 has been changed to Sliced Beef

The value of item1 is:
Name: Sliced Beef
Number in stock: 32
Price: 129
Distributor: Bob's Distribution
UPC: 123456789

The value of item2 is:
Name: Sliced Beef
Number in stock: 32
Price: 129
Distributor: Bob's Distribution
UPC: 123456789

```
Problem
Algorithms
Java
Interpreter
Hardware
```

Figure 6.11: Output of sample program for references
(code\reference1\reftest1.out)

Do you see anything odd about that output? I certainly do! Let's start from the beginning. We assign the value 3 to an int variable called x. Then we set another int variable called y to the value that x has. When we display the values of these variables, both of them have the value 3, which is certainly reasonable. Then we change the value of x to 2. The last step of this part of the program displays the values of x and y again, and as you would expect, x is 2 and y is still 3.

The second part of the program performs a seemingly similar operation with a couple of StockItems. First, we give item1 a value, the m_Name field of which is "Chunky Chicken". Then we display that StockItem, and the name is indeed "Chunky Chicken". Then we assign item2 the value of item1 by the statement item2 = item1;. Then we display the value of item2, which naturally enough shows its name as "Chunky Chicken".

The next statement is the one that uses SetName to change the name in item1 to "Sliced Beef", which as we have seen is quite a simple operation. Then we display the value of item1, which of course now has the name "Sliced Beef". So far, so good.

Now we come to the tricky part (to put it mildly): When we display the value of item2, it also has the name "Sliced Beef"! This is not the way the primitive variables behaved in the earlier part of this program, and is not obviously correct. Is there a bug in this program?

Problem
Algorithms
Java
Interpreter
Hardware

Referred Pain

No, that's the way Java works. The problem is that item1 and item2, like all other variables of user-defined types, aren't really objects; they are *references* to objects. That is, they are just middlemen that pass along all of our method calls and field references to the "real" objects, which are forever inaccessible to us in any other manner.

Okay, so they're not the real objects; why does that matter? Because the meaning of "item2 = item1;" is "make item2 refer to the same object as item1". In other words, rather than item1 and item2 each having their own object with its own fields, they share one object that has one set of fields.

That's why we get the output that we do from that test program; when we change "item1", we're really changing the object it refers to, which is the same object that item2 refers to. When we display "item1" and "item2", what we're really displaying is the same object through two different references.

Of course, there are situations in which this behavior is undesirable, and where we must be able to separate such "Siamese twins". We can do this by writing a method called clone that will actually create a new object with the same value as an existing object. Then we can assign that new object to our other reference and thus avoid the problem of sharing data when we don't want to. Luckily, in this book we will be able to avoid this complication, as we will not encounter any circumstances in which sharing an object in this way is erroneous.

However, there are plenty of circumstances in the real world where sharing data *is* a problem. Unfortunately, in those cases the clone method doesn't really solve the problem fully, because we can still use = by accident when we should use clone and end up with improperly shared data. This is called *aliasing*, and it is a common source of serious, difficult-to-find errors in large programs where it's almost impossible to keep track of all of the places that a given object is being referred to.

I consider this a major flaw in the design of Java, because it is an inescapable fact of life that programmers make errors. Java was intended to be safer than many other existing languages; that is, it should be harder to make mistakes in Java than in other languages. The ease with which aliasing errors can be generated in Java is inconsistent with that goal.

At the moment, however, there's nothing that can be done about it, so let's move on to the next part of our discussion of references and objects: how we actually create an object to assign to a reference.

Problem
Algorithms
Java
Interpreter
Hardware

Objection Sustained

What is the purpose of the statement item1 = new StockItem("Chunky Chicken",32,129,"Bob's Distribution","123456789");? It uses a Java facility called new to mark off a segment of memory that can be used to hold the fields that make up a StockItem object, as well as some supporting information that connects that object with its methods. As soon as that memory area has been assigned, the StockItem constructor is called to initialize the newly created StockItem object to the appropriate values; this object is then assigned to the StockItem reference item1.

Once a particular area of memory has been assigned to an object, it won't be used for any other purpose until we're done with it. Of course, this leads to the question of how the Java interpreter knows when we're done using the object; do we have to use another facility called something like old to tell Java it can reuse that memory?

In many other languages, we would indeed need to do that, but in Java it's handled automatically by a process known as **garbage collection**. Whenever most of the memory available for objects is in use, the **garbage collector** combs through memory to find objects that no longer have any references. Any such objects are "garbage" and the memory they occupy can therefore be "collected" (made available for reuse).

Garbage collection was included in the Java language because it is regrettably common for programmers in other languages (such as C and C++) to forget to tell the system when they are done with a piece of memory, so that it can be reused. This error is called a **memory leak**, and it's a particularly insidious kind of error, because the program seems to work correctly unless it is run for a long enough time that it uses up all the available memory and stops working.

Now let's go back and look at a statement that we've skipped: StockItem item1;. This statement doesn't create a StockItem object; as we've just seen, to do that we have to write a statement that uses new to allocate memory for that object.Instead, it creates a reference to a StockItem, which can be made to refer to an actual StockItem when we have one to refer to. In the meantime, it is an uninitialized variable, that is, one that hasn't been assigned a value. If we try to do anything with such a variable other than assign it a value, our program won't compile, just as it won't compile if we have any other variables that haven't been assigned values.

Problem
Algorithms
Java
Interpreter
Hardware

We're ready to continue with the next phase of our StockItem project. We've covered all of the methods and fields of the StockItem class, but you may be wondering how we can use this class to keep track of all of the items in the store. Surely we aren't going to have a separately named StockItem variable for each one.

Array of Hope

This is another application for our old friend the array; specifically, we need an array of StockItems to store the data for all the StockItems in the store. In a real application we would need to be able to vary the number of elements in the array, unlike our previous use of arrays. After all, the number of items in a store can vary from time to time. However, in our example program we'll ignore this complication and just use an array that can hold 100 StockItems. Even with this limitation, we will have to keep track of the number of items that are in use, so that we can store each new StockItem in its own array element and maintain a count of how many there are in the array at the moment. Finally, we need something to read the data for each StockItem from the inventory file where it's stored when we're not running the program.

Susan had some questions about these details of the test program.

> **Susan**: In the paragraph where you are talking about the number of items, I am a little confused. That is, do you mean the number of different products that the store carries or the quantity of an individual item available in the store at any given time?

> **Steve**: The number of different products, which is the same as the number of StockItems. Remember, each StockItem represents any number of objects of that exact description.

> **Susan**: So what you're referring to is basically all the inventory in the store at any given period of time?

> **Steve**: Exactly.

> **Susan**: What do you mean by "need something to read the data" and "where it's stored when we're not running the program." I don't know what you are talking about; I don't know where that place would be.

> **Steve**: Well, where is the data when we're not running the program? The disk. Therefore, we have to be able to read the information for the StockItems from the disk when we start the program.

> **Susan**: Okay, that makes sense now.

> **Steve**: I'm glad to hear it.

Problem
Algorithms
Java
Interpreter
Hardware

Figure 6.12 is a program that shows the code necessary to read the data for the StockItem array into memory when the program starts up.

To use the debugger for this program, follow the instructions in the section titled "Using the debugger" in the file "\readme.txt" on the CD in the back of the book. These instructions assume that you've installed the examples on drive C:, so that the location of this program is "c:\whosj\code\itemtst2".

```
import WAJ.*;
import java.io.*;

public class Itemtst2
{
static final int MaxItems = 100;

    public static void main( String args[ ] )
    {
        FileInputStream ShopInfo;

        try
        {
            ShopInfo = new FileInputStream("shop2.in");
        }
        catch (FileNotFoundException e)
        {
            System.out.println("Can't open file \"shop2.in\"");
            return;
        }

        int i;
        int InventoryCount;
        boolean Result;

        StockItem[ ] AllItems;
        AllItems = new StockItem[MaxItems];

        for (i = 0; i < MaxItems; i ++)
          {
              AllItems[i] = new StockItem();
              Result = AllItems[i].Read(ShopInfo);
              if (Result == false)
                    break;
          }

        InventoryCount = i;

        for (i = 0; i < InventoryCount; i ++)
              {
                  AllItems[i].Display();
              }

    }
}
```

Problem
Algorithms
Java
Interpreter
Hardware

Figure 6.12: Reading and displaying an array of StockItems
(code\itemtst2\itemtst2.java)

This program has a number of new features that need examination. First, the statement static final int MaxItems = 100; is new. This defines a *constant*: a data item that is like a variable except that its value can't change. Rather than get into the details of the static final keywords, which aren't particularly relevant here, you can think of that as a phrase meaning "we're defining a constant". We will use this MaxItems constant rather than the number "100" to specify the number of items in an array of StockItems; this is better programming practice because the next programmer to come along will be able to see that it's not just a coincidence that the number of array elements is the same as the number of times we want to execute a loop. Also, if that number ever needs to change, we would only have to change it in one place (the definition of MaxItems) rather than in several places in the program. This makes maintenance easier and less error prone.

The next new feature of this program is the addition of the java.io.* package to the list of packages we're using, which is required if we want to read data from a file (or write data to a file, for that matter).[8] The way we do this is to create a FileInputStream reference and assign it an object that is connected to a file. In this case, we create the FileInputStream reference called ShopInfo in the statement FileInputStream ShopInfo;, and we're going to connect it to the file named shop2.in when we create the FileInputStream object it refers to.

Before we can create that object, though, we have to stop and consider some possible problems when dealing with file input and output.

```
Problem
Algorithms
Java
Interpreter
Hardware
```

An Exceptional Opportunity

Whenever we try to use a file, we may encounter an error. For example, if we try to open a file to read from it, it may not exist, or we may not have permission to open it. If we try to read from it, it may not have any more data in it, or there may be some kind of operating system error in the process (bad sectors, etc.). If we try to open a file to write to it, there may not be any more space on the disk, or we may not have permission to create it.[9]

---

8. I haven't defined the meaning of the * in a package name before, so this is a good time to do it: It means "I want to use everything in the package that it's affixed to, not just part of it". In this case, the name java.io.* tells the compiler that we want to be able to use everything in the java.io package rather than just some of its contents. This is similar to the use of * when asking for a directory listing, where it serves as a "wild card" that will match anything.

9. Of course, other operations can have errors of this sort as well; for example, when we try to create an object, we may run out of memory. For now, though, let's stick with I/O errors.

Different programming languages provide different mechanisms for programmers to handle these problems and other similar ones. In C, for example, when you request an operation that can fail, you're supposed to check the return value to see whether it is okay. However, this approach has a number of drawbacks. First, it's very easy to write your program without such checks on the theory that you'll add them later, "when you have time"; needless to say, that happy eventuality rarely comes to pass. Second, having lots of error checks in your program can quickly transform a simple program into a complicated, hard-to-follow mess. Third, if you're using the return value to indicate success or failure, you can't also use it to convey the result of the operation. I'm sure there are other drawbacks to this method, but those should be enough to convince a reasonable person that a better way would be desirable!

In Java, there is a better way, called **exception handling**. An exception is an unexpected event that occurs during the execution of a program, or in other words, an error. The idea behind exception handling can be expressed by the old saying: "Hope for the best, but prepare for the worst." In other words, rather than trying to handle every possible error condition in the normal flow of a program, we assume that everything will work all right. If it doesn't, we have a fallback plan to handle the error.

Problem
Algorithms
Java
Interpreter
Hardware

Of course, this new approach to error handling gives us a new set of concepts and constructs to deal with. Let's start by examining the next non-blank line of our test program (6.12), which consists of the keyword **try**. The controlled block of a try statement is called, reasonably enough, a **try block**.

Better Read than Dead

There's only one statement in this try block, ShopInfo = new FileInputStream("shop2.in");. This statement creates a FileInputStream object, attaches it to the file shop2.in, and makes this object the current object for the ShopInfo reference.

Actually, that description has left out something important. What it should say is that this statement *attempts* to create that object and attach it to the file shop2.in. What happens if that file doesn't exist?

In that case, the next part of the exception-handling mechanism comes into play, in the form of the **catch** statement that immediately follows the controlled block of the try. While a try statement doesn't have any arguments, a catch statement has one, which specifies the type of exception that it can catch.[10] This catch statement handles an exception of the FileNotFoundException type.

As is usual with method arguments, this argument also has a name. In this case, we won't actually be using the exception object, but if we wanted to, we could refer to it by the name e, since that's what we called it in the argument list of the catch.

Instead of using the contents of the exception object, our catch block just displays an error message telling us about the error and then executes a return statement. Since we are already in the main method, this return will cause the program to stop running.

Susan had some questions about exception handling.

> **Susan**: About catch. If you get an error, then the program just ends? Otherwise, this is just ignored?

> **Steve**: If you get an exception and there is no catch block that catches that type of exception in the current method, then the error propagates to the calling method, if there is one. If the current method is main, then the program ends.
>
> However, if there is an appropriate catch block in the current method, then it catches the exception and can decide what to do about it. Usually this is to display an error message and quit, but in some cases it can fix the problem that caused the exception so that processing can continue.

Problem
Algorithms
Java
Interpreter
Hardware

We'll get back to exceptions very shortly, but for now let's continue with our program (Figure 6.12) under the assumption that the file shop2.in exists and our attempt to open it is successful. In that case, we'll continue by creating three variables named i, InventoryCount, and Result, which we will use in keeping track of the number of elements read and whether we have reached the end of the file.[11]

Next, we create an array called AllItems to hold the references to all the StockItem objects that will hold the real information about the items in the store, and fill those StockItems in with information read from the file.

---

10. Actually, any catch statement can catch more than one type of exception, as is explained in Chapter 8, but that's a complication we can overlook for the moment.

11. This is an example of the fact that we can create variables wherever we want to, not just at the beginning of a method as we have been doing so far. There are two schools of thought on where to create variables if you have a choice: one says that it's easier to find the variables if they're always at the top of the method, and the other says that it's easier to find them if they are created shortly before they are used. Of course, in some cases you might not have enough information to know that you will need a particular variable until after you have executed some code in the method; obviously in such cases you won't be able to create the variables at the beginning of the method.

To make that last step more intelligible, I think some diagrams showing how an array works in more detail might be in order. Figure 6.13 is the first installment, showing what the AllItems array might look like when it is first created by the statement StockItem[ ] AllItems;.

```
Address    Name

12300000   StockItem[ ] AllItems
```

Figure 6.13: An uninitialized array of StockItem references

The box that will hold the value of the AllItems variable is blank to indicate that the AllItems array doesn't refer to anything at the moment. You see, an array in Java is actually a reference, just as a user-defined variable is. That is, just as we must use a reference to access a user-defined variable, we must use a reference to access a set of elements. Until we assign an actual set of elements to an array, it has no value and therefore cannot be used.

Therefore, the next step is to use the statement AllItems = new StockItem[MaxItems]; to assign the AllItems array a set of 100 elements, each of which is a reference to a StockItem; the elements of this array will refer to the StockItems we will read in from the file. Figure 6.14 illustrates what the AllItems array might look like at that point, omitting the 95 elements between element 3 and element 98, inclusive; after all, I'm not being paid by the page!

Problem
Algorithms
Java
Interpreter
Hardware

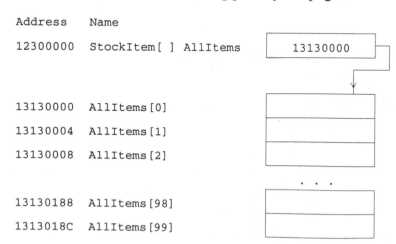

```
Address    Name

12300000   StockItem[ ] AllItems        13130000



13130000   AllItems[0]

13130004   AllItems[1]

13130008   AllItems[2]
                                            . . .

13130188   AllItems[98]

1313018C   AllItems[99]
```

Figure 6.14: An array of uninitialized StockItem references

As was the case with the array itself, the blank boxes indicate that we haven't initialized the array elements yet, so they don't refer to anything.

Now we're up to the beginning of the for loop in Figure 6.12. As usual in Java, the first index that we will use is 0. We want to continue the loop until we have read either 100 items or all of the data in the file, whichever comes first. We handle the former condition in the for loop header by stopping when i is not less than 100; the latter condition will be handled in the loop, as we'll see in a moment.

The next statement is AllItems[i] = new StockItem();. We have to do this to create the object for the ith reference in the AllItems array before we can do anything with that object. Remember that merely creating the array of references doesn't mean that those references refer to anything, and in fact they don't refer to anything until we make them do so. But what would happen if we forgot to assign an object to each reference in the AllItems array before we use it?

Nothing Ventured, Nothing Gained

If we did forget to assign an object to each reference before trying to use it, we would get an exception. If we didn't handle that exception ourselves, then we would get the default error message, which looks like this:

ERROR: java.lang.NullPointerException

telling us that we have tried to use a **null reference**.[12]

However, we won't get that error here because we've remembered to initialize our references before using them. After the first execution of this loop, therefore, the array might look something like Figure 6.15 (omitting most of the fields in the StockItem to keep the diagram relatively simple).

Of course, the reason that the name and number of items in stock are "" and 0, respectively, is that the default constructor StockItem(),

```
Problem
Algorithms
Java
Interpreter
Hardware
```

---

12. In case you're wondering why the error message says "NullPointer" rather than "NullReference", I'm not sure, but I can guess. A Java reference is very similar to a C **pointer**, and the Java designers probably had named this exception before they changed the term "pointer" to "reference". Of course, this doesn't answer the question of why they would change the term in the first place, but I think that was a marketing decision made so that Sun could claim that "Java has no pointers".

which we've used to create the StockItem, sets those fields to those values.

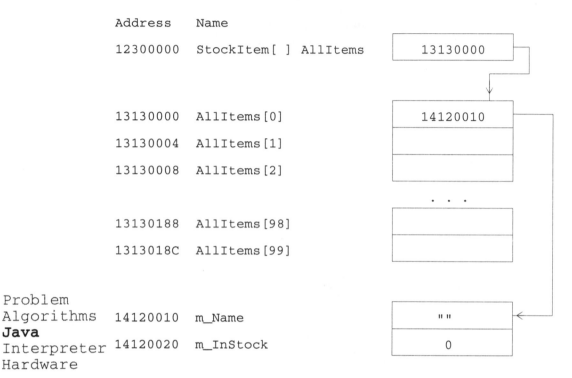

Figure 6.15: An array of StockItem references, with the first reference initialized

Now we're up to the statement Result = AllItems[i].Read(ShopInfo);. This statement calls the method Read (shown in Figure 6.17), which I've added to the StockItem class. This method reads data from a FileInputStream, in this case ShopInfo, into its StockItem object, in this case AllItems[i]. After that statement has been executed, the AllItems array might look like Figure 6.16.

As you can see, the first StockItem in the AllItems array has now been set up properly. Of course, the same process has to be applied to the rest of the StockItems in the AllItems array before it can be used in the rest of the program.

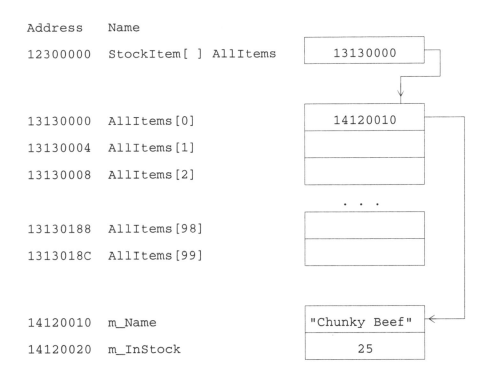

```
Address      Name

12300000     StockItem[ ] AllItems          13130000


13130000     AllItems[0]                    14120010

13130004     AllItems[1]

13130008     AllItems[2]

                                              . . .

13130188     AllItems[98]

1313018C     AllItems[99]



14120010     m_Name                       "Chunky Beef"

14120020     m_InStock                         25
```

Figure 6.16: An array of StockItem references, with the first StockItem set up for use

Problem
Algorithms
Java
Interpreter
Hardware

This whole process was anything but obvious to Susan.

Susan: How does just adding the package java.io.* enable you to read data in from a file?

Steve: The package java.io.* contains the FileInputStream class.

Susan: Where did the FileInputStream class come from?

Steve: It's one of the standard classes that comes with the compiler.

Susan: Your only reference to this is just "The way we do this is to create a FileInputStream object that is 'attached' to a file when the object is constructed". If this is just something that you wrote to aid this program that we don't have to worry about at this time, then please mention this.

Steve: I didn't write it, but we don't have to worry about it. I'll explain it to the minimum extent necessary.

Susan: Where did java.io come from and how did it get there? Who defined it and when was it written? And how did you know it was there?

Steve: It is defined in the Java language. Since we're using Visual J++, a Microsoft compiler/interpreter, I imagine it was written by programmers at Microsoft. As to how I knew it was there, I looked it up in a book. If you want to do any serious programming in Java, you'll need a reference book. I recommend *Java in a Nutshell*, by David Flanagan, published by O'Reilly & Associates. Although it won't teach you Java, it does have a list of every class and method that was defined in the Java language at the time the book was published.

Figure 6.17 is the implementation of the new Read method.

Problem
Algorithms
Java
Interpreter
Hardware

```
boolean Read(FileInputStream s)
{
        DataInputStream dis = new DataInputStream(s);
        String tempInStock;
        String tempPrice;

        try
        {
            m_Name = dis.readLine();
            tempInStock = dis.readLine();
            tempPrice = dis.readLine();
            m_Distributor = dis.readLine();
            m_UPC = dis.readLine();
        }
        catch (IOException e)
        {
            System.out.println(e);
            return false;
        }

        if (m_UPC == null)
            return false;

        m_InStock = Integer.parseInt(tempInStock);
        m_Price = Integer.parseInt(tempPrice);

        return true;
}
```

Figure 6.17: The Read method for the StockItem class (from code\itemtst2\StockItem.java)

This is the first time we've used the boolean type. Expressions and variables of that type are limited to the two values true and false. We've been using the terms true and false to refer to the result of a logical expression such as if (x < y); similarly, a boolean variable or method return value can be either true or false. In this case, Read needs to inform its caller of whether it has read data from the file (true) or has failed in that attempt (false); therefore, a boolean return value is a good choice.

Susan wasn't initially convinced of the advantages of using boolean.

> **Susan**: How does boolean work? How does it differ from int, where you could just compare two numbers and if they don't match you get a false and if they do match you get a true?
>
> **Steve**: I don't understand your question.
>
> **Susan**: Yes, you do. Why is boolean any better than if and else?
>
> **Steve**: That's like asking, "Why is a bank better than a supermarket?" They aren't in competition. The if and else keywords allow us to determine what will be executed based on some condition; a boolean variable is used to remember whether some condition is true or false.
>
> **Susan**: No, what I mean is why should we use boolean rather than int for a return value? We could make 0 mean false and 1 mean true.
>
> **Steve**: That is in fact the way that C does it, but C++ has added an equivalent bool data type. The reason for this addition is to allow the compiler to tell you when you've made a mistake by trying to return a value other than true or false. If you used an int return type, you could return 6 instead of either 0 or 1, and the compiler wouldn't be able to tell that it was an error, whereas with boolean it can.
>
> **Susan**: Okay, I think I have that now.
>
> **Steve**: Good.

```
Problem
Algorithms
Java
Interpreter
Hardware
```

Now let's continue with the statement DataInputStream dis = new DataInputStream(s);. The purpose of this statement is to allow us to read data from the FileInputStream called s, which is the argument that our caller passed us for that purpose. As you may recall, that FileInputStream was connected to a file called shop2.in, which means that when we read data from s, we are really reading it from shop2.in.

However, in order to read data from a FileInputStream, we have to use it to create a DataInputStream, as we do in the current statement.

The discerning reader will notice I haven't explained exactly what a DataInputStream is and how it differs from a FileInputStream. Unfortunately, I can't do that, because it involves yet another facet of Java that we won't be able to cover in this book. Thus, you'll just have to take my word for it that we have to create a DataInputStream from a FileInputStream before we can read data from the file connected to the FileInputStream.

Even aside from this detail, this Read method is pretty complicated. Why is this?

I Take Exception to That Statement

Problem
Algorithms
Java
Interpreter
Hardware

The main reason is that reading from a file can cause a type of exception called a **checked exception**, which means one that the compiler insists that you deal with when writing your methods. There are two ways you can satisfy this requirement. First, by stating in the header of your method that it may throw this type of exception, and second, by handling it via the try/catch mechanism. The purpose of this requirement is to make sure that the user of a method knows exactly what checked exceptions can result from calling that method; if it doesn't declare any, it won't throw any. However, there are (at least) two things I haven't explained: Why are some exceptions checked, and what other kinds are there?

A checked exception is one that the design of Java assumes can only happen at certain reasonably predictable places in your program; therefore, you are required to let the callers of your methods know about the possibility of its being thrown if you don't handle it yourself. An example of a condition that causes checked exceptions is trying to open a nonexistent file for reading.

On the other hand, an **unchecked exception** is one that the design of Java assumes can happen virtually anywhere in your program, so it wouldn't make sense to force you to specify that your methods can throw such an exception. Examples of conditions that cause unchecked exceptions are attempting to use a null reference, trying to access an element of an array that is past the end of the array, and the like. We can handle unchecked exceptions in our methods if we wish, but we don't have to; whether or not we handle them, we don't have to declare that we will throw them, because any method is permitted to throw them.[13]

As you might expect, Susan wanted to explore the logical consequences of exception handling in general, and the notion of two classes of exceptions in particular.

Susan: Why do you need exception handling in Read?

Steve: Because the readLine method can throw checked exceptions. In Java, the compiler requires that any methods that call other methods that can throw checked exceptions either handle those exceptions or declare that they can also throw those exceptions.

Susan: Why bother with unchecked exceptions then?

Steve: You only have to deal with them if you want to give better error messages than the default ones that happen if you ignore them.

Susan: Why are these custom error messages better than default error messages?

Steve: Because when you write your own error messages, you know more about the situation where the error occurred than the person who wrote the package containing the code where the error really occurred. After all, the package designer doesn't know how you're using the code in the package.

Problem
Algorithms
Java
Interpreter
Hardware

Susan: What is dis? I am serious.

Steve: It's short for *DataInputStream*, because that's the type of variable that it is.

Susan: Is reading variables in from dis what the whole try block does?

Steve: Yes, that's what this try block does. Of course, other try blocks do other things.

Susan: So then there is no general statement that you can make about all try blocks?

Steve: The general statement might be "if you're worried about the possibility of an exception in a section of code, you can use a try block to

---

13. If you find the distinction between these categories far from obvious, you're not alone. I consider the division into checked and unchecked exceptions fairly arbitrary; you just have to look up which is which, or let the compiler tell you when you've called a method that might throw a checked exception.

handle it." While just about every section of code *could* throw an exception, you can ignore that possibility in many cases. However, some sections of code can throw a checked exception; in that case, you have to decide whether you want to handle that exception or pass it back to the calling method. If you want to handle the exception yourself, you have to use a try block.

However, that isn't the only time that you would use a try block: in general, you would also use it for code that you're concerned might throw an unchecked exception, where you want to handle such an exception yourself rather than relying on the system's default exception handling.

The easiest thing to do, at least when you're starting out, is to ignore exceptions when you're writing your code. If you don't handle a checked exception, the compiler will give you an error telling you that you have to do something about it, and you can deal with it then.

Problem
Algorithms
Java
Interpreter
Hardware

In the case of the Read method, IOException is a checked exception, which means we have to do something about it in our method. In this case, we want to handle it ourselves, so we use a try block to surround the statements that try to read from the file, because they might throw an IOException. If there is a problem, then the catch block displays an error message and returns false (meaning there is no more data to be read).

Note that in this case we're using the default error message that comes with the exception, in the statement System.out.println(e);. This is a handy feature of the exceptions that come with Java: they all have error messages in them, and will display those error messages via println. That means that we don't have to write our own error messages for these exceptions as long as we're content with the default ones.

If we preferred to have our callers handle this exception rather than handling it ourselves, we could change the header of our Read method to indicate that it can throw an IOException; that would make the header boolean Read(FileInputStream s) throws IOException. In that case, we could write our method without worrying about the possibility that such an exception could occur; of course, the users of our method might not be happy at our foisting the exception handling off on them!

Assuming that we don't have any exceptions while reading data, each statement inside the try block will read one line from the file. The statements that read data for String fields (i.e., m_Name, m_Distributor, and m_UPC) can simply store data read from the file directly into the corresponding variable. However, this won't work for our int fields; instead, they have to be converted from Strings to numeric values, which we'll do at the end of the routine.

As you probably have guessed, Susan had some questions about this whole concept.

Susan: How does Read make Shopinfo go get data?

Steve: Well, the argument s is a reference to the FileInputStream object provided by the caller; in this case, the FileInputStream object to which s refers is Shopinfo. That FileInputStream is connected to the file shop2.in.

Susan: How come this Read method is a boolean type? I would think it would return data being read from a file.

Steve: You would think so, wouldn't you? I love it when you're logical. However, it actually reads data from a file into the object for which it was called, then tells its caller whether that read was successful. Therefore, its appropriate return type is boolean.

Susan: So the DataInputStream object is a transfer mechanism? That is, DataInputStream s; would read data from a file named s?

Steve: Yes, it's a transfer mechanism. However, DataInputStream s; would create a DataInputStream called s that was not connected to any file. In this case, we're creating the DataInputStream called dis and specifying the FileInputStream that it actually uses to go get the data.

Susan: OK. A DataInputStream just reads data from a file. It doesn't care which file until you specify it, either when you create it or later?

Steve: Right.

Susan: What does this mean without System.in? Is it just the same thing, only you can't call it System.in because System.in is for primitive use and this is a class?

Steve: The s takes the place of System.in, because we want to read from s, not System.in.

Susan: Am I right that null is used if you can't read a whole item?

Steve: Close, but not quite. If we try to read something from a file when there isn't anything left, we will get a null rather than whatever we were expecting. In that case. we return false.

```
Problem
Algorithms
Java
Interpreter
Hardware
```

There is another point that we haven't examined yet, though: how this routine determines that it's finished reading from the input file. With keyboard input, we process each line separately when it's typed in, but that won't do the job with a file, where we want to read all the items in until we get to the end of the file.

We handle this detail by checking whether the value for m_UPC is null, that is, a null reference. This is what the readLine method of DataInputStream returns when there is nothing left in the file.[14] When this occurs, we simply return false to inform our caller that we were unsuccessful in reading the StockItem that they wanted us to get.

Once we have read all of the data for the current StockItem, we have to convert the m_InStock and m_Price values from their String form as read from the file into int values so we can calculate with them. This is the task of the next two lines, m_InStock = Integer.parseInt(tempInStock); and the corresponding line for m_Price. The Integer.parseInt method is a handy feature that is provided by the standard package Java.lang to allow us to determine the numeric value of a String that is supposed to represent a number.[15]

Reading between the Lines

Problem
Algorithms
Java
Interpreter
Hardware

Now that we're done with the Read method, let's get back to our main program (Figure 6.12). At this point, we have to check whether our most recent attempt to read a StockItem from shop2.in was successful. We use the return value from Read to do this. If Read was able to read all the data for a StockItem, the answer will be true; otherwise, it will be false. How do we use this information?

We use it to decide whether to execute a break **statement**. This is a loop control device that interrupts processing of a loop. The flow of control passes to the next statement after the end of the controlled block of the for statement.[16]

The loop will terminate in one of two ways. Either 100 records have been read, in which case i will be 100; or the end of the file is reached, in which case i is the number of records that have been read successfully.

---

14. In case you were wondering why we don't get an exception when we try to read data that isn't in the file, so am I.

15. By the way, if the String in fact does not represent a valid numeric value, we'll get a BadNumberFormat exception. The reason we don't have to catch or declare this exception in our method is that it is an unchecked exception. We aren't handling this exception here or in the main program; therefore, if it occurs, our program will terminate with an "unhandled exception" error.

16. The break statement can also terminate execution of a while loop, as well as some other types of control mechanisms that we won't get to.

Susan had some questions about the implementation of this program.

Susan: Where did break come from?

Steve: It's another keyword like for; it means to terminate the loop that is in progress.

Susan: I do not understand what is actually happening with the program at this time. When is break implemented? Is it just to end the reading of the entire file?

Steve: We have to stop reading data when there is no more data in the file. The break statement allows us to terminate the loop when that occurs.

Susan: What do you mean that the loop will terminate either by 100 records being read or when the end of the file is reached? Isn't that the same thing?

Steve: It's the same thing only if there are exactly 100 records in the file.

Susan: So you mean when there are no more records to be read? So that the loop won't continue on till the end with nothing to do?

Steve: Exactly.

Susan: So does i just represent the number of records in the file?

Steve: Actually, it's the number of records that we've read.

Susan: Well, the program sounded like there were indeed 100 records in the file. However, I see that in practice that might change, and why you would therefore need to have a break.

Steve: You obviously understand this.

```
Problem
Algorithms
Java
Interpreter
Hardware
```

Whether there are 100 records in the file or fewer than that number, obviously the number of items in the array is equal to the current value of i. Or is it?

Don't Fence Me In

Let's examine this a bit more closely. It's actually quite easy to make a mistake when writing code that counts items, believing that you have one more or one less than the actual number of items. In fact, this error is common enough to have a couple of widely known nicknames: an **off-by-one error**, also known as a **fence post error**. The former name should be fairly evident, but the latter name may require some explanation. First, let's try it as a "word problem". If you have to put up a fence 100 feet long, and each section of the fence is 10 feet long, how many sections of fence do you need? Obviously, the answer is 10. Now how many fence posts do you need? 11. The confusion caused by counting fence posts when you should be counting segments of the fence (and vice versa) is the cause of a fence post error.

That's fine as a general rule, but what about this specific example? Well, let's start out by supposing that we have an empty file, so the sequence of events in the upper loop is as follows:

Problem
Algorithms
Java
Interpreter
Hardware

1. Set i to 0.
2. Is i less than 100? If not, exit. If so, continue.
3. Use the Read method to try to read a record into the ith element of the AllItems array.
4. Check the return value from Read to find out whether we've tried to read past the end of the file.
5. If so, execute the break statement to exit the loop.

The answer to the question in step 4 is that in fact nothing was read, so we do execute the break and leave the loop. The value of i is clearly 0 here, because we never went back to the top of the loop; since we haven't read any records, setting InventoryCount to i works in this case.

Now let's try the same thing, but this time assuming that there is one record in the file. Here's the sequence of events:

1. Set i to 0.
2. Is i less than 100? If not, exit. If so, continue.
3. Use the Read method to try to read a record into the ith element of the AllItems array.
4. Check the return value from Read to find out whether we've tried to read past the end of the file.
5. If so, execute the break statement to exit the loop. In this case, we haven't run off the end of the file, so we go back to the top of the loop, and continue as follows:

6.   Increment i to 1.
7.   Is i less than 100? If not, exit. If so, continue.
8.   Use the Read method to try to read a record into the AllItems array.
9.   Check the return value from Read to find out whether we've tried to read past the end of the file.
10. If so, execute the break statement to exit the loop.

The second time through, we do execute the break. Since i is 1, and the number of elements read was also 1, it's correct to set the count of elements to i.

It should be pretty clear that this same logic applies to all the possible numbers of elements up to 99. But what if we have 100 elements in the file? Relax, I'm not going to go through these steps 100 times, but I think we should start out from the situation that would exist after reading 99 elements, and see if we get the right answer in this case too. After the 99th element has been read, i will be 99; we know this from our previous analysis that indicates that whenever we start executing the statements in the controlled block of the loop, i is always equal to the number of elements previously read. So here's the 100th iteration of the loop:

Problem
Algorithms
Java
Interpreter
Hardware

1.   Use the Read method to try to read a record into the AllItems array.
2.   Check the return value from Read to find out whether we've tried to read past the end of the file.
3.   If so, execute the break statement to exit the loop.
4.   Otherwise, increment i to 100.
5.   Is i less than 100? If not, exit. If so, continue.

Since i is not less than 100, we exit.

At this point, we've read 100 records and i is 100, so these two numbers are still the same. Therefore, we can conclude that setting InventoryCount equal to i when the loop is finished is correct; we have no fence post error here.

Susan wasn't sure why I was hammering this fence post thing into the ground.

> **Susan**: Why are you always saying that "it's correct to set the count of elements to i"?

> **Steve**: Because I'm showing how to tell whether or not we have a fence post error. That requires a lot of analysis.

Actually, this whole procedure we've just been through reminds me of the professor who claimed that some point he was making was obvious. This was questioned by a student, so the professor spent ten minutes absorbed in calculation and finally emerged triumphantly with the news that it was indeed obvious.

To use the debugger for this program, follow the instructions in the section titled "Using the debugger" in the file "\readme.txt" on the CD in the back of the book. These instructions assume that you've installed the examples on drive C:, so that the location of this program is "c:\whosj\code\itemtst2". You'll see that it indeed prints out each StockItem object read from the file.

Can I Help You?

Of course, this isn't all we want to do with the items in the store's inventory. Since we have a working means of reading and displaying the items, let's see what else we might want to do with them. Here are a few possible transactions at the grocery store:

Problem
Algorithms
Java
Interpreter
Hardware

1. George comes in and buys 3 bags of marshmallows. We have to adjust the inventory for the sale.
2. Sam wants to know the price of a can of string beans.
3. Judy comes in looking for chunky chicken soup; there's none on the shelf where it should be, so we have to check the inventory to see if we're supposed to have any.

All of these scenarios require the ability to find a StockItem object given some information about it. Let's start with the first example, which we might state as a programming task in the following manner: "Given the UPC from the bag of marshmallows, and the number of bags purchased, adjust the inventory by subtracting the number purchased from the previous quantity on hand."

Here's a further breakdown of the steps needed to do this:

1. Take the UPC from the item.
2. Look through the inventory list to find an item with that UPC.
3. When you find it, subtract the number purchased from its m_InStock.

Figure 6.18 is a program that looks as though it should solve this problem. Does it?

```
import WAJ.*;
import java.io.*;

public class Itemtst3
{
    static final int MaxItems = 100;

    public static void main( String args[ ] )
    {
        FileInputStream ShopInfo;

        StockItem[ ] AllItems;
        AllItems = new StockItem[MaxItems];

        int i;
        int InventoryCount;
        int OldInventory;
        int NewInventory;
        String PurchaseUPC;
        String ItemName;
        int PurchaseCount;
        boolean Found;
        boolean Result;

        try
        {
            ShopInfo = new FileInputStream("shop2.in");
        }
        catch (IOException e)
        {
            System.out.println("Can't open file \"shop2.in\"");
            return;
        }

        for (i = 0; i < MaxItems; i ++)
        {
            AllItems[i] = new StockItem();
            Result = AllItems[i].Read(ShopInfo);
            if (Result == false)
                break;
        }
```

Problem
Algorithms
Java
Interpreter
Hardware

Figure 6.18: Trying to update inventory (code\itemtst3\itemtst3.java)

```
InventoryCount = i;
System.out.print("What is the UPC of the item? ");
PurchaseUPC = RWVar.readString(System.in);
Found = false;

for (i = 0; i < InventoryCount; i ++)
    {
    if (PurchaseUPC == AllItems[i].m_UPC)
        {
        Found = true;
        break;
        }
    }

if (Found == true)
    {
    OldInventory = AllItems[i].m_InStock;
    ItemName = AllItems[i].m_Name;

    System.out.print("There are currently "  + OldInventory);
    System.out.println(" units of " + ItemName + " in stock.");
    System.out.print("How many items were sold? ");
    PurchaseCount = RWVar.readInt(System.in);

    AllItems[i].m_InStock -= PurchaseCount;
    System.out.println("The inventory has been updated.");

    NewInventory = AllItems[i].m_InStock;
    System.out.print("There are now "  + NewInventory);
        System.out.println(" units of " + ItemName + " in stock.");
    }
else
    System.out.println("Can't find that item. Please check UPC");

    }
}
```

Problem
Algorithms
Java
Interpreter
Hardware

Figure 6.18 continued

There's nothing really new here except for the use of a boolean variable, and the -= operator that the program uses to adjust the inventory; -= is just like +=, except that it subtracts the right-hand value from the left-hand variable, whereas += adds.

We've already seen that the boolean type can be useful as a return value from a function that simply needs to tell its user whether it succeeded or failed. Much the same is true of boolean variables such as Found in 6.17: its purpose is to record whether or not we have been successful in finding the StockItem that we're looking for. Since the only two possible answers to that question are true and false, a boolean variable is ideal for the task.

However, we'll have to wait a bit to analyze the use of Found, because if you compile this program, you'll find that it is not valid. The problem is that we're trying to access private fields of the StockItem class, namely m_UPC, m_Name, and m_InStock, from the method main. Since main is not a method of StockItem, this is not allowed. You'll get a number of error messages from the compiler, which should look something like this:

E:\whosj\code\Itemtst3\Itemtst3.java(46,34) : error J0147: Cannot access private member 'm_UPC' in class 'StockItem' from 'void main(String[ ] args)'
E:\whosj\code\Itemtst3\Itemtst3.java(55,30) : error J0147: Cannot access private member 'm_InStock' in class 'StockItem' from 'void main(String[ ] args)'
E:\whosj\code\Itemtst3\Itemtst3.java(56,26) : error J0147: Cannot access private member 'm_Name' in class 'StockItem' from 'void main(String[ ] args)'
E:\whosj\code\Itemtst3\Itemtst3.java(63,15) : error J0147: Cannot access private member 'm_InStock' in class 'StockItem' from 'void main(String[ ] args)'
E:\whosj\code\Itemtst3\Itemtst3.java(66,30) : error J0147: Cannot access private member 'm_InStock' in class 'StockItem' from 'void main(String[ ] args)'

Does this mean that we can't accomplish our goal of updating the inventory? Not at all. It merely means that we have to do things "by the book" rather than going in directly and reading or changing fields that belong to the StockItem class. Of course, we could theoretically "solve" this access problem by simply making these fields public rather than private. However, this would allow anyone to mess around with the internal variables in our StockItem objects, which would defeat one of the main purposes of using classes in the first place: that the users of a class can ignore the internal workings of its objects and merely use them according to the class interface. The implementation of the class is our responsibility, not theirs.

As it happens, we can easily solve our access problem without exposing the implementation of our class to the user. All we have to do is to add a couple of new methods called CheckUPC and DeductSaleFromInventory to the StockItem class; the first of these allows us to check whether a given UPC belongs to a given StockItem, and the second allows us to adjust the inventory level of an item.

Susan had another suggestion as to how to solve this problem, as well as a question about why I hadn't anticipated it in the first place.

Problem
Algorithms
Java
Interpreter
Hardware

Susan: How do CheckUPC and DeductSaleFromInventory help keep from exposing the implementation of our class to the user?

Steve: Because the user has to call one of our methods to get the information rather than reaching into the fields to read or modify the data. Thus, we can change our implementation by, for example, preventing a sale of more items than the number in stock.

Susan: I don't understand how this works. Is it that you are putting the variables in the methods and this way the user doesn't get to use them?

Steve: As long as the variables are listed as private, the user can't use them in his program. Instead, if the user wants to do something with an object, he has to call a method of that object.

Susan: So then all these new methods do is to act as a go-between linking the StockItem class and the inventory update program to compare data that is privately held in the StockItem class?

Steve: Yes, the new methods are designed to make the private data available in a safe manner. I think that's the same as what you're saying.

Problem
Algorithms
Java
Interpreter
Hardware

Susan: If you wanted to change the program, why didn't you just do it in the first place instead of breaking it down in parts like this?

Steve: Because that's not the way it actually happens in real life.

Susan: Do you think it is less confusing to do that, and also does this act as an example of how you can modify a program as you see the need to do it?

Steve: Right on both counts.

Figure 6.19 shows the new, improved class definition. The declarations of the two new methods CheckUPC and DeductSaleFromInventory should be pretty easy to figure out: CheckUPC takes the UPC that we want to find and compares it to the UPC in its StockItem, then returns true if they match and false if they don't. Here's another good use for the boolean data type; the only possible results of the CheckUPC method are that the UPC in the StockItem matches the one we've supplied (in which case we return true) or it doesn't match (in which case we return false). DeductSaleFromInventory takes the number of items sold and subtracts it from the previous inventory. But where did those other two methods GetInventory and GetName come from?

```
import WAJ.*;
import java.io.*;

class StockItem
{
private int m_InStock;
private int m_Price;
private String m_Name;
private String m_Distributor;
private String m_UPC;

StockItem()
{
    m_InStock = 0;
    m_Price = 0;
    m_Name = "";
    m_Distributor = "";
    m_UPC = "";
}

StockItem(String Name, int InStock, int Price, String Distributor, String UPC)
{
    m_InStock = InStock;
    m_Price = Price;
    m_Name = Name;
    m_Distributor = Distributor;
    m_UPC = UPC;
}

void Display()
{
    System.out.println("Name: " + m_Name);
    System.out.println("Number in stock: " + m_InStock);
    System.out.println("Price: " + m_Price);
    System.out.println("Distributor: " + m_Distributor);
    System.out.println("UPC: " + m_UPC);
    System.out.println();
}

boolean Read(InputStream s)
{
    DataInputStream dis = new DataInputStream(s);
    String tempInStock;
    String tempPrice;

    try
        {
        m_Name = dis.readLine();
        tempInStock = dis.readLine();
```

Problem
Algorithms
Java
Interpreter
Hardware

Figure 6.19: An enhanced StockItem class (code\itemtst4\stockitem.java)

```
                tempPrice = dis.readLine();
                m_Distributor = dis.readLine();
                m_UPC = dis.readLine();
                }
            catch (IOException e)
                {
                System.out.println("Problem reading from file \"shop2.in\"");
                return false;
                }

            if (m_UPC == null)
                return false;

            try
                {
                m_InStock = Integer.parseInt(tempInStock);
                m_Price = Integer.parseInt(tempPrice);
                }
            catch (NumberFormatException e)
                {
                System.out.println("Bad number format in file \"shop2.in\"");
                return false;
                }

            return true;
            }

        boolean CheckUPC(String ItemUPC)
            {
            if (m_UPC.equals(ItemUPC))
                    return true;
            return false;
            }

        void DeductSaleFromInventory(int QuantitySold)
            {
            m_InStock -= QuantitySold;
            }

        int GetInventory()
            {
            return m_InStock;
            }

        String GetName()
            {
            return m_Name;
            }
        }
```

Problem
Algorithms
Java
Interpreter
Hardware

Figure 6.19 continued

The Customer Is Always Right

I added those methods because I noticed that the "itemtst" program wasn't very user friendly. Originally it followed these steps:

1.   Ask for the UPC.
2.   Ask for the number of items purchased.
3.   Search through the list to see whether the UPC is legitimate.
4.   If so, adjust the inventory.
5.   If not, give an error message.
6.   Exit.

What's wrong with this picture? Well, for one thing, why should the program make me type in the number of items sold if the UPC is no good? Also, it never told me the new inventory or even what the name of the item was. It may have known these things, but it never bothered to inform me. So I changed the program to work as follows:

1.   Ask for the UPC.
2.   Search through the list to see whether the UPC was legitimate.
3.   If not, give an error message and exit.
4.   If the UPC was OK, then
    a.   Display the name of the item and the number in stock.
    b.   Ask for the number of items purchased.
    c.   Adjust the inventory.
    d.   Display a message with the name of the item and number of remaining units in inventory.
5.   Exit.

Problem
Algorithms
Java
Interpreter
Hardware

To do this, I needed those two new methods GetInventory and GetName, so as you've seen I added them to the class definition. Let's go over these new methods (Figure 6.19).

Most of the code in these methods is pretty simple, but there's one little twist in CheckUPC that I want to make sure you understand: how we compare String variables. As I've already mentioned, we can't just use the normal == that we use with ints and the other primitive types to compare two Strings. Instead, we have to use a method called equals. Why is this, and what happens if we use == anyway?

According to the authors of *The Java Programming Language*, one of whom was the originator of the language, "Using equality operators on String objects does not work as expected. Given String objects str1 and str2, str1==str2 tests whether str1 and str2 refer to the same String object. It does *not* test whether they have the same contents. Content equality is tested using String.equals, described in Chapter 8." (p. 116, emphasis in the original)

That explains what happens if we use == by accident. However, it doesn't explain **why** the String class works that way. The answer is that this is another example of the fact that in Java objects of class type do not act like primitive types; instead, we must always refer to objects via references to those objects. Thus, when we compare str1 and str2 in the quoted example, we are really comparing the references str1 and str2, not the objects they refer to. Comparing references tells us only whether they refer to the same objects, which isn't what we want to know.

Now that I've explained why == doesn't work correctly when we're comparing objects of a class type (including String), let's get back to our example, which is getting to be enough like a real program that I'm going to start using the term *application program* (or equivalently, *application*) to refer to it sometimes. As is generally true of Java programs, the responsibility for doing the user's work is divided up into a main program (or application program) and a set of more general classes (sometimes called *infrastructure* classes) used by the application. In this case, itemtst4.java is the main program, or application program, whereas the other file (StockItem.java) is the infrastructure. Figure 6.20 shows the new, improved version of our application, which updates the inventory and actually tells the user what it's doing.

Problem
Algorithms
Java
Interpreter
Hardware

```java
import WAJ.*;
import java.io.*;

public class Itemtst4
{
    static final int MaxItems = 100;

    public static void main( String args[ ] )
    {
        FileInputStream ShopInfo;

        StockItem[ ] AllItems;
        AllItems = new StockItem[MaxItems];

        int i;
        int InventoryCount;
        int OldInventory;
```

Figure 6.20: Updating StockItem inventory (code\itemtst4\itemtst4.java)

```
int NewInventory;
String PurchaseUPC;
String ItemName;
int PurchaseCount;
boolean Found;
boolean Result;

try
{
    ShopInfo = new FileInputStream("shop2.in");
}
catch (IOException e)
{
    System.out.println("Can't open file \"shop2.in\"");
    return;
}

for (i = 0; i < MaxItems; i ++)
    {
        AllItems[i] = new StockItem();
        Result = AllItems[i].Read(ShopInfo);
        if (Result == false)
            break;
    }

InventoryCount = i;
System.out.print("What is the UPC of the item? ");
PurchaseUPC = RWVar.readString(System.in);
Found = false;

for (i = 0; i < InventoryCount; i ++)
    {
        if (AllItems[i].CheckUPC(PurchaseUPC) == true)
            {
            Found = true;
            break;
            }
    }

if (Found == true)
    {
    OldInventory = AllItems[i].GetInventory();
    ItemName = AllItems[i].GetName();
```

Problem
Algorithms
Java
Interpreter
Hardware

Figure 6.20 continued

```
System.out.print("There are currently " + OldInventory);
System.out.println(" units of " + ItemName + " in stock.");
System.out.print("How many items were sold? ");
PurchaseCount = RWVar.readInt(System.in);

AllItems[i].DeductSaleFromInventory(PurchaseCount);
System.out.println("The inventory has been updated.");
NewInventory = AllItems[i].GetInventory();
System.out.print("There are now " + NewInventory);
    System.out.println(" units of " + ItemName + " in stock.");
}
    else
        System.out.println("Can't find that item. Please check UPC");

}
}
```

Figure 6.20 continued

This code should be pretty easy to follow; it simply implements the first item purchase scenario I outlined in the section titled "Can I Help You?".

Problem
Algorithms
Java
Interpreter
Hardware

To use the debugger for this program, follow the instructions in the section titled "Using the debugger" in the file "\readme.txt" on the CD in the back of the book. These instructions assume that you've installed the examples on drive C:, so that the location of this program is "c:\whosj\code\itemtst4".

When the program asks for a UPC, you can use 7904886261, which is the (made-up) UPC for "antihistamines". When the program asks you for a transaction code, type S for "sale" or P for "price check", and then hit ENTER.

Next Customer, Please?

Now let's consider what might be needed to handle some of the other possibilities, starting with the second scenario in that same list. To refresh your memory, here it is again: "Sam wants to know the price of a can of string beans".

How would this be expressed as a programming task? Perhaps in this way: "Given a UPC, look up the price of the item in the inventory".

Here is a set of steps to solve this problem:

1.   Ask for the UPC.
2.   Search through the list to see whether the UPC is legitimate.
3.   If not, give an error message and exit.
4.   If the UPC is OK, then display the name and price of the item.
5.   Exit.

Have you noticed that this solution is very similar to the solution to the first problem? For example, the search for an item with a given UPC is exactly the same. It seems wasteful to duplicate code rather than using the same code again, and in fact we've seen how to avoid code duplication by using a method.

This is a good idea, except that the search method can't be a method of StockItem, because we don't have the right StockItem yet; if we did, we wouldn't need to search for it. Therefore, we have to create a new class that contains a field that is an array of StockItems and write the search routine as a method of this new class; the new method would look through its array to find the StockItem we want. Then we can use the methods of StockItem to do the rest of the work.

Susan had some questions about having to create a new class to find a StockItem.

Susan: I am not sure if I truly understand the problem as to why you can't search StockItem as a method.

Steve: A method of StockItem always accesses a particular StockItem.[17] However, our problem is that we don't know which StockItem we want; therefore, a method in the StockItem class, which necessarily applies to a particular StockItem, won't solve our problem.

Susan: I don't understand, "because we don't have the right StockItem yet". Yes we do, it is "string beans".

Steve: Which StockItem is that? Is it the first element of AllItems, or the third, or the 37th? Or is it even in the AllItems array at all? Until we can determine which one it is (or if we even have it), we can't use it.

Figure 6.21 shows the class definition for this new class, called Inventory.

Problem
Algorithms
Java
Interpreter
Hardware

---

17. This is not strictly true. In fact, as we'll see in the next chapter, it is possible to have a method called a *static method*, which does not refer to any particular object of a class. However, such methods aren't applicable here, so I'll just ignore their existence for the time being.

```
import WAJ.*;
import java.io.*;

class Inventory
{
static final int MaxItems = 100;
private int m_StockCount;
private StockItem[ ] m_Stock;

Inventory()
{
   m_Stock = new StockItem[MaxItems];
   m_StockCount = 0;
}

int LoadInventory(FileInputStream s)
{
    int i;
    boolean Result;

    for (i = 0; i < MaxItems; i ++)
       {
       m_Stock[i] = new StockItem();
       Result = m_Stock[i].Read(s);
       if (Result == false)
          break;
       }

    m_StockCount = i;
    return m_StockCount;
}

StockItem FindItem(String UPC)
{
    int i;
    boolean Found = false;

    for (i = 0; i < m_StockCount; i ++)
        {
        if (m_Stock[i].CheckUPC(UPC) == true)
            {
            Found = true;
            break;
            }
        }

    if (Found == true)
        return m_Stock[i];
    return null;
}
}
```

Problem
Algorithms
Java
Interpreter
Hardware

Figure 6.21: Inventory class (code\itemtst5\Inventory.java)

Here's the next installment of that discussion of searching for a StockItem.

> **Susan**: Ugh. I know we have gone over this but I don't understand why it doesn't know it is there if it has a UPC.

> **Steve**: What are the referents of the three occurrences of "it" in that sentence? That might help me answer, because I can't find my secret decoder ring.

> **Susan**: Why StockItem can't search string beans even though it has a UPC.

> **Steve**: The StockItem class cannot have a method that looks for a StockItem, because to call a StockItem method, you need a StockItem variable. Once you have that variable, you don't need to look for it. Let's say we have an array of StockItems called AllItems. In that case, to call a StockItem method, you would have to pick one of the StockItems in that array to call it on. Once you have the StockItem you're looking for, you don't need to search for it.
>   However, you *can* have a class such as Inventory, each of whose objects contains an array of StockItems. Then that class can have a method that searches for a particular StockItem in the array of StockItems in a given Inventory object.

> **Susan**: Oh, then so far that is all our program is able to do? It is unable to locate one item of all possible items and display it just from the UPC code? In fact that is what we are trying to accomplish, right?

> **Steve**: Exactly.

Problem
Algorithms
Java
Interpreter
Hardware

Susan also wasn't sure what the purpose of the LoadInventory method was.

> **Susan**: What does the code int LoadInventory (FileInputStream s) do? Does it just give you an object named LoadInventory that reads a file that has an argument named s? I don't get this.

> **Steve**: That's quite close. The line you're referring to is the declaration of a method named LoadInventory, which takes a reference to a FileInputStream. The implementation of the method, as you'll see shortly, reads StockItem records from the file connected to the FileInputStream.

Once that was cleared up, she had some questions about the way the FindItem method works, including its interface.

Susan: Is the argument UPC to the FindItem method a String because it is returning the name of a stock item?

Steve: That's the input to the FindItem method, not its output; therefore, it's not "returning" anything. Or did I misunderstand your question?

Susan: Let's see if I even know what I was asking here. OK, how about this: I wanted to know why UPC was a String and not an int, since a UPC is usually a number. In this case, it will be returning a name of a "found item", so that is why it is a String, right?

Steve: No, it's because the UPC is ten digits, which is too many to fit in an int. There actually is another type of number in Java, a long, that is big enough. However, we're not using the UPC in calculations anyway, so we might as well store it as a String.

Susan: Oh, OK. So a String is useful for storing numbers that are somewhat lengthy as long as you don't calculate with those numbers. They are nothing more than "numerical words"?

Steve: Exactly.

Problem
Algorithms
Java
Interpreter
Hardware

Most of this should be fairly self-explanatory by this point. We start out with the default constructor which makes an empty Inventory. Figure 6.22 has the implementation for the default constructor.

```
Inventory()
{
    m_Stock = new StockItem[100];
    m_StockCount = 0;
}
```

Figure 6.22: Default constructor for Inventory class (from code\itemtst5\Inventory.java)

There's nothing complex here; we're initializing the m_Stock variable to a newly constructed array of 100 StockItems and the number of active StockItems to 0. The latter, of course, is because we haven't yet read any data in from the file.

Then we have a couple of handy methods. The first is LoadInventory, which will take data from a FileInputStream and store it in its Inventory object, just as we did directly in our application itemtst4.java.

Susan had a question about this.

Susan: How did you know that you were going to need to use a FileInputStream again?

Steve: Because we're reading data from a file into an array of StockItems, and reading data from a file is what FileInputStreams are for.

Figure 6.23 shows the implementation of LoadInventory.

```
int LoadInventory(FileInputStream s)
{
    int i;
    boolean Result;

    for (i = 0; i < 100; i ++)
        {
            m_Stock[i] = new StockItem();
            Result = m_Stock[i].Read(s);
            if (Result == false)
                break;
        }

    m_StockCount = i;
    return m_StockCount;
}
```

Figure 6.23: The LoadInventory method for the Inventory class (from
code\itemtst5\Inventory.java)

Problem
Algorithms
Java
Interpreter
Hardware

Now we're up to the FindItem method (Figure 6.24). Its declaration, StockItem FindItem(String UPC), is pretty simple: It takes an argument of type String which contains the UPC that we're looking for. Its implementation is pretty simple too: It will search the Inventory object for the StockItem that has that UPC and return a reference to that StockItem, which can then be interrogated to find the price or whatever other information we need.

However, there's a serious design issue here: What should this method return if the UPC doesn't match the UPC in any of the StockItem entries in the Inventory object? The application program has to be able to determine whether or not the UPC is found. In the original program this was no problem, because the main program maintained that information itself. But in this case, the method FindItem has to communicate success or failure to the caller somehow.

Of course, we could use a return value of true or false to indicate whether the UPC is found, but we're already using the return value to return the StockItem to the calling method.

Nobody's Home

There's one more possibility. We can return a null reference, which will indicate that we couldn't find the StockItem we were looking for.

I like this solution, because when the method terminates, the application program has to test something anyway to see if the desired StockItem was found; why not test whether the returned reference is a null reference? This solution also has the advantage of avoiding changes to our implementation of StockItem: We can test whether a reference is null by using == to compare it to null with the expression if (FoundItem == true).

Let's hear from Susan on the topic of method return values.

> **Susan**: This is something I have not thought about before: When you call a method where does the return value go?

> **Steve**: Wherever you put it. If you say x = sum(weight);, then the return value goes into x. If you just say sum(weight);, then it is discarded.

> **Susan**: Why is it discarded?

Problem
Algorithms
Java
Interpreter
Hardware

> **Steve**: If you don't use it, the compiler assumes you aren't interested in it.

> **Susan**: So the return value can be used in only one place?

> **Steve**: Yes, unless you save it in a variable, in which case you can use it however you like.

Figure 6.24 shows the implementation of FindItem, which uses CheckUPC to check whether the requested UPC is the one in the current item and returns a null reference if the desired UPC isn't found in the inventory list.

Now that we've solved the problem of finding an object given its UPC in a more general way, we can also directly apply this same lookup method to the previous problem of updating the inventory. In that case, after we get a reference to the correct StockItem and update its inventory via DeductSaleFromInventory, we're done; since FoundItem is a reference to the StockItem object that we're interested in, we have actually updated that object by calling DeductSaleFromInventory.

```
StockItem FindItem(String UPC)
{
    int i;
    boolean Found = false;

    for (i = 0; i < m_StockCount; i ++)
        {
        if (m_Stock[i].CheckUPC(UPC) == true)
            {
            Found = true;
            break;
            }
        }

    if (Found == true)
        return m_Stock[i];

    return null;
}
```

Figure 6.24: FindItem method for Inventory class (from
code\itemtst5\invent1.java)

Here's my interchange with Susan on the implementation of this
method:

> **Susan**: About the first if statement, if (m_Stock[i].CheckUPC(UPC) == true):
> Does that mean if you find the UPC you are looking for, then the
> program breaks and you don't need to continue looking? In that case,
> what does the statement Found = true; do? It looks as if you are setting
> Found to the value true.

> **Steve**: That's right. If we've found the item we're looking for, then
> Found will have been set to true, so we'll return the real item; otherwise,
> we'll return a null StockItem to indicate that we couldn't find the one
> requested.

> **Susan**: Also, I am confused about why we are working on the actual
> object. I thought that was the opposite, that everything is a reference to
> some object in Java.

> **Steve**: Yes, everything (other than a primitive variable) is a reference to
> an object in Java. That's precisely why, when we are working on a
> StockItem from the AllItems array, we are actually working on the original
> object, not on a copy. Because a StockItem variable is just a pointer to a
> StockItem object, copying a StockItem variable results in another StockItem
> variable that points to the same StockItem object that the first StockItem

Problem
Algorithms
Java
Interpreter
Hardware

variable pointed to. Thus, when we access the StockItem object through the newly created StockItem variable, we are actually accessing the same StockItem object that the original StockItem variable referred to. This means that when we have modified the StockItem by, for example, reducing the number of items in its stock, we have actually modified the original StockItem object that the AllItems array element referred to, not a copy of it, and therefore the object the array element refers to has been changed. This is a case where the situation in Figures 6.7 through 6.9 is actually what we want, rather than an error.

The application program needs one more method to be added to the interface of StockItem to retrieve the price from the object once we have found it. This additional method, GetPrice(), is shown in Figure 6.25.

```
int GetPrice()
{
      return m_Price;
}
```

Figure 6.25: The implementation of GetPrice (from code\itemtst5\StockItem.java)

Problem
Algorithms
Java
Interpreter
Hardware

We're almost ready to examine the revised test program. First, though, let's take a look at the class definitions of the StockItem and Inventory classes all in one place. The definition of StockItem is in Figure 6.26.

```
import WAJ.*;
import java.io.*;

class StockItem
{
private int m_InStock;
private int m_Price;
private String m_Name;
private String m_Distributor;
private String m_UPC;
```

Figure 6.26: Current implementation for StockItem class (code\itemtst5\StockItem.java)

```
StockItem()
{
    m_InStock = 0;
    m_Price = 0;
    m_Name = "";
    m_Distributor = "";
    m_UPC = "";
}

StockItem(String Name, int InStock, int Price, String Distributor, String UPC)
{
    m_InStock = InStock;
    m_Price = Price;
    m_Name = Name;
    m_Distributor = Distributor;
    m_UPC = UPC;
}

void Display()
{
    System.out.println("Name: " + m_Name);
    System.out.println("Number in stock: " + m_InStock);
    System.out.println("Price: " + m_Price);
    System.out.println("Distributor: " + m_Distributor);
    System.out.println("UPC: " + m_UPC);
    System.out.println();
}

boolean Read(InputStream s)
{
    DataInputStream dis = new DataInputStream(s);
    String tempInStock;
    String tempPrice;

    try
      {
      m_Name = dis.readLine();
      tempInStock = dis.readLine();
      tempPrice = dis.readLine();
      m_Distributor = dis.readLine();
      m_UPC = dis.readLine();
      }
    catch (IOException e)
      {
      System.out.println(e);
      return false;
      }
```

Problem
Algorithms
Java
Interpreter
Hardware

Figure 6.26 continued

```
        if (m_UPC == null)
           return false;

        try
           {
           m_InStock = Integer.parseInt(tempInStock);
           m_Price = Integer.parseInt(tempPrice);
           }
        catch (NumberFormatException e)
           {
           System.out.println(e);
           return false;
           }

        return true;
    }

    boolean CheckUPC(String ItemUPC)
    {
        if (m_UPC.equals(ItemUPC))
            return true;

        return false;
    }
```

Problem
Algorithms
Java
Interpreter
Hardware

```
    void DeductSaleFromInventory(int QuantitySold)
    {
        m_InStock -= QuantitySold;
    }

    int GetInventory()
    {
        return m_InStock;
    }

    String GetName()
    {
        return m_Name;
    }

    int GetPrice()
    {
        return m_Price;
    }

    }
```

Figure 6.26 continued

And Figure 6.27 contains the implementation for Inventory.

```
import WAJ.*;
import java.io.*;

class Inventory
{
static final int MaxItems = 100;
private int m_StockCount;
private StockItem[ ] m_Stock;

Inventory()
{
   m_Stock = new StockItem[MaxItems];
   m_StockCount = 0;
}

int LoadInventory(FileInputStream s)
{
    int i;
    boolean Result;

    for (i = 0; i < MaxItems; i ++)
       {
       m_Stock[i] = new StockItem();
       Result = m_Stock[i].Read(s);
       if (Result == false)
          break;
       }

    m_StockCount = i;
    return m_StockCount;
}

StockItem FindItem(String UPC)
{
    int i;
    boolean Found = false;

    for (i = 0; i < m_StockCount; i ++)
        {
        if (m_Stock[i].CheckUPC(UPC) == true)
            {
            Found = true;
            break;
            }
        }

    if (Found == true)
        return m_Stock[i];
    return null;
}
}
```

Problem
Algorithms
Java
Interpreter
Hardware

Figure 6.27: Latest Inventory class (code\itemtst5\Inventory.java)

Testing, 1, 2, 3. . .

To finish this stage of the inventory control project, Figure 6.28 is the revised test program that uses the Inventory class rather than doing its own search through an array of StockItems.

```java
import WAJ.*;
import java.io.*;

public class Itemtst5
{
    public static void main( String args[ ] )
    {
        FileInputStream ShopInfo;
        String PurchaseUPC;
        int PurchaseCount;
        String ItemName;
        int OldInventory;
        int NewInventory;
        Inventory MyInventory = new Inventory();
        StockItem FoundItem;
        String TransactionCode;

        try
        {
            ShopInfo = new FileInputStream("shop2.in");
        }
        catch (IOException e)
        {
            System.out.println("Can't open file \"shop2.in\"");
            return;
        }

        MyInventory.LoadInventory(ShopInfo);

        System.out.print("What is the UPC of the item? ");
        PurchaseUPC = RWVar.readString(System.in);

        FoundItem = MyInventory.FindItem(PurchaseUPC);
        if (FoundItem == null)
            {
            System.out.println("Can't find that item. Please check UPC.");
            return;
            }
```

Problem
Algorithms
Java
Interpreter
Hardware

Figure 6.28: Updated inventory application (code\itemtst5\itemtst5.java)

```
OldInventory = FoundItem.GetInventory();
ItemName = FoundItem.GetName();

System.out.print("There are currently " + OldInventory);
System.out.println(" units of " + ItemName + " in stock.");

System.out.print("Please enter transaction code as follows:\n");
System.out.print("S (sale), C (price check): ");
TransactionCode = RWVar.readString(System.in);

if (TransactionCode.equals("C") || TransactionCode.equals("c"))
    {
    System.out.println("The name of that item is: " + ItemName);
    System.out.println("Its price is: " + FoundItem.GetPrice());
    }
else if (TransactionCode.equals("S") || TransactionCode.equals("s"))
    {
    System.out.print("How many items were sold? ");
    PurchaseCount = RWVar.readInt(System.in);

    FoundItem.DeductSaleFromInventory(PurchaseCount);
    System.out.println("The inventory has been updated.");

    NewInventory = FoundItem.GetInventory();

    System.out.print("There are now " + NewInventory + " units of ");
    System.out.println(ItemName + " in stock.");
    }

    }
}
```

Problem
Algorithms
Java
Interpreter
Hardware

Figure 6.28 continued

This program can perform either of two operations, depending on what the user requests. Once the UPC has been typed in, the user is prompted to type either "C" for price check or "S" for sale. Then an if statement selects which of the two operations to perform. The code for the S (i.e., sale) operation is the same as it was in the previous version of this application, except that, of course, at that time it was the only possible operation, so it wasn't controlled by an if statement. The code for the C (i.e., price check) operation is new, but it's very simple; it just displays both the item name and the price.

The only part of the program that might not be obvious at this point is the expression in the if statement that determines whether the user wants to enter a price check or sale transaction. The first part of

the test is if (TransactionCode.equals("C") || TransactionCode.equals("c")). The ||
is the "logical or" operator. An approximate translation of this
expression is "if at least one of the two expressions on its right or left
is true, then produce the result true; if they're both false, then produce
the result false".[18] In other words, this if statement will be true if the
TransactionCode variable is either C or c. Why do we have to check for
either a lower or upper case letter, when the instructions to the user
clearly state that the choices are C or S?

This is good practice because users generally consider upper and
lower case letters to be equivalent. Of course, as programmers, we
know that the characters c and C are completely different; however,
we should humor the users in this harmless delusion. After all,
they're our customers!

Susan had a couple of questions about this program.

> **Susan**: What does the following output statement mean: System.out.print("S
> (sale), C (price check): ");? I am not clear as to what this is doing.

> **Steve**: Nothing special; the prompt S (sale), C (price check) is just to notify
> the user what his or her choices are.

Problem
Algorithms
Java
Interpreter
Hardware

> **Susan**: OK, so the line with the || is how you tell the computer to
> recognize upper case as well as lower case to have the same meaning?

> **Steve**: Yes, that's what we're doing here.

> **Susan**: So what do you call those || thingys?

> **Steve**: They're called "vertical bars". The operator that is spelled || is
> called a "logical OR" operator, because it results in the value true if
> either the left-hand **or** the right-hand expression is true (or if both are
> true).

> **Susan**: What do you mean by using else and if in the line else if
> (TransactionCode.equals("S") || TransactionCode.equals("s"))? I don't believe I
> have seen them used together before.

> **Steve**: You may be right. However, it's not that complicated: As always,
> the else means that we're specifying actions to be taken if the original if

---

18. The reason it's only an approximate translation is that there is a special rule in Java
governing the execution of the || operator: If the expression on the left is true, then the answer
is known to be true and the expression on the right will not be executed. The reason for this
short-circuit evaluation rule is that in some cases you may want to write a right-hand
expression that will only be legal if the left-hand expression is true.

isn't true. The second if merely checks whether another condition is true and executes its controlled block if that is the case.

To use the debugger for this program, follow the instructions in the section titled "Using the debugger" in the file "\readme.txt" on the CD in the back of the book. These instructions assume that you've installed the examples on drive C:, so that the location of this program is "c:\whosj\code\itemtst5".

When the program asks for a UPC, you can use 7904886261, which is the (made-up) UPC for "antihistamines". When the program asks you for a transaction code, type S for "sale" or P for "price check", and then hit ENTER.

Paging Rosie Scenario

By this point, you very understandably might have gotten the notion that we have to make changes to our classes every time we need to do anything slightly different in our application program. In that case, where's the advantage of using classes instead of just writing the whole program in terms of ints, chars, and so on?

Well, this is your lucky day. It just so happens that the next (and last) scenario we are going to examine requires no more methods at all; in fact, we don't even have to change the application program. Here it is, for reference: "Judy comes in looking for chunky chicken soup; there's none on the shelf where it should be, so we have to check the inventory to see if we're supposed to have any".

Problem
Algorithms
Java
Interpreter
Hardware

The reason we don't have to do anything special for this scenario is that we're already displaying the name and inventory for the item as soon as we find it. Of course, if we hadn't already handled this issue, there are many other ways that we could solve this same problem. For example, we could use the Display method of StockItem to display an item as soon as the UPC lookup succeeds, rather than waiting for the user to indicate what operation our application is supposed to perform.

For that matter, we'd have to consider a number of other factors in writing a real application program, even one that does such a simple task as this one. For example, what would happen if the user indicated that 200 units of a particular item had been sold when only 100 were in stock? Also, how would we find an item if the UPC isn't available? The item might very well be in inventory somewhere, but the current implementation of Inventory doesn't allow for the possibility of looking up an item by any information other than the UPC.

Although these topics and many others are essential to the work of a professional programmer, they would take us too far afield from our purpose in this book, which is to teach you how to program using Java. Therefore, we will leave them for another day (and another book). Now let's review what we've covered in this chapter.

Review

The most important concept in this chapter is the idea of creating user-defined data types. In Java, this is done by defining a class for each such data type. Each class has a class *definition*, which both describes the behavior that the class displays to the "outside world" (i.e., other unrelated methods), and tells the compiler how to perform those behaviors. A data item of a class type is called an *object*.

A class is defined in terms of the methods and variables of which the class is composed; the latter are called *fields* to distinguish them from local variables that don't belong to a particular object.

```
Problem
Algorithms
Java
Interpreter
Hardware
```

Of course, one obvious question is why we need to make up our own variable types. What's wrong with char, int, and the rest of the primitive types built into Java? The answer is that it's easier to write an inventory control program, for example, if we have data types representing items in the stock of a store, rather than having to express everything in terms of the primitive types. An analogy is the universal preference of professionals for communicating in technical jargon rather than "plain English": Jargon conveys more information, more precisely, in less time.

The idea of using objects as the fundamental building blocks of programming is the basis of the "object-oriented programming" paradigm.[19]

Then we examined how creating classes differs from using classes, as we have been doing throughout the book. A fairly good analogy is that creating your own classes is to using classes as writing a program is to using a program.

Next, we went through the steps needed to actually create a new class; our example is the StockItem class, which is designed to allow

---

19. Purists may not approve of this use of the term *object-oriented programming*, as I'm not using this term in its strictest technical sense. However, since we are using objects and classes as our central organizing ideas, using the term *object-oriented* seems reasonable to me in this context.

tracking of inventory for a small grocery store. These steps include writing the class definition, writing the program that uses the class, compiling both, and running the final program.

Then we moved from the general to the specific, analyzing the particular data and methods that the StockItem class needed to perform its duties in an application program. The fields needed for each StockItem object included the name, count, distributor, price, and UPC. Of course, merely having these fields doesn't make a StockItem object very useful, if it can't do anything with them. This led us to the topic of what methods might be needed for such a class.

Next, we looked at the first version of a class definition for StockItem (Figure 6.2) which tells the user (and the compiler) exactly what operations objects of this class can perform and how these operations work. Some items of note in this construct are these:

1. The *access specifiers* public and private, which control access to the implementation of a class by methods not in the class. Fields and methods marked as public are available for use by outside methods, whereas fields and methods marked as private are usable only by methods of the same class.

2. The definitions of the *constructor* methods, which construct a new object of the class. The first noteworthy point about constructors is that they have the same name as the class, which is how the compiler identifies them as constructors. The second point of note is that there can be more than one constructor for a given class; all constructors have the same name, and are distinguished by their argument lists. This facility, called *method overloading*, is applicable to Java methods in general, not just constructors. That is, you can have any number of methods with the same name as long as they have different argument lists; the difference in argument lists is enough to make the compiler treat them as different methods. In this case, we have written two constructors: the default constructor, which is used to create a StockItem when we don't specify an initial value, and a constructor that has arguments to specify values for all of the fields.

3. The declaration of a "normal" method (that is, a method that is not a constructor) named Display, which as its name indicates, is used to display a StockItem on the screen.

4. The declaration of the fields of StockItem, which are used to keep track of the information for a specific object of the StockItem class.

Problem
Algorithms
Java
Interpreter
Hardware

Next, we examined the default constructor for the StockItem class: StockItem(), which simply sets the values of the fields in a newly constructed StockItem to either 0 or "", whichever is appropriate for their type.

The next topic we visited was the scope of fields, which is class scope. Each object of a given class has one set of fields; these fields live as long as the object does. These fields can be accessed from any method of the same class as though they were global variables.

Then we examined how the default constructor was actually used in the example program, in the statement item1 = new StockItem();. This led to a discussion of the fact that the person who writes a class isn't always the person who uses it. One reason for this is that the skills required to write a program using a class are not the same as those required to create the class in the first place.

Next, we covered the other constructor for the StockItem class. This one has arguments specifying the values for all of the fields that make up the data part of the class.

Then we got to the next-to-the-last method of the first version of the StockItem class: the Display method, which as its name indicates is used to display the contents of a StockItem on the screen. This method uses the preexisting ability of System.out to display the ints and Strings that hold the contents of the StockItem. The return type of this method is a type we hadn't seen before, void, which simply means that there is no return value from this method. We don't need a return value from the Display method because we call it solely for its *side effect*: displaying the value of its StockItem on the screen.

Next, we took up the private items in the StockItem class definition, namely, the fields. We covered two reasons why it is a good idea to keep the fields private: First, it makes debugging easier, because only the methods can modify the fields; second, we can change the names or types of our fields or delete them from the class definition much more easily if we don't have to worry about what other methods might be relying on them. While we were on the subject of the fields of StockItem, I also explained how we could use an int to store a price: By expressing the price in cents, rather than dollars and cents, any reasonable price could be stored in such a variable.

The final method in this version of the StockItem class was SetName, which changes the name of the StockItem for which it is called. I used this method to show that variables that seem to be class objects really aren't; instead, they are *references* to those objects. This is very important because if we change an object through a reference, all references to that variable will now refer to that changed object. This

Problem
Algorithms
Java
Interpreter
Hardware

is not how primitive variables behave, and it is a rich source of subtle program errors, so it's important to understand this point fully.

As we continued with the analysis of how the StockItem objects would be used, we discovered that our example program actually needed an array of such objects, one for each different item in the stock. We also needed some way to read the information for these StockItem objects from a disk file, so we wouldn't have to type it in every time we started the program up. So the next program we examined provided this method via a Java class we hadn't seen before: FileInputStream (for input from a file). We also added a new method called Read to use this new class to read information for a StockItem from the file containing that information.

This led to a discussion of *exception handling*, which is the Java mechanism that is used to deal with unexpected results. In this case, we had to handle the possibility that the file we were trying to open might not exist.

Then we got to the question of how we could tell when there was no data left in the input file; the answer was that the Read method could determine this by checking whether it received a null reference instead of the data it was requesting from the file. Read transmitted that information back to its caller by returning a value of the boolean type: true if it had succeeded in reading data from the file and false otherwise. We used a false return value from Read to trigger a break statement, which terminates whatever loop contains the break. In this case, the loop was the one that read data from the input file, so the loop would stop whenever we got to the end of the input file or when we had read 100 records, whichever came first.

This led to a detailed investigation of whether the number of records read was always calculated correctly. The problem under discussion was the potential for a *fence post error*, also known as an *off-by-one error*. After careful consideration, I concluded that the code as written was correct.

Having cleared up that question, we proceeded to some other scenarios that might occur in the grocery store for which this program theoretically was being written. All of the scenarios we looked at had a common requirement: to be able to look up a StockItem, given some information about it. We first tried to handle this requirement by reading the UPC directly from each StockItem object in the array. When we found the correct StockItem, we would display and update the inventory for that StockItem. However, this didn't compile, because we were trying to access private fields of a StockItem object from outside that class, which is illegal. Although we could have changed those fields from private to public, that would

Problem
Algorithms
Java
Interpreter
Hardware

directly contradict the reason that we made them private in the first place; that is, to prevent external methods from interfering in the inner workings of our StockItem objects. Therefore, we solved the problem by adding some new methods (DeductSaleFromInventory and CheckUPC) to manipulate the inventory information for a StockItem and check the UPC of a StockItem, respectively.

While I was making these changes, I noticed that the original version of the test program wasn't very helpful to its user; it didn't tell the user whether the UPC was any good, the name of the item, or how much inventory was available for sale. So I added some more methods (GetInventory and GetName) to allow this more "user-friendly" information to be displayed.

Then we progressed to the second of the grocery store scenarios, in which the task was to find the price of an item, given its UPC. This turned out to be very similar to the previous problem of finding an item to update its inventory. Therefore, it was a pretty obvious step to try to make a method out of the "find an item by UPC" operation, rather than writing the code for the search over again. However, this couldn't be a method of StockItem, because the whole idea of this method was to locate a StockItem. A method of StockItem needs a StockItem object to work on, but we didn't have the StockItem object yet.

Problem
Algorithms
Java
Interpreter
Hardware

The solution was to make another class, called Inventory, which had methods to load the inventory information in from the disk file (LoadInventory) and search it for a particular StockItem (FindItem). Most of this class was pretty simple, but we did run into an interesting design question: What should the FindItem method return if the UPC didn't match anything in the inventory? After some consideration, I decided to use a null reference; that is, a reference that doesn't refer to any actual object.

Then we updated the test program to use this new means of locating a StockItem. Since the new version of the test program could perform either of two methods (price check or sale), we also added some output and input statements to ask the user what he wanted to do. To make this process more flexible, we allowed the user to type in either an upper or lower case letter to select which method to perform. This brought up the use of the "logical OR" operator || to allow the controlled block of an if statement to be executed if either (or both) of two expressions is true. We also saw how to combine an else with a following if statement, when we wanted to select among more than two alternatives.

At this point, we noted that changing the StockItem that we got from the FindItem changed the actual StockItem in the array; the reason is that we have a copy of a reference to the actual StockItem object, and copying a reference produces another reference that refers to the same object as the first reference. Therefore, we are not working on a copy of the object, but on the original object.

This brought us to the final scenario, which required us to look up the inventory for an item, given its UPC. As it happened, we had already solved that problem by the simple expedient of displaying the name and inventory of the StockItem as soon as it was located.

Finally, I mentioned a few other factors, such as alternative means of looking up an item without knowing its UPC, that would be important in writing a real application program, and noted that we couldn't go into them here due to space limitations.

Exercises

1. In a real inventory control program, we would need to do more than merely read the inventory information from a disk file, as we have done in this chapter. We'd also want to be able to write the updated inventory back to the disk file via a FileOutputStream object, which is exactly like a FileInputStream object except that it allows us to write to a file rather than reading from one. You can use the RWVar.println methods that write ints and Strings to actually do the output. Modify the class descriptions of the StockItem and Inventory classes to include two new methods, Write and StoreInventory, that are needed in those respective classes to support this new ability.

Problem
Algorithms
Java
Interpreter
Hardware

An answer to the preceding exercise can be found at the end of the chapter.

2. Suppose that the store that is using our inventory control program adds a new pharmacy department. Most of their items are nonprescription medications that can be handled with the StockItem class we've already created, but their prescription drug items need to be handled more carefully. This means that the DeductSaleFromInventory member function has to ask for a password before allowing the sale to take place. Create a DrugStockItem class that enforces this new rule.
3. The store also needs some way to keep track of its employees' hours so it can calculate their pay. We'll assume that the employees are paid their gross wages, ignoring taxes. These wages are calculated as follows:

a.   Managers are paid a flat amount per week, calculated as their hourly rate multiplied by 40 hours.

b.   Hourly employees are paid a certain amount per hour, no matter how many hours are worked (i.e., overtime is not paid at a higher rate).

Write an Employee class that allows the creation of Employee objects with a specified hourly wage level and either "manager" or "hourly" salary rules. The pay for each object is to be calculated via a CalculatePay member function that uses the "manager" or "hourly" category specified when the object was created. You should use the float data type to store the pay rate and to calculate the total pay; this data type behaves just like an int except that it can store values with fractional parts as well as whole numbers.

Conclusion

Problem
Algorithms
Java
Interpreter
Hardware

In this chapter, we've delved into the concepts and implementations of classes and objects, which are the constructs that make Java an object-oriented language. Of course, we have only scratched the surface of these powerful topics; in fact, we'll spend the rest of this book on the fundamentals of classes and objects. Unfortunately, it's impossible to cover these constructs and all of their uses in any one book, no matter how long or detailed it may be, and I'm not going to try to do that. Instead, we'll continue with our in-depth examination of the basics of object-oriented programming. In the next chapter, we'll continue by seeing how we can extend our StockItem class to handle items with expiration dates.

Answers to Exercises

1.   Figure 6.29 shows the implementation of the Write method for StockItem.

```
void Write(OutputStream s)
{
    try
    {
      DataOutputStream ostr = new DataOutputStream(s);
      RWVar.println(ostr,m_Name);
      RWVar.println(ostr,m_InStock);
      RWVar.println(ostr,m_Price);
      RWVar.println(ostr,m_Distributor);
      RWVar.println(ostr,m_UPC);
    }
    catch (IOException e)
    {
      System.out.println(e);
    }

}
```

Figure 6.29: The Write method for the StockItem class (from
code\itemtst6\StockItem.java)

Figure 6.30 is the implementation of the StoreInventory method of the
Inventory class.

```
void StoreInventory(OutputStream s)
{
    int i;

    for (i = 0; i < m_StockCount; i ++)
      {
      m_Stock[i].Write(s);
      }
}
```

Problem
Algorithms
Java
Interpreter
Hardware

Figure 6.30: The StoreInventory method for the Inventory class (from
code\itemtst6\Inventory.java)

As you can see, neither of these is tremendously complex or, for
that matter, very different from its counterpart used to read the data
in from the file in the first place.

Finally, Figure 6.31 shows the changes needed to the application
program to write the updated inventory back to a new file.

```
FileOutputStream NewShopInfo;

try
    {
    NewShopInfo = new FileOutputStream("shop2.out");
    }
catch (IOException e)
    {
    System.out.println("Can't open file \"shop2.out\"");
    return;
    }

MyInventory.StoreInventory(NewShopInfo);
}
```

Figure 6.31: The changes to the application program (from
code\itemtst6\itemtst6.java)

Of course, in a real program, it would probably be better to write
the updated inventory back to the original file, so that the next time
we ran the program, the updated inventory would be used. However,
in the case of a test application, it's simpler to avoid modifying the
input file so we can run the same test again if necessary.

Problem
Algorithms
Java
Interpreter
Hardware

To use the debugger for this program, follow the instructions in the
section titled "Using the debugger" in the file "\readme.txt" on the
CD in the back of the book. These instructions assume that you've
installed the examples on drive C:, so that the location of this
program is "c:\whosj\code\itemtst6".

When the program asks for a UPC, you can use 7904886261,
which is the (made-up) UPC for "antihistamines". When the program
asks you for a transaction code, type S for "sale" or P for "price
check", and then hit ENTER.

Susan had a question about this exercise.

Susan: What is the purpose of Write and StoreInventory?

Steve: Write writes a StockItem to a file; StoreInventory writes all of the
StockItems in an Inventory to a file.

Susan: Oh. So all we were doing before was reading and not writing?

Steve: Correct.

Chapter 7

Stocking Up

In this chapter we'll start to build on our previous StockItem class by using another of the primary organizing principles of Java: **inheritance**. First, let's define a few terms and then take a look at the objectives for the chapter.

Definitions

Inheritance is the definition of one class as a more specific version of another class which has been previously defined. This process is also called **extending** a class. The newly defined class is called the **derived class** (or sometimes the **subclass**), whereas the previously defined class is called the **base class** (or sometimes the **superclass**). In this book, we will use the terms "base class" and "derived class". The derived class inherits all of the fields and regular methods from the base class. Inheritance is one of the primary organizing principles of object-oriented programming.

A **regular method** is any method that is *not* a constructor. A *derived* class inherits all regular methods (such as the Display method of the StockItem class) from its *base* class.

A method in a derived class is said to **override** a base class method if the derived class method has the same *signature* (name and argument types) as the base class method. The derived class method will be called instead of the base class method when the method is called for an object of the derived class. A method in a derived class with the same name as a method in the base class but with a different *signature* does *not* override the base class method. Instead, both the derived class method and the base class method are available for use with objects of the derived class.[1]

For example, the method Reorder(OutputStream s) may be defined in a base class (StockItem) and in a derived class (DatedStockItem); when Reorder is called for an object of the base class StockItem, the base class version of Reorder will be called, and when Reorder is called for an object of the derived class DatedStockItem, the derived class version of Reorder will be called. This behavior of Java allows a derived class to supply the same functionality as a base class but implement that functionality in a different way.

The keyword **protected** is an access specifier. When present in a base class definition, it allows derived class methods access to members in the base class part of a derived class object, while preventing access by other methods outside the base class.

The **base class part** of a derived class object is an unnamed component of the derived class object whose fields and methods are accessible as though they were defined in the derived class, so long as they are either public or protected.

```
Problem
Algorithms
Java
Interpreter
Hardware
```

A **static method** is a method that can be called without reference to an object of its class. Because such a method call is not connected with any particular object of its class, a static method cannot refer to fields of the class.

Objectives for This Chapter

By the end of this chapter, you should:

1. Understand how we can use *inheritance* to create a new class by adding new methods or fields to those provided by an existing class.
2. Understand how methods of a derived class can override methods of the base class when objects of the derived class are involved.

---

1. C++ programmers should note this significant difference between the handling of inheritance in C++ and Java.

Under Control

Before we get to the details of our extensions to the StockItem class, let's expand a bit on the first objective as it applies to this particular case.

There are two reasons to use *inheritance*. The first is to create a new class that has all of the capabilities of an existing class, while adding capabilities that are unique to the new class. In such a case, objects of the new class are clearly not equivalent to objects of the preexisting class, which means that the user of these classes has to know which class any given object belongs to so that he or she can tell which operations that object can perform.[2] Therefore, it does not make sense to be able to substitute objects of the derived class for objects of the base class. We could call this "inheritance for extension"; it's illustrated by one of the Employee class exercises in this chapter.

In the current case, however, we'll be using inheritance to create a new class called DatedStockItem that will be exactly like the StockItem class except that its items will have expiration dates. As a result, objects of this class will behave, as far as the application programmer is concerned, just like objects of the StockItem class. Of course, to create an object of this class, the expiration date for the object must be provided, but once such an object exists, its user can view it in exactly the same way as an object of the base class, which makes this an example of "inheritance for re-implementation". In such a case, it is reasonable to be able to substitute objects of the derived class for those of the base class, and we will see how to do that in the next chapter.

Problem
Algorithms
Java
Interpreter
Hardware

Susan wanted to know the difference between these two reasons for using inheritance.

Susan: I just don't get what inheritance for extension is.

Steve: Well, there are two different reasons to create a new class by inheritance. The first reason is that the old class can't do everything that we want it to do because it is missing some methods that we need. In that case, our new class will have new methods to provide those new features that we need. Clearly, this means that we will need to distinguish the new class from the old in our programs, because the old

---

2. As elsewhere in this book, the user of a class means the application programmer who is using objects of the class to perform work in his or her program, not the "end user" who is using the finished program.

class doesn't have the features we want. This is "inheritance for extension".

The second reason to create a new class by inheritance is that we like the features of the old class but we need to implement them somewhat differently to handle a new situation. In that case, we don't need to add new methods to the derived class; all we need to do is to re-implement the same methods differently. In this case, we can view the old and new classes as interchangeable in our application program. This is "inheritance for re-implementation."

Before we can substitute objects of one class for those of another one, we'll need to learn how to create a new class by extending an existing class such as the StockItem class.

There are a few minor changes between the final version of the StockItem class from Chapter 6 and the first one in this chapter (code\Itemtst20\StockItem.java) that we should get out of the way before moving on. I've renamed the method Display to FormattedDisplay, which is more descriptive, and added a new method called Reorder and a couple of new fields called m_MinimumStock and m_MinimumReorder, whose purpose we'll see shortly. Of course, the arguments to the "normal" constructor have been updated to reflect these two new fields. Figure 7.1 shows the new class definition file.

Problem
Algorithms
Java
Interpreter
Hardware

Susan had some questions about this program.

Susan: Why do you add a + to the code in the FormattedDisplay method?

Steve: Because we want to display both the name and the value of each variable.

Susan: Yes, I know, but I forgot how that is done.

Steve: We want to tell the user not only the name, price, and so on for each StockItem, but which field is which. Therefore, we have to write a title for each field as we're displaying it. The title of the field is a literal String (e.g., "Name"), whereas the value of the field is the contents of a String variable (e.g., the contents of m_Name). Thus, to display the values along with titles, you need both the literal String and the contents of the field. That is, you have to write something like System.out.println("Name: " + m_Name);. The "+" means "stick the value of the second expression onto the end of the value of the first expression", so if the value of m_Name is "Chunky Chicken", the whole line will be "Name: Chunky Chicken".

```
import WAJ.*;
import java.io.*;

class StockItem
{
private int m_InStock;
private int m_Price;
private int m_MinimumStock;
private int m_MinimumReorder;
private String m_Name;
private String m_Distributor;
private String m_UPC;

StockItem()
{
    m_InStock = 0;
    m_Price = 0;
    m_MinimumStock = 0;
    m_MinimumReorder = 0;
    m_Name = "";
    m_Distributor = "";
    m_UPC = "";
}

StockItem(String Name, int InStock, int Price, int MinimumStock,
int MinimumReorder, String Distributor, String UPC)
{
    m_InStock = InStock;
    m_Price = Price;
    m_MinimumStock = MinimumStock;
    m_MinimumReorder = MinimumReorder;
    m_Name = Name;
    m_Distributor = Distributor;
    m_UPC = UPC;
}

void FormattedDisplay(OutputStream s)
{
    RWVar.println(s,"Name: " + m_Name);
    RWVar.println(s,"Number in stock: " + m_InStock);
    RWVar.println(s,"Price: " + m_Price);
    RWVar.println(s,"Minimum stock: " + m_MinimumStock);
    RWVar.println(s,"Minimum reorder: " + m_MinimumReorder);
    RWVar.println(s,"Distributor: " + m_Distributor);
    RWVar.println(s,"UPC: " + m_UPC);
}
```

Problem
Algorithms
Java
Interpreter
Hardware

Figure 7.1: The latest StockItem class (code\Itemtst20\StockItem.java)

```java
boolean Read(InputStream s)
{
    DataInputStream dis = new DataInputStream(s);
    String tempInStock;
    String tempPrice;
    String tempMinimumStock;
    String tempMinimumReorder;

    try
    {
        m_Name = dis.readLine();
        tempInStock = dis.readLine();
        tempPrice = dis.readLine();
        tempMinimumStock = dis.readLine();
        tempMinimumReorder = dis.readLine();
        m_Distributor = dis.readLine();
        m_UPC = dis.readLine();
    }
    catch (IOException e)
    {
        System.out.println(e);
        return false;
    }

    if (m_UPC == null)
        return false;

    m_InStock = Integer.parseInt(tempInStock);
    m_Price = Integer.parseInt(tempPrice);
    m_MinimumStock = Integer.parseInt(tempMinimumStock);
    m_MinimumReorder = Integer.parseInt(tempMinimumReorder);

    return true;
}

void Write(OutputStream s)
{
    try
    {
        RWVar.println(s,m_Name);
        RWVar.println(s,m_InStock);
        RWVar.println(s,m_Price);
        RWVar.println(s,m_MinimumStock);
        RWVar.println(s,m_MinimumReorder);
        RWVar.println(s,m_Distributor);
        RWVar.println(s,m_UPC);
    }
```

Problem
Algorithms
Java
Interpreter
Hardware

Figure 7.1 continued

```java
        catch (IOException e)
            {
            System.out.println(e);
            }
    }
boolean CheckUPC(String ItemUPC)
{
    if (m_UPC.equals(ItemUPC))
            return true;
    return false;
}

void DeductSaleFromInventory(int QuantitySold)
{
    m_InStock -= QuantitySold;
}

int GetInventory()
{
    return m_InStock;
}

String GetName()
{
    return m_Name;
}

int GetPrice()
{
    return m_Price;
}

void Reorder(OutputStream s)
{
    int ActualReorderQuantity;

    if (m_InStock < m_MinimumStock)
        {
        ActualReorderQuantity = m_MinimumStock - m_InStock;
        if (m_MinimumReorder > ActualReorderQuantity)
            ActualReorderQuantity = m_MinimumReorder;

        RWVar.print(s,"Reorder " + ActualReorderQuantity + " units of ");
        RWVar.print(s,m_Name + " with UPC " + m_UPC);
        RWVar.println(s," from " + m_Distributor);
        }
    }
}
```

```
Problem
Algorithms
Java
Interpreter
Hardware
```

Figure 7.1 continued

Claiming an Inheritance

Now let's work out the details of a particular extension to this inventory control program: calculating how much of each item has to be ordered to refill the stock. I've chosen the imaginative name ReorderItems for the method in the Inventory class that will perform this operation.

The new ReorderItems method is pretty simple. Its behavior can be described as follows: For each element in the StockItem array in the Inventory object, call its method Reorder to generate an order if that StockItem object needs to be reordered.

Of course, this analysis neglects a number of considerations that would be relevant in a real program; however, it has some resemblance to the real algorithm, which is good enough for our purposes.

Figure 7.2 shows the implementation of the ReorderItems method in the Inventory class.

```
void ReorderItems(OutputStream s)
{
    int i;

    for (i = 0; i < m_StockCount; i ++)
        m_Stock[i].Reorder(s);
}
```

Problem
Algorithms
Java
Interpreter
Hardware

Figure 7.2: The ReorderItems method for the Inventory class (from code\itemtst20\Inventory.java)

That could hardly be much simpler: As you can see, it merely tells each StockItem element in the m_Stock array to execute its Reorder method. Now let's see what that Reorder method needs to do:

1. Check to see if the current stock of that item is less than the desired minimum.
2. If we are below the desired stock minimum, then order the amount needed to bring us back to the stock minimum, unless that order amount is less than the minimum allowable quantity from the distributor. In the latter case, order the minimum allowable reorder quantity.
3. If we are not below the desired stock minimum, do nothing.

To support this new Reorder method, we'll use the new data items m_MinimumStock and m_MinimumReorder, which I added to the first version of the StockItem class definition in this chapter. As I've already mentioned, the normal constructor for a StockItem has two additional arguments to initialize these two new fields.

Figure 7.3 shows the code for the Reorder method.

```java
void Reorder(OutputStream s)
{
    int ActualReorderQuantity;

    if (m_InStock < m_MinimumStock)
        {
        ActualReorderQuantity = m_MinimumStock - m_InStock;
        if (m_MinimumReorder > ActualReorderQuantity)
            ActualReorderQuantity = m_MinimumReorder;

        RWVar.print(s,"Reorder " + ActualReorderQuantity + " units of ");
        RWVar.print(s,m_Name + " with UPC " + m_UPC);
        RWVar.println(s," from " + m_Distributor);
        }
}
```

Figure 7.3: The Reorder method for the StockItem class (from
code\Itemtst20\StockItem.java)

```
Problem
Algorithms
Java
Interpreter
Hardware
```

There's nothing particularly difficult about this code, which implements the reordering algorithm in a very straightforward manner.

1. If the number of units in stock is less than the minimum number desired, we calculate the number needed to bring the inventory back to the minimum.
2. However, the number we want to order may be less than the minimum number that we are allowed to order; the latter quantity is specified by the variable m_MinimumReorder.
3. If the value of m_MinimumReorder is more than the number we actually needed, then we have to substitute the minimum quantity for that previously calculated number.
4. Finally, we display the order for the item. Of course, if we already have enough units in stock, we don't have to reorder anything, so we don't display anything in that case.

A Dated Approach

Now we want to add one wrinkle to this algorithm: handling items that have expiration dates. This actually applies to a fair number of items in a typical grocery store, including dairy products, meats, and even dry cereals. To keep things as simple as possible, we'll assume that whenever we buy a batch of some item with an expiration date, all of the items of that type have the same date. When we get to the expiration date of a given StockItem, we send back all of the items and reorder as though we had no items in stock.

The first question to answer is how to store the expiration date. My first inclination was to use our old friend, the int, to store each date as a number representing the number of days from, for example, January 1, 1990 to the date in question. Since there are approximately 365.25 days in a year, the range of an int extends approximately 5 1/2 million years into the future, which is good enough for our purposes; perhaps by that time we'll all be eating food pills that don't spoil.

Problem
Algorithms
Java
Interpreter
Hardware

However, storing a date as a number of days since a *base date* such as January 1, 1990 does require a means of translating from a "normal" date format like "September 4, 1995" into a number of days from the base date, and vice versa. Owing to the peculiarities of our Gregorian calendar (primarily the different numbers of days in different months and the complication of leap years), this is not a trivial matter, and is a distraction from our goal here. Is there a simpler way to store and use dates that will still allow us to determine whether a given date is before or after another date?

As a matter of fact, there is. Suppose we represent a date as an int of the form YYYYMMDD, where YYYY is the year, MM is the month number, and DD is the day number within the month.[3] Then we can compare two of these "date numbers" and be sure that the one with a lower numeric value will represent the earlier date. Why is this?

Here's the analysis:

1. Of two dates with different year numbers, whichever has the higher year number is the later date. Thus, if we compare two "date numbers" that have different year portions, the one with the higher year number will represent a later date.

---

3. As I mentioned in Chapter 4, we need to allocate 4 digits for the year to ensure that the program will still work after the end of 1999.

2. Of two dates with the same year number but different month numbers, whichever has the higher month number is a later date. Of course, this is just the same reasoning as step 1.
3. Of two dates having the same year and month numbers, whichever has the higher day number is later.

Now all we have to do is figure out how to generate a date number, and we're all set. Luckily, this is pretty easy; Figure 7.4 shows how to do this, using a static method. That's just a method that we can call without having to specify an object that it should operate on. This should make sense because today's date is the same for all objects.[4]

```
protected static int Today()
{
    Date d = new Date();
    int year;
    int day;
    int month;
    int TodaysDate;

    year = d.getYear()+1900;
    month = d.getMonth()+1;
    day = d.getDate();

    TodaysDate = year * 10000 + month * 100 + day;

    return TodaysDate;
}
```

Problem
Algorithms
Java
Interpreter
Hardware

Figure 7.4: The Today method for the DatedStockItem class (from code\Itemtst21\DatedStockItem.java)

To make sense of this method, you should know that the default constructor for Date creates a Date object that represents the current date. It's also important to know that the year part of a Date object is returned as a number of years since 1900, the month as a number 0 through 11 (why not 1 through 12?), and the day as a number 1 through 31. So the first part of the algorithm just gets those values and adjusts them to make sense as part of an 8-digit "date number". Then we combine these individual parts as follows:

1. Multiplying the year by 10000 to produce a number with 4 trailing zeroes (to leave room for the month and day).

---

4. At least if we ignore relativistic effects, which we can do pretty safely in this situation.

2.   Multiplying the month by 100 to produce a number with 2 trailing zeroes (to leave room for the day).
3.   Leaving the day alone.

Finally, we add these three pieces to produce an 8-digit date number that we can store as an int and can compare to other date numbers to see which represents an earlier date.

Apparently my explanation of static methods wasn't clear enough for Susan.

> **Susan**: I am not sure exactly what static is. How is it different from void?

> **Steve**: It's almost but not quite entirely unlike void. A void method is just one that doesn't return a value. On the other hand, a static method is one that we can call without supplying an object. That is, unlike the Display method, where we have to say, for example, "item1.Display();", with a static method like Today, we can just say Today();.

> **Susan**: Okay, so void doesn't return a value, and static doesn't have an object to call, but does return something.

> **Steve**: A method can be both static and void (as main is). In that case, you don't need an object to call it, and it doesn't return anything.

Problem
Algorithms
Java
Interpreter
Hardware

Now that we've figured out that we can store the expiration date as an int, how do we arrange for it to be included in the StockItem object? One obvious solution is to make up a new class called, say, DatedStockItem, by copying the definition of StockItem, adding a new field m_Expires, and modifying the copied Reorder method to take the expiration date into account. However, doing this would create a maintenance problem when we had to make a change that would affect both of these classes; we'd have to make such a change in two places. Just multiply this nuisance by ten or twenty times, and you'll get a pretty good idea of how program maintenance has acquired its reputation as difficult and tedious work.

Susan had some questions about the idea of program maintenance.

> **Susan**: What kind of change would you want to make? What is maintenance? What is a typical thing that you would want to do to some code?

> **Steve**: Any kind of change. For example, if we decided that an int wasn't the right kind of variable to hold the price, then we would have to change its definition to some other type.

Since one of the purposes of object-oriented programming is to reduce the difficulty of maintenance, surely there must be a better way to create a new class "just like" StockItem but with an added field and a modified method to use it.

Ancestor Worship

In fact, there is; it's called **inheritance**. We can define our new class called DatedStockItem with a notation that it inherits (or *derives*) from StockItem. This makes StockItem the *base* class (sometimes referred to as the superclass), and our new class DatedStockItem the *derived* class (sometimes referred to as the subclass). By doing this, we are specifying that a DatedStockItem includes every data member and regular method that a StockItem has. Since DatedStockItem is a separate class from StockItem, we can also add whatever other methods and data we need to handle the differences between StockItem and DatedStockItem.

I think a picture might help here. Let's start with a simplified version of the StockItem class, illustrated in Figure 7.5.

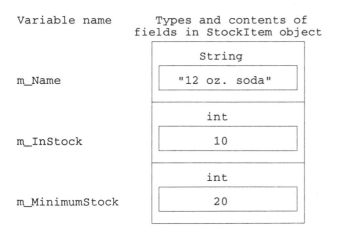

Figure 7.5: A StockItem object

Problem
Algorithms
Java
Interpreter
Hardware

A simplified version of a DatedStockItem object might look as depicted in Figure 7.6.

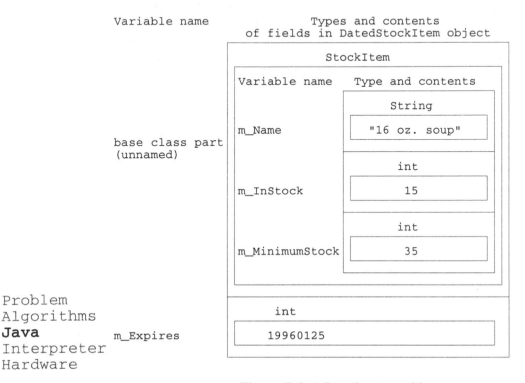

Problem
Algorithms
Java
Interpreter
Hardware

Figure 7.6: A DatedStockItem object

As you can see, an object of the new DatedStockItem class effectively contains a StockItem as part of its data. In fact, this "base class part" of a DatedStockItem accounts for most of the data of a DatedStockItem; all we've added is a data member called m_Expires.[5]

In fact, a derived class object always contains all of the variables and "regular" methods in the base class because the derived class object effectively has an object of the base class embedded in it, as indicated in Figure 7.6.[6] We can access those fields and methods that

---

5. This diagram and all the others that depict object layouts are purely schematic; there's no guarantee that an object looks anything like these pictures. However, objects behave pretty much as though they did look this way, which is good enough for our purposes.

6. The reason that I prefer the terms base class and derived class to superclass and subclass, respectively, is that a derived class contains at least all the fields and methods of the base class and usually contains at least one added field or method. The terms *sub* and *super* generally indicate "less" and "more", respectively, so I find it confusing to call the class with less functionality the superclass and the one with greater functionality the subclass.

are part of the base class part of our derived class object exactly as though they were defined in the derived class object, so long as their access specifiers are either public or protected. Although the public and private access specifiers have been part of our arsenal of tools for some time, we haven't used protected before; we'll see shortly that the sole purpose of the protected access specifier is to allow methods of a derived class unfettered access to methods and variables of the base class part of an object of that derived class, while protecting those methods and variables from use by unrelated classes.

Of course, as noted above, we don't have to rely solely on the facilities we inherit from our base class; we can also add whatever new methods or variables we need to provide the new functionality of the new class. As you will see, we don't want or need to add any public methods in the present case, because our goal is to allow the application programmer to treat objects of the new DatedStockItem class as being equivalent to objects of the StockItem class. In order to reach this goal, these two classes must have the same behavior, which means that they must have the same public methods.

Instead of adding new public methods, we will *override* the base class version of Reorder by writing a new version of Reorder for our DatedStockItem class. Our new method, which has the same signature as the base class method Reorder, will use the new data member m_Expires. Since the base class version of Reorder has been overridden by the derived class Reorder method, the latter method will be called whenever the user's program calls the Reorder method of a DatedStockItem.

Problem
Algorithms
Java
Interpreter
Hardware

Why do we want to override the base class method Reorder rather than writing an entirely new method with a new name? Precisely because our goal is to allow the user to be able to use stock items with and without dates interchangeably; if StockItem and DatedStockItem had different names for their reordering method, then the user would have to call a different method depending on which type the object really was, which would defeat our attempt to make them interchangeable.

Before we get into the details of the Reorder method in the DatedStockItem class, I should explain in more detail what I mean by "regular method". A regular method is one that is *not* a constructor. For example, Reorder(OutputStream s) is a regular method of the DatedStockItem class, whereas DatedStockItem() is a constructor and therefore not a regular method.

If the concepts I've just introduced aren't immediately obvious to you, you're not alone. Here's the discussion I had with Susan on this matter:

Susan: Are inheritance and derivation the same thing?

Steve: Yes. To say that A inherits from B is the same as saying that A is derived from B.

Susan: Why don't you want to add any methods to DatedStockItem?

Steve: Because a DatedStockItem should act just like a StockItem; this won't be the case if we add new methods that the class user can see. Instead of adding new public methods, we'll write a new version of the Reorder method we already have.

Susan: Huh? Why do you have to use a new version? It is supposed to act just like a StockItem.

Steve: Yes, it is supposed to act "just like" a StockItem. However, that means that it has to do the "same" things differently; in particular, reordering items is different when you have to send things back because their expiration dates have passed. However, this difference in implementation is not important to the application program, which can treat DatedStockItems just like StockItems.

Problem
Algorithms
Java
Interpreter
Hardware

Susan: Why is the term "override" used here? The derived class method is called for an object of the derived class, so I don't see how it "overrides" the base class method with the same signature.

Steve: What would happen if we didn't write the derived class method? Then the base class method would be called for a derived class object. Therefore the derived class method is overriding the previously existing base class method.

Susan: The first thought that came to mind was, why can't we just add some new methods and member variables to a class instead of making a derived class? So do you use inheritance here to make a point or is it vital to achieve what we want to achieve?

Steve: If you added more methods, then StockItem would not be StockItem as it is and needs to be. You could write another class like StockItem which would be more labor intensive, and it would have to do everything that the original Reorder does and add the expiration dates. If you are going to use Java properly, then it is vital to use inheritance to avoid these problems.

Susan: Is it the expiration date which makes it necessary to make a derived class?

Steve: Yes.

Susan: Explain again how the regular method is not a constructor.

Steve: I'm not sure what you mean by this question. A "regular" method is simply any method that isn't a constructor. For example, Display is a regular method.

Susan: Then I am confusing a method with a constructor. Look at your definition for a constructor in the glossary. It says, "A constructor is a *method* that creates new objects..."

Steve: Yes, and a Lexus™ is an automobile. Does that mean that every automobile is a Lexus? A constructor is a particular kind of method: the kind that makes a new object of a given class. Other methods, which don't create new objects, aren't constructors: Those are the "regular" methods I've been talking about.

Susan: The nomenclature doesn't make sense. If constructors are methods then regular methods should be called non-constructors, or constructors should be called irregular methods. I am confused by the wording.

Steve: Sorry, I didn't make it up. There are two kinds of methods, constructors and "other". Since there are generally more "other" methods than constructors, we refer to the "other" methods as "regular".

Problem
Algorithms
Java
Interpreter
Hardware

In other words, when we write a derived class (in this case, DatedStockItem), it does not inherit the constructors from the base class (in this case, StockItem); instead, we have to write our own constructors for the derived class, if we don't want to rely on the compiler-generated versions in the derived class. Why is this?

It's because base class constructors are called automatically to construct the base class part of the derived class object; therefore, all we have to worry about in our derived class is handling the newly added parts of that class. We'll see exactly how and when these base class constructors are called as we go through the corresponding derived class methods.

Susan didn't buy this idea of having to write our own constructors for the derived class.

Susan: What is a compiler-generated version and why is it bad?

Steve: It's the version of the constructor generated by the compiler. It's not always bad, but sometimes we can't use it, for one of two reasons: First, because the compiler doesn't know which base class constructor we want to call to initialize the base class part of the derived class object.

Second, because the compiler doesn't know how we want to initialize the new fields we've added in creating the derived class.

Susan: What if your derived class needs a regular constructor, what do you do then?

Steve: You write one that does the right thing, as we do with DatedStockItem in this chapter.

Susan: But if the base class constructors are similar to the derived class ones, couldn't you use them?

Steve: We actually do use the base class constructors indirectly; the compiler will always call a base class constructor when a derived class constructor is executed. However, any new member variables added to the derived class will have to be handled in the derived class constructors.

Susan: But why can't you ever use the base class constructors as they are? Why do you always have to write derived class versions?

Steve: Because the new class will almost always have new variables. Clearly, the constructor for the base class cannot know what to do with a new variable added in the derived class; therefore, we will need a new constructor in the derived class.

Problem
Algorithms
Java
Interpreter
Hardware

Susan: So anything not inherited that is added to a derived class then has to be handled as a separate entity than the stuff in the base class part of the derived class? UGH!!!!

Steve: Yes, but just the new stuff has to be handled separately; whatever is inherited from the base class can be handled by the base class methods. After all, *someone* has to write the code to handle the new member variables; the compiler can't read our minds!

However, there is one change that we have to make to our previous definition of StockItem to make it a suitable base class; we have to change the *access specifiers* for its fields from private to protected. By this point, you should be familiar with the meaning of private: Any fields or methods that are marked as private can be referred to only by methods of the same class, whereas all other methods are prohibited from accessing those private fields or methods. On the other hand, marking methods or member data of a class as public means that any method, whether or not a member of that class, can access those public methods or data. That seems to take care of all the possibilities, so what is protected good for?

Protection Racket

Fields and methods that are listed as protected are treated the same as though they were private, with one important exception: Methods of derived classes can access these fields and methods when they occur as the base class part of a derived class object.

Susan had a couple of questions about the notion of a base class part of a derived class object.

> **Susan**: What do you mean by "base class part of the derived class object"? I am fuzzy here.

> **Steve**: Every DatedStockItem (derived) object effectively contains an unnamed StockItem (base class) object, because DatedStockItem is derived from StockItem. This is what allows us to avoid duplicating the data and code from the base class in the derived class.

> **Susan**: If fields have names, why doesn't the base class part?

> **Steve**: Because it is an inherent part of the derived class object. As such, you can access its fields, methods, and so on (assuming that they're not private) as though they were part of the derived class object.

In the current case, we've seen that a DatedStockItem is "just like" a StockItem with one additional field and some other additions and changes that aren't relevant here. The important point is that every DatedStockItem contains everything that a StockItem contains; for example, every DatedStockItem has a m_MinimumStock field included in it, because the StockItem class has a m_MinimumStock field, and we're defining a DatedStockItem as being derived from StockItem. Logically, therefore, we should be able to access the value of the m_MinimumStock field in our DatedStockItem; however, if that field is declared as private, we can't. The private access specifier doesn't care about inheritance; since DatedStockItem is a different class from StockItem, private fields and methods of StockItem wouldn't be accessible to methods of DatedStockItem, even though the fields of StockItem are actually present in every DatedStockItem! That's why we have to make those variables protected rather than private.

It wasn't obvious to Susan why we need protected at all.

> **Susan**: I don't understand why if DatedStockItem has those member variables it would not be able to access them if they were specified as private in the base class.

Problem
Algorithms
Java
Interpreter
Hardware

Steve: Because the compiler wouldn't let DatedStockItem methods access them; private variables are private even if they are part of the base class part of a derived class object. That's why protected was invented in the first place.

Now that we've have cleared up that point (I hope), we have to consider the question of when to use protected versus private fields. Because private fields of the base class cannot be accessed directly by derived class methods, we have to decide whether we want any derived classes to be able to access fields of the base class part of the derived class object when we define the base class; if we do, we have to use the protected access specifier for those fields. If we don't do that and later discover that we need access to those variables in a derived class, then we will have to change the definition of the base class so that the variables are protected rather than private. Such changes are not too much trouble when we have written all of the classes involved, but they can be extremely difficult or even impossible when we are trying to derive new classes from previously existing classes written by someone else.

Problem
Algorithms
Java
Interpreter
Hardware

However, protected variables and methods have some of the drawbacks of public variables and methods, because anyone can derive a new class that uses those variables or methods. Once they have done that, any changes to those variables or methods will cause their code to break. Hence, making everything protected isn't an unalloyed blessing.

Another possibility is to use protected methods to allow access to private fields in the base class part, rather than using protected fields for the same purpose. I haven't investigated this approach enough to render a definitive opinion, but at first glance it appears to provide the advantages of protected variables while being less likely to cause maintenance problems down the road.

The moral of the story is that it's easier to design classes for our own use and derivation than for the use of others; even though we could go back and change our class definitions to make them more flexible, that alternative may not be available to others. The result may be that our classes will not meet their needs.

Apparently this explanation wasn't as comprehensible as I thought it was.

Susan: I don't get your moral of the story. Sorry.

Steve: The moral is that when designing classes that may be used by others as base classes, we have to know whether *they* will ever need access to our fields. If we are in charge of all of the classes, we can change the access specifiers easily enough, but that's not a very good solution if someone else is deriving new classes from our classes.

Stock Footage

Because the next version of StockItem is identical to the previous version except for changing its fields from private to protected, I won't waste the space on reproducing the whole class definition: instead, Figure 7.7 shows the changed field definitions.

```
protected int m_InStock;
protected int m_Price;
protected int m_MinimumStock;
protected int m_MinimumReorder;
protected String m_Name;
protected String m_Distributor;
protected String m_UPC;
```

Figure 7.7: protected fields in StockItem (from code\itemtst21\StockItem.java)

After clearing that up, let's look at the class definition of DatedStockItem, shown in Figure 7.8.[7]

Problem
Algorithms
Java
Interpreter
Hardware

```
import WAJ.*;
import java.io.*;
import java.util.*;

class DatedStockItem extends StockItem
{
protected int m_Expires;

DatedStockItem(String Name, int InStock, int Price, int MinimumStock,
int MinimumReorder, String Distributor, String UPC, String Expires)
{
    super(Name,InStock,Price,MinimumStock,
        MinimumReorder,Distributor,UPC);

    m_Expires = Integer.parseInt(Expires);
}
```

Figure 7.8: Implementation for DatedStockItem
(code\itemtst21\DatedStockItem.java)

---

7. I know there are some constructs in this file that haven't been covered yet, such as super, but rest assured that we'll get to them shortly.

```java
DatedStockItem()
{
    m_Expires = 0;
}

protected static int Today()
{
    Date d = new Date();
    int year;
    int day;
    int month;
    int TodaysDate;

    year = d.getYear()+1900;
    month = d.getMonth()+1;
    day = d.getDate();

    TodaysDate = year * 10000 + month * 100 + day;

    return TodaysDate;
}

void Reorder(OutputStream s)
{
    if (m_Expires < Today())
    {
        RWVar.print(s,"Return " + m_InStock + " units of ");
        RWVar.print(s,m_Name + " with UPC " + m_UPC);
        RWVar.println(s, " to " + m_Distributor);
        m_InStock = 0;
    }

    super.Reorder(s);
}

void FormattedDisplay(OutputStream s)
{
    RWVar.println(s, "Expiration Date: " + m_Expires);
    super.FormattedDisplay(s);
}
```

Problem
Algorithms
Java
Interpreter
Hardware

Figure 7.8 continued

```
boolean Read(InputStream s)
{
    DataInputStream dis = new DataInputStream(s);
    String tempExpires;

    try
      {
      tempExpires = dis.readLine();
      }
    catch (IOException e)
      {
      System.out.println(e);
      return false;
      }

    super.Read(s);

    if (m_UPC == null)
       return false;

    m_Expires = Integer.parseInt(tempExpires);

    return true;
}

void Write(OutputStream s)
{
    try
      {
      RWVar.println(s,m_Expires);
      }
    catch (IOException e)
      {
      System.out.println(e);
      }

    super.Write(s);
}
}
```

```
Problem
Algorithms
Java
Interpreter
Hardware
```

Figure 7.8 continued

Most of this should be pretty familiar by now. However, there are a couple of constructs here that we haven't seen before. The first one is in the class header: DatedStockItem extends StockItem. I'm referring specifically to the expression extends StockItem, which states that this class, DatedStockItem, is derived from StockItem.

Before we get into the implementation of the DatedStockItem class, let's take a look back at the other new feature of the Today method (Figure 7.4): the notion of a static method.

Getting static

The static modifier means that we don't have to specify an object for the method to apply to. Thus, we can refer to the static method called Today by just its name. Within DatedStockItem methods, that means writing "Today();" is sufficient; if we wanted to call Today() from a method of another class, we would have to refer to it by its full name: DatedStockItem.Today().[8] This is clearly different from the normal use of a method, where we specify the method along with the object to which it applies; for example, soup.GetInventory();. What is the advantage of a static method?

The advantage is precisely that we can call it without needing an object to call it for. In this case, the value of today's date is not dependent on any DatedStockItem object; therefore, it's quite handy to be able to call Today() without referring to any object of the DatedStockItem class.

Problem
Algorithms
Java
Interpreter
Hardware

There's one other thing here that we haven't seen before: Today() is a protected method, which means that it is accessible only to methods of DatedStockItem and descendants of DatedStockItem, just as a protected field is. The reason that we want to keep this method from being called by application programs is the same reason that we protect fields by restricting access: to reserve the right to change its name, return value, or argument types. Since application code can't access this method, they can't depend on its interface.

Now that we've taken care of the new method Today, let's take a look at the other methods of the DatedStockItem class that differ significantly from their counterparts in the base class StockItem; these are the constructors, the Reorder method, and FormattedDisplay.

Let's start with the default constructor, which of course is called DatedStockItem() (Figure 7.9). It's a very short method, but there's a bit more here than meets the eye.

---

8. The . notation here is analogous to the use of the . to specify a reference and a method or field of that reference in an expression such as item1.Display(). In such cases, the type of the object to which the reference refers is sufficient to determine which method should be called; in the case of a static method, however, there is no reference to help with this determination. Therefore, we have to specify the class to which the method belongs explicitly.

```
DatedStockItem()
{
    m_Expires = 0;
}
```

Figure 7.9: Default constructor for DatedStockItem (from
code\itemtst21\DatedStockItem.java)

A very good question here is "what happens to the base class part
of the object?" This is taken care of by the default constructor of the
StockItem class, which will be invoked by default to initialize that part
of this object. The following is a general rule: Any base class part of a
derived class object will automatically be initialized when the derived
class object is created at run time, by calling a base class constructor.
By default, the base class default constructor will be called when we
don't specify which base class constructor we want to execute. In
other words, the code in Figure 7.9 is translated by the compiler as
though it were the code in Figure 7.10.

```
DatedStockItem()
{
    super();
    m_Expires = 0;
}
```

Problem
Algorithms
Java
Interpreter
Hardware

Figure 7.10: How the compiler interprets the default constructor for
DatedStockItem (from code\itemtst21\DatedStockItem.java)

The statement super(); specifies which base class constructor we
want to use to initialize the base class part of the DatedStockItem object.
In this case, we're calling the default constructor for the base class,
StockItem.

You probably won't be surprised to hear that Susan had some
questions about this idea of calling the base class constructor.

Susan: Would super stand for supersede?

Steve: Good guess, but it actually stands for "superclass", which is the
official Java term for "base class".

Susan: I don't understand your "good question". What do you mean by
base class part?

Steve: The base class part is the embedded base class object in the
derived class object.

Susan: So derived classes use the default constructor from the base classes?

Steve: They always use some base class constructor to construct the base class part of a derived class object. By default, they use the default constructor for the base class object, but you can specify which base class constructor you want to use.

Susan: If that is so, then why are you writing one for DatedStockItem?

Steve: Because the base class constructor only constructs the base class part. The rest of the derived class object has to be constructed too, and that job is handled by the derived class constructor.

Susan: Let me see if I can get this straight. The derived class will use a base class default constructor unless you specify otherwise.

Steve: Correct so far.

Susan: Under what circumstances wouldn't the base class constructor be called?

Problem
Algorithms
Java
Interpreter
Hardware

Steve: *Some* base class constructor will always be called to initialize the base class part; the only question is which constructor is to be called, and what arguments should be used to call it. We can use super to select the constructor and to specify the arguments.

Susan: It just doesn't "know" to go to the base class as a default unless you tell it to?

Steve: No, it always goes to the base class; the question is which base class constructor is called.

Susan: Ugh. Put this super thing down as necessary to let the derived class know which constructor you are using. This is not clear.

Steve: Okay, here's another way of stating the same point: If you don't want the base class part to be initialized by the base class default constructor, you have to use the super keyword to specify which base class constructor you want to use.

Whether we allow the compiler to call the default base class constructor automatically, as in Figure 7.9, or explicitly specify that it's the one we want, as in Figure 7.10, the path of execution for the default DatedStockItem constructor is as illustrated in Figure 7.11.

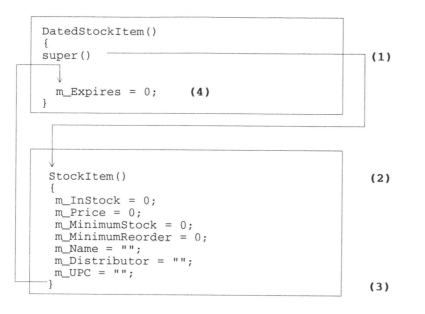

```
DatedStockItem()
{
super()  ─────────────────────────────────────┐   (1)
   │
   ↓
   m_Expires = 0;        (4)
}
```

```
StockItem()                                        (2)
{
 m_InStock = 0;
 m_Price = 0;
 m_MinimumStock = 0;
 m_MinimumReorder = 0;
 m_Name = "";
 m_Distributor = "";
 m_UPC = "";
}                                                  (3)
```

Figure 7.11: Constructing a default DatedStockItem object

Problem
Algorithms
Java
Interpreter
Hardware

At step **(1)** the DatedStockItem calls the default constructor for StockItem, which starts in step **(2)** by initializing all the variables in the StockItem class to their default values. Once the default constructor for StockItem is finished, in step **(3)**, it returns to the DatedStockItem constructor. In step **(4)**, that constructor finishes the initialization of the DatedStockItem object by initializing m_Expires to the default String value.

This is fine as long as the base class default constructor is the one we want to use to construct the base class part of the DatedStockItem object. However, if that constructor doesn't do what we want, we can specify which base constructor we wish to call, as shown in the "normal" constructor for the DatedStockItem class (Figure 7.12).

Susan wanted to know why the base class constructor wouldn't do what we wanted.

Susan: Where you say, "if that constructor doesn't do what we want", why wouldn't it? I don't get the negative part of this.

Steve: Because there can be more than one base class constructor. The default one is only appropriate when we don't know the data for the base class object, as is the case in our derived class default constructor. With our derived class "normal" constructor, we *do* know the data for the base class object and therefore have to call the "normal" constructor for the base class rather than the default constructor.

```
DatedStockItem(String Name, int InStock,
int Price, int MinimumStock,
int MinimumReorder, String Distributor,
String UPC, String Expires)
{
    super(Name,InStock,Price,MinimumStock,
        MinimumReorder,Distributor,UPC);

    m_Expires = Integer.parseInt(Expires);
}
```

Figure 7.12: Normal constructor for DatedStockItem (from code\itemtst21\DatedStockItem.java)

As before, we have to use super to specify the base class constructor. For the "normal" DatedStockItem constructor, we use the statement

```
super(Name, InStock, Price, MinimumStock, MinimumReorder, Distributor, UPC);
```

Problem
Algorithms
Java
Interpreter
Hardware

to call the corresponding "normal" base class constructor to initialize the base class part of the DatedStockItem object. This means that the StockItem part of the DatedStockItem object will be initialized exactly as though it were being created by the corresponding constructor for StockItem. Figure 7.13 illustrates how this works.

At step **(1)** the DatedStockItem "normal" constructor is entered. In step **(2)**, that constructor calls the "normal" constructor for StockItem, which constructs the base class part of a DatedStockItem exactly as though it had been created by calling the StockItem constructor with the arguments Name, InStock, Price, MinimumStock, MinimumReorder, Distributor, and UPC. These arguments, of course, are the corresponding arguments of the DatedStockItem constructor, so in effect we are just passing them through to the base class constructor. Once the "normal" constructor for StockItem is finished, in step **(3)**, it returns to the DatedStockItem constructor. In step **(4)**, that constructor finishes the initialization of the DatedStockItem object by initializing m_Expires to the value of the argument Expires.

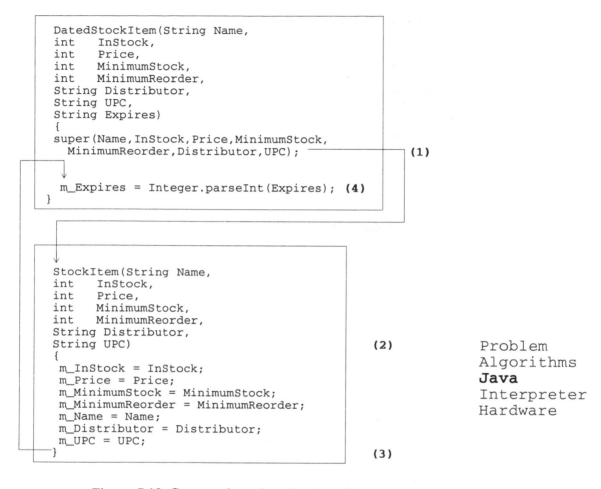

```
DatedStockItem(String Name,
int    InStock,
int    Price,
int    MinimumStock,
int    MinimumReorder,
String Distributor,
String UPC,
String Expires)
{
super(Name,InStock,Price,MinimumStock,
  MinimumReorder,Distributor,UPC);                    (1)


  m_Expires = Integer.parseInt(Expires);    (4)
}
```

```
StockItem(String Name,
int    InStock,
int    Price,
int    MinimumStock,
int    MinimumReorder,
String Distributor,
String UPC)                                           (2)
{
 m_InStock = InStock;
 m_Price = Price;
 m_MinimumStock = MinimumStock;
 m_MinimumReorder = MinimumReorder;
 m_Name = Name;
 m_Distributor = Distributor;
 m_UPC = UPC;
}                                                     (3)
```

```
Problem
Algorithms
Java
Interpreter
Hardware
```

Figure 7.13: Constructing a DatedStockItem object

As you can see by these examples, using super allows us to call the base class constructor to initialize the base class object, which in turn means that our derived class constructor won't have to keep track of the details of the base class. This is an example of one of the main benefits claimed for object-oriented programming: We can confine the knowledge of the details of a class to the methods of that class, which simplifies maintenance efforts. In this case, after calling the base class constructor via super, the only task left for the DatedStockItem constructor is to initialize the field m_Expires.

Susan had some questions about exactly how this works.

Susan: How does all the information of (3) get into (4)? And exactly what part of the code here calls the base class constructor? I don't see which part it is.

Steve: The information from (3) gets into the derived class DatedStockItem object in the upper part of the diagram because the DatedStockItem object contains a base class part consisting of a StockItem object. That's the object that is being initialized by the call to the base class constructor caused by the super keyword in the following line:

super(Name, InStock, Price, MinimumStock, MinimumReorder, Distributor, UPC);

There's another reason that we should use super rather than trying to initialize the fields of the base class part of our object directly: It's much safer. If we initialized the base class variables ourselves, and if the base class definition were later changed to include some new variables initialized according to arguments to the normal constructor, we might very well neglect to modify our derived class code to initialize the new variables. On the other hand, when we use super to call a base class constructor, and its arguments change (as they presumably will if new variables need to be initialized), a derived class constructor that calls that constructor will no longer compile. That will alert us to the changes that we have to make.

Problem
Algorithms
Java
Interpreter
Hardware

Reordering Priorities

Now that we have dealt with the constructors, let's take a look at the Reorder method (Figure 7.14).

```
void Reorder(OutputStream s)
{
    if (m_Expires < Today())
        {
        RWVar.print(s,"Return " + m_InStock + " units of ");
        RWVar.print(s,m_Name + " with UPC " + m_UPC);
        RWVar.println(s, " to " + m_Distributor);
        m_InStock = 0;
        }

    super.Reorder(s);
}
```

Figure 7.14: Reorder method for DatedStockItem (from
code\itemtst21\DatedStockItem.java)

We have added some new code that checks whether the expiration date on the current batch of product is before today's date; if so, we create an output line indicating that the batch is to be returned. But what about the "normal" case for which the base class Reorder method is perfectly suitable? That's handled by the line super.Reorder(s);, which calls the Reorder method in the StockItem class by using the super keyword to specify that we want to call the Reorder method in our base class. If we just wrote Reorder(s), that would call the method that we're in again, a process known as *recursion*. Recursion has its uses in certain complex programming situations, but we can do without it in this book. In this case, of course, it would not do what we wanted, as we have already handled the possibility of expired items; we need to deal with the "normal" case of running low on stock, which is handled very nicely by the base class Reorder method.

We should not pass by this method without noting one more point; the only reason that we can access m_InStock and the other fields of the StockItem base class part of our object is that those fields of StockItem were declared protected rather than private; had they been declared private, we wouldn't be able to access them in our DatedStockItem methods, even though every DatedStockItem object would still have such fields.

Susan wanted a clarification of this point.

Problem
Algorithms
Java
Interpreter
Hardware

> **Susan**: I can't picture the statement "even though every DatedStockItem object would still have such fields." I don't get it.

> **Steve**: Well, every DatedStockItem has a StockItem base class part, and that base class part contributes its member variables to the DatedStockItem.

What about FormattedDisplay? There's nothing that should be very unfamiliar in that method, which is illustrated in Figure 7.15.

```
void FormattedDisplay(OutputStream s)
{
    RWVar.println(s, "Expiration Date: " + m_Expires);
    super.FormattedDisplay(s);
}
```

Figure 7.15: FormattedDisplay method for DatedStockItem (from code\itemtst21\DatedStockItem.java)

As in the case of Reorder, we handle the new field that we've added and defer the rest to the base class method via a super method call. Of course, if we just wrote that line as FormattedDisplay(s) rather than as

super.FormattedDisplay(s), the DatedStockItem method called
FormattedDisplay method would be called rather than the StockItem
FormattedDisplay method, which wouldn't work very well because
that's the same method that's making the call!

Now that we've seen all the pieces, let's take a look at how they all
fit together. Figure 7.16 shows the main program that reads
DatedStockItems from a file and displays them.

```
import WAJ.*;
import java.io.*;

public class Itemtst21
{
    public static void main( String args[ ] )
    {
        FileInputStream ShopInfo;
        FileOutputStream ReorderInfo;
        Inventory MyInventory = new Inventory();

        try
        {
            ShopInfo = new FileInputStream("shop21.in");
        }
        catch (IOException e)
        {
            System.out.println("Can't open file \"shop21.in\"");
            return;
        }

        MyInventory.LoadInventory(ShopInfo);

        try
        {
            ReorderInfo = new FileOutputStream("shop21.reo");
        }
        catch (IOException e)
        {
            System.out.println("Can't open file \"shop21.reo\"");
            return;
        }

        MyInventory.ReorderItems(ReorderInfo);
    }
}
```

Problem
Algorithms
Java
Interpreter
Hardware

Figure 7.16: Test program for DatedStockItem (code\itemtst21\itemtst21.java)

To use the debugger for this program, follow the instructions in the
section titled "Using the debugger" in the file "\readme.txt" on the

CD in the back of the book. These instructions assume that you've installed the examples on drive C:, so that the location of this program is "c:\whosj\code\itemtst21".

Now we have a good solution to the creation of stock items with dates. But what we originally wanted was to be able to mix StockItem and DatedStockItem objects in the same array. Have we accomplished that goal?

As a matter of fact, we have. However, to understand exactly how this works, we'll need to go into the depths of Java a bit further, which is the task of the next chapter. First, though, it's time to review what we've learned in this chapter.

Review

We started out the chapter by adding some new methods to the StockItem class and the Inventory class that were missing from the final versions of these classes in Chapter 6, including a method called ReorderItem that can be called for an Inventory object to produce a reordering report. This method calls a Reorder method for each StockItem in its StockItem array to calculate how many items of that StockItem need to be ordered, based on the desired stock and the current stock.

Problem
Algorithms
Java
Interpreter
Hardware

Then we built on the previous StockItem class by adding an expiration date. Rather than copying all of the old code and class definitions, we made use of a concept that is essential to the full use of Java for object-oriented programming, namely, *inheritance*. Inheritance is a method of constructing one class (the *derived* class) by specifying how it differs from another class (the *base* class), rather than writing it from scratch. We used inheritance to create a new DatedStockItem class that had all of the capabilities of the StockItem class and added the ability to handle items with expiration dates.

In the process, we wrote a new Reorder method with the same signature as the base class method of the same name. This is called *overriding* the base class method. When the method with that signature is called via an object of the base class, the base class method will be called; on the other hand, when the method with that signature is called via an object of the derived class, the derived class method will be called. This allows a derived class to supply the same functionality as a base class but implement that functionality in a different way.

The reason why a derived class object can do anything that a base class object can do is that a derived class object effectively contains an object of the base class, called the *base* class *part* of the derived class object.[9] This base class part is very similar to a field in the derived class, but it is not the same, for two reasons:

1. A field always has a name, whereas the base class part does not.
2. The base class definition can give derived class methods privileged access to some fields and methods of the base class part of an object of the derived class, by marking those fields and methods protected.

In the process of writing the new Reorder method for the DatedStockItem class, we saw how we could store a date as an int that allowed comparison of two dates to see which was later. To do this, we needed to create an eight-digit number representing the date as YYYYMMDD; that is, a four-digit year number, a two-digit month number, and a two-digit day number.

After the discussion of creating these "date numbers", we continued by examining the default constructor of the DatedStockItem class. Although this is an extremely short method, consisting of a lone assignment statement, there is more to it than meets the eye. The default constructor deals only with the newly added field m_Expires, but behind the scenes, the base class part of the DatedStockItem object is being initialized by the default constructor of the base class, i.e., StockItem(). The rule is that a base class constructor will *always* be called for the base class part of a derived class object; if we don't specify which base class constructor we want to use, the default constructor for the base class will be used. If we do want to select the constructor for the base class part, we can do it by an explicit call to that base class constructor via the super keyword. In our "normal" constructor for DatedStockItem, we used this construct to call the corresponding constructor for the base class (see Figures 7.12 and 7.13).

Then we looked at the Reorder method for the DatedStockItem class, which included code to request the return of any items that were past their expiration date and called the base class Reorder method to handle the rest of the job, again using the super keyword; this time, we used it to specify the base class method rather than the same named method in DatedStockItem.

At that point, we had a working DatedStockItem class, but we hadn't investigated what happens if we mix StockItem and DatedStockItem

Problem
Algorithms
Java
Interpreter
Hardware

---

9. Whether or not a derived class object actually contains a base class object is an implementation detail that may vary from one Java compile to another; however, this is not visible to the programmer, who can proceed as though this is always the case.

objects in the same array; we'll find out how that works in the next chapter.

Exercises

1. Rewrite the DrugStockItem class that you wrote in Chapter 6, using derivation from the StockItem class.
2. Rewrite the Employee class that you wrote in Chapter 6 as two classes, the base Manager class and a Hourly class derived from the base class. The CalculatePay method for each of these classes should use the appropriate method of calculating the pay for each class; in particular, this method doesn't need an argument specifying the number of hours worked for the Manager class, whereas the corresponding method in the Hourly class does need such an argument. Because the CalculatePay methods in these two classes don't have the same arguments, objects of these classes cannot be treated as though they were of the same class; therefore, this is an example of inheritance for extension.
3. What happens if you call the CalculatePay method for an Hourly object with a float argument? Why?

Problem
Algorithms
Java
Interpreter
Hardware

Conclusion

In this chapter we have extended the functionality provided in the StockItem class by deriving a new class called DatedStockItem, based on StockItem. However, we have not yet seen how to use objects of these two classes interchangeably. In Chapter 8, we will see exactly how to do that.

Chapter 8

Pretty Poly

At the end of the previous chapter, we had created a DatedStockItem class by *inheritance* from the StockItem class, adding an expiration date field. This was a fine solution to the problem of creating a new class based on the existing StockItem class without rewriting all of the already functioning code in that class. As we will see in this chapter, these two classes can also be used interchangeably in an application program, which is an application of the third and final major organizing principle that characterizes object-oriented programming: **polymorphism**. Once we have defined some terms and objectives for this chapter, we'll get right to the explanation of how polymorphism works.

Definitions

Static typing means determining the exact type of a data item when the program is compiled. Note that this has no particular relation to the keyword static.

Dynamic typing means delaying the determination of the exact type of a data item until run time, rather than fixing that type at compile time as in *static typing*. Java uses dynamic typing for user-defined types and static typing for primitive types.

Polymorphism is the major organizing principle in Java that allows us to implement several classes whose objects can be used interchangeably by the user of these classes. In Java, variables of user-defined types are polymorphic, because they can refer to objects of different classes at run time (dynamic typing). The word "polymorphism" is derived from the Greek words "poly", meaning "many", and "morph", meaning "form". In other words, the same behavior is implemented in different forms.

Objectives for This Chapter

By the end of this chapter, you should:

1. Understand how *polymorphism* allows objects of a number of different classes to be treated interchangeably by the user of these classes.
2. Understand the Java mechanisms that allow polymorphism to work.

Polymorphism

Problem
Algorithms
Java
Interpreter
Hardware

To select the correct method to be called based on the actual type of an object at run time, Java uses **polymorphism**. Polymorphic behavior of our StockItem and DatedStockItem classes means that we can, for example, mix StockItem and DatedStockItem objects in an array and have the right Reorder method be executed for each object in the array.

Why would we want to do this? Because the objects of these two classes perform the same operation, although in a slightly different way. In our example, a DatedStockItem acts just like a StockItem, except that it has an additional data field and produces different reordering information. Because neither of these differences significantly affects the way that the application program uses objects of these two classes, it is handy to be able to mix objects of these two types in the application program without having to worry about which class each object belongs to except when creating an individual item (at which time we have to know whether the item has an expiration date or not).

When we create an array, we have to specify the type of the elements of that array. However, in the present case we want to be able to store a mixture of StockItem and DatedStockItem objects in that array. How do we specify the type of that array, when we don't know the type of each element?

If we specify the array to contain StockItem references, those references will be able to store objects of both of these types. The reason is that Java allows a derived class object to be assigned to a reference of its base class. Moreover, the exact method to be executed for any given method call will be determined by the actual type of the object to which the reference refers, rather than being based on the declared type of the reference. This implies that the selection of the method to be called is postponed to run time rather than being determined at compile time; clearly, if the actual run-time type of the object determines which version of the method is called, the compiler can't select the method at compile time.

Susan had some questions about polymorphism.

Susan: Explain how polymorphism is different from inheritance. Recap that the three organizational principles of object-oriented programming are:
1. encapsulation
2. inheritance
3. polymorphism

Steve: Sure. Encapsulation is just the idea that the user of a class shouldn't have to know how it works, just what it does. Therefore, we should keep our fields private (or at least protected) so we can change them, delete them, or add new ones whenever we want.

Problem
Algorithms
Java
Interpreter
Hardware

Inheritance is the definition of one class in terms of another, so that we don't have to write the common code used by several classes over and over again. Instead, we can reuse existing code where it is appropriate and write new code only where we need to make the new class behave differently from the old one.

Polymorphism is the idea that two or more classes can vary only in their implementation while presenting the same appearance to their users. In such a case, we want to be able to write our application programs so that we don't care which class each object belongs to. For example, we might have an array of StockItem references, each of which might actually refer to either a StockItem or a DatedStockItem, and the application programmer can process each item in the same way without having to write special code to say, "if it's a StockItem, do this; otherwise, if it's a DatedStockItem, do this." Of course, objects of different types will have to execute different code sometimes, but by using polymorphism the compiler can determine which method to call rather than putting that burden on the application programmer.

Susan: Why do you write a new version of Reorder instead of adding a new public method?

Steve: So that the application program can treat StockItems and DatedStockItems in the same way. If they had different method names, then they wouldn't seem the same to the user program.

Susan: But what if the two versions of Reorder were exactly the same, couldn't you just declare them public?

Steve: If they had different names, then the user program would still have to distinguish between them, which is what we're trying to avoid.

Susan: Yes, but if they were exactly the same and the names were the same, couldn't they be used anywhere just by making them public? I thought that this was the whole idea not to have to rewrite these things.

Steve: They are public. The point is that StockItem's version of Reorder and DatedStockItem's version of Reorder accomplish the same result in different ways, so the user of objects of either of these classes should be able to just call Reorder and get the correct method executed without having to worry about which one that is.

Susan: I don't get it. You say that both Reorders are exactly the same but then you say that they work in different ways. I don't like that.

Steve: They do the same thing, but in different ways, appropriate to the type of object they do it for.

Problem
Algorithms
Java
Interpreter
Hardware

Susan: Okay, I guess that makes sense. But what else do StockItem and DatedStockItem share besides the names of the methods?

Steve: The derived class contains all of the fields and methods of the base class, along with others it adds.

Susan: See, the word "derived" is confusing. If a DatedStockItem is derived from a StockItem, one tends to think in a linear approach as in a family tree, which isn't quite right. It would be better to think of DatedStockItem as a fruit like a plum, with the pit being the StockItem that is the core of the object.

Steve: Or maybe like a chocolate-covered cherry, with a fruit inside another kind of food, rather than a pit and an edible part.

Susan: So is it correct to say that polymorphism is the same as interchangeable inheritance classes, otherwise inheritance is used side by side (i.e., either/or)?

Steve: Yes, that's correct.

But exactly how does polymorphism help us with our Reorder method? Let's take a look at what happens when we create objects of both StockItem and DatedStockItem classes, and access them through StockItem and DatedStockItem references, in Figure 8.1.

```
import WAJ.*;

public class Polytest
{
    public static void main( String args[ ] )
    {
        StockItem SI = new StockItem("soup",32,100,40,
            15,"Bob's Distribution","1234567890");

        DatedStockItem DSI = new DatedStockItem("milk",
            10,15,40,20,"Phil's Distribution",
            "9876543210","19950110");

        SI.Reorder(System.out);
        System.out.println();

        DSI.Reorder(System.out);
        System.out.println();

        SI = new DatedStockItem("steak",90,95,30,
            20,"Sam's Stuff","1212343456","19960110");

        SI.Reorder(System.out);
        System.out.println();
    }
}
```

```
Problem
Algorithms
Java
Interpreter
Hardware
```

Figure 8.1: Polymorphism test program (code\polytest\polytest.java)

To use the debugger for this program, follow the instructions in the section titled "Using the debugger" in the file "\readme.txt" on the CD in the back of the book. These instructions assume that you've installed the examples on drive C:, so that the location of this program is "c:\whosj\code\polytest".

Figure 8.2 shows the output of this test program.

```
Reorder 15 units of soup with UPC 1234567890 from Bob's Distribution

Return 10 units of milk with UPC 9876543210 to Phil's Distribution
Reorder 40 units of milk with UPC 9876543210 from Phil's Distribution

Return 90 units of steak with UPC 1212343456 to Sam's Stuff
Reorder 30 units of steak with UPC 1212343456 from Sam's Stuff
```

Figure 8.2: Polymorphism test program output (code\polytest\polytest.out)

According to our rules, the correct answer is to return 90 units of steak and reorder 30, because the previous stock has expired. Therefore, the program is working correctly. But how can we call the DatedStockItem version of Reorder through a StockItem reference?

Poly Anna

Because when we call a method through a base class reference, the method that will be executed will be the one defined in the class of the actual object to which the reference points, not the one defined in the class of the reference.[1]

This means that the compiler can't decide exactly which methods will be called for an object referred to by a StockItem, because the actual object may be a descendant of StockItem rather than an actual StockItem; in that case, we will want the method defined in the derived class (e.g., DatedStockItem) to be called even though the reference is declared to point to an object of the base class (e.g., StockItem).

Since the actual type of the object for which we want to call the method isn't available at compile time, another way must be found to determine which method should be called. The most logical place to store this information is in the object itself, because after all we already need to know where the object is located in order to call the method for it. So whenever a method call is compiled, the compiler translates that call into instructions that use the information in the object to determine at run time which version of the method will be called.[2]

If every object needed to contain the addresses of all its methods, that might make objects a lot larger than they would otherwise have to be. However, this is not necessary, because all objects of the same class have the same methods. Therefore, the addresses of all of the methods for a given class are stored in a method address table, which we'll call an **mtable** for short. Every object of a given class contains the address of the mtable for that class.

As you might imagine, Susan had some questions about mtables.

Susan: Are mtables customized for each class?

Problem
Algorithms
Java
Interpreter
Hardware

---

1. In case you would like a picture of this, there's one coming up, in Figure 8.7.

2. Actually, there are times when the compiler can tell at compile time what the type of the object will have to be at run time; in that case, it can generate more efficient ways to call methods on that object. However, we can ignore this detail in our analysis, because it never makes any difference in the way our programs work.

Steve: Yes.

Susan: Where do they come from, how are they created, and how do they work?

Steve: The compiler creates them based on the class definition, and all they do is store the addresses of the methods for that class, so that the compiler can generate code that will select the correct method for the object being referred to at run time.

Susan: I don't get this mtable stuff; why is it here again?

Steve: To allow the program to find the correct Reorder method at run time.

Susan: And does this just point the Reorder method in the proper direction at run time?

Steve: Yes.

Susan: Is the mtable in the object?

Steve: No, the address of the mtable is in the object. Putting the whole mtable in the object would waste a lot of space if there were very many methods.

```
Problem
Algorithms
Java
Interpreter
Hardware
```

Susan: How is an mtable made? Is it created only when there is a derived class?

Steve: No, every class has an mtable associated with it, because that's the usual way to find the methods for that class. Sometimes the compiler can figure out what methods are going to be called at compile time, but that isn't true in general. Therefore, an mtable is required for every class.

Susan: This stuff is beyond "UGH!"; it is just outrageous and I can't believe that you understand it.

Steve: It's a dirty, lousy job, but somebody has to do it.

Thus, a simplified version of a StockItem object, including its mtable, might look something like Figure 8.3.[3]

---

3. Of course, all of the "memory addresses" in this and the succeeding figures are arbitrary; the real addresses are assigned by the interpreter when the program is executed.

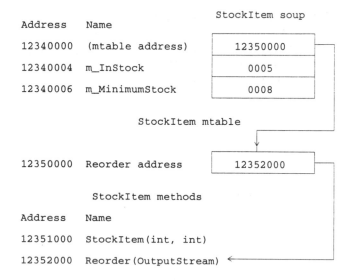

Figure 8.3: A simplified StockItem object

On the other hand, a simplified version of a DatedStockItem object might look like Figure 8.4.

Problem
Algorithms
Java
Interpreter
Hardware

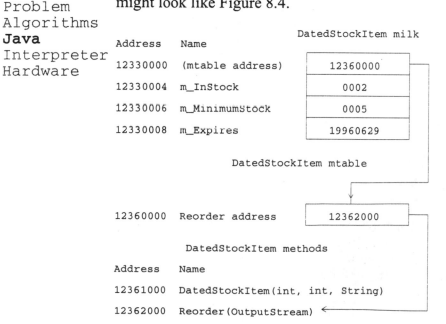

Figure 8.4: A simplified DatedStockItem object

Given these pictures of StockItem and DatedStockItem objects, let's examine the behavior of three method call examples, one for each legal combination of references and objects. First, Figure 8.5 shows what happens when Reorder is called for a StockItem object through a StockItem variable named SI (short for "stock item").

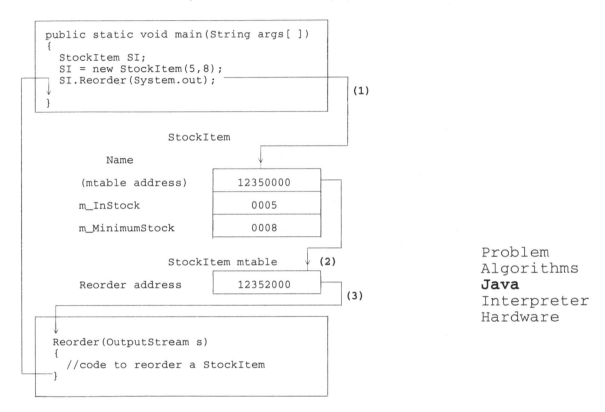

```
public static void main (String args [ ])
{
    StockItem SI;
    SI = new StockItem(5,8);
    SI.Reorder(System.out);
}
```
(1)

```
            StockItem

    Name

    (mtable address)        12350000

    m_InStock               0005

    m_MinimumStock          0008

            StockItem mtable        (2)

    Reorder address         12352000
                                        (3)

    Reorder(OutputStream s)
    {
        //code to reorder a StockItem
    }
```

Problem
Algorithms
Java
Interpreter
Hardware

Figure 8.5: Calling the Reorder method of StockItem through a StockItem reference to a StockItem object

Step **(1)** gets the mtable pointer from the StockItem object to which SI refers. Step **(2)** gets the address of the Reorder method from that mtable. Then step **(3)** uses that address to call the StockItem version of Reorder. At the end of that method, it returns to the next statement in the main program. So the net result of the call illustrated in Figure 8.5 is that the StockItem version of Reorder is called, which is what we want in this situation.

Next, Figure 8.6 shows what happens when Reorder is called for a DatedStockItem object through a DatedStockItem reference.

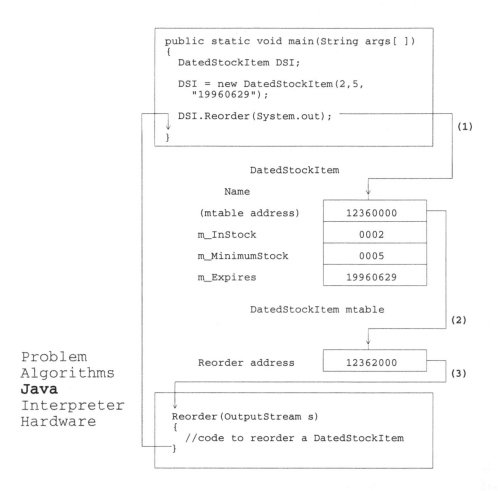

```
public static void main(String args[ ])
{
  DatedStockItem DSI;

  DSI = new DatedStockItem(2,5,
    "19960629");

  DSI.Reorder(System.out);
}
```
(1)

DatedStockItem

Name

(mtable address)   12360000

m_InStock   0002

m_MinimumStock   0005

m_Expires   19960629

DatedStockItem mtable
(2)

Problem
Algorithms
Java
Interpreter
Hardware

Reorder address   12362000
(3)

```
Reorder(OutputStream s)
{
   //code to reorder a DatedStockItem
}
```

Figure 8.6: Calling the Reorder method of DatedStockItem through a
DatedStockItem reference

Step **(1)** gets the mtable pointer from the DatedStockItem object to which DSI refers. Step **(2)** gets the address of the Reorder method from that mtable. Then step **(3)** uses that address to call the DatedStockItem version of Reorder. At the end of that method, it returns to the next statement in the main program. So the net result of the call illustrated in Figure 8.6 is that the DatedStockItem version of Reorder is called, which is what we want in this situation.

Finally, Figure 8.7 shows what happens when Reorder is called for a DatedStockItem object through a StockItem reference. This is where polymorphism pays off, because we can use a base class reference to refer to a derived class object, and the correct method for that derived class object will be called anyway.

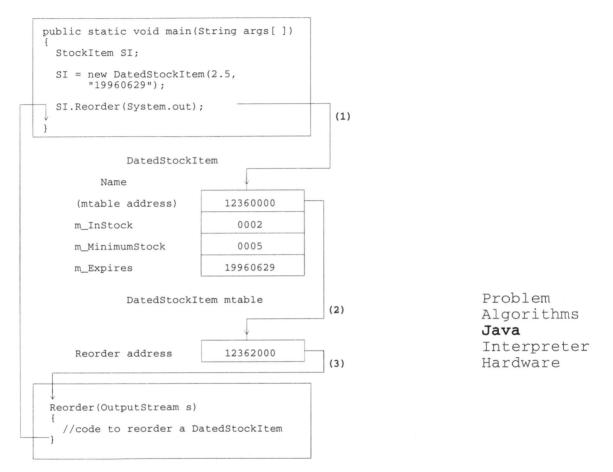

Figure 8.7: Calling the Reorder method of DatedStockItem through a StockItem reference

Step **(1)** gets the mtable pointer from the DatedStockItem object to which SI refers. Step **(2)** gets the address of the Reorder method from that mtable. Then step **(3)** uses that address to call the DatedStockItem version of Reorder. At the end of that method, it returns to the next statement in the main program. So the net result of the call illustrated in Figure 8.7 is that the correct method, DatedStockItem.Reorder, is called even though the type of the reference through which it is called is StockItem.

To translate this into what I hope is understandable English, the call to the Reorder method in any of these figures might be expressed as follows:

1. Get the mtable address from the object referred to by SI.
2. Since Reorder is the first defined method, retrieve its address from the first method address slot in the mtable.
3. Execute the method at that address.

What happens if we add another method, say Write, to the StockItem class, after the Reorder method? The new method will be added to the mtables for both the StockItem and DatedStockItem classes.

Susan had some questions about mtables.

> **Susan**: What do you mean by added to both mtables? Do StockItem and DatedStockItem each have their own?

> **Steve**: Yes.

> **Susan**: If so, then why are the numbers of their addresses so similar? They are just different addresses of the same mtable?

Problem
Algorithms
Java
Interpreter
Hardware

> **Steve**: In the StockItem case, I've given the starting address as 12350000, and in the DatedStockItem case, as 12360000. These are the addresses I made up for the two mtables.

> **Susan**: How does the mtable get the address for the new StockItems?

> **Steve**: It's the other way around. The constructor for each class has code added to it by the compiler to fill in the mtable address for the objects of that class. Therefore, each StockItem, when it is created by the constructor, has its mtable address filled in by that compiler-generated code.

By following this sequence, you can see that while both versions of Reorder are referred to via the same relative position in the StockItem and DatedStockItem mtables, the particular version of Reorder that is executed will depend on which mtable the object points to. Since all objects of the same class have the same methods, all StockItem objects will point to the same StockItem mtable, and all DatedStockItem objects will point to the same DatedStockItem mtable.

To make this more tangible, if we added another method to the StockItem class, its layout might look something like Figure 8.8.

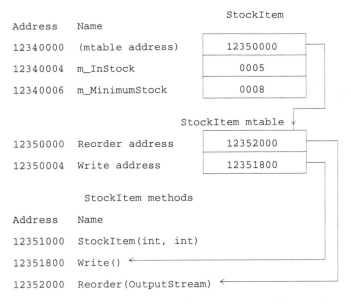

Figure 8.8: A simplified StockItem object with two methods

The situation for a DatedStockItem object might look like Figure 8.9.

Problem
Algorithms
Java
Interpreter
Hardware

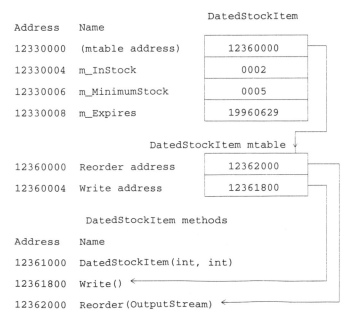

Figure 8.9: A simplified DatedStockItem object with two methods

As you can see, the new method has been added to both mtables, so that a call to Write through a base class reference will call the correct method.

A Pointed Reminder

Now let's see how we can use polymorphism in an application program to handle a mix of StockItem and DatedStockItem objects. Figure 8.10 shows how to do this.

```
import WAJ.*;

public class Polytest2
{
    public static void main( String args[ ] )
    {
        StockItem[ ] x = new StockItem[2];

        x[0] = new StockItem("3-ounce cups",71,78,40,
              15,"Bob's Distribution","1234567890");

        x[1] = new DatedStockItem("milk",76,87,40,
               20,"Phil's Distribution","9876543210","19970719");

        System.out.println("A StockItem: ");
        x[0].Write(System.out);
        System.out.println();

        System.out.println("A DatedStockItem: ");
        x[1].Write(System.out);
        System.out.println();
    }
}
```

Problem
Algorithms
Java
Interpreter
Hardware

Figure 8.10: Mixing StockItem and DatedStockItems in a single array
(code\polytest2\polytest2.java)

The first item of note in this program is the statement StockItem[ ] x = new StockItem[2];, which creates an array of StockItem references. The elements of this array can refer to any mixture of StockItems and DatedStockItems, because we can assign objects of either of those types to a base class reference, which in this case is a StockItem reference. Once we have the array of StockItem references, we use new, together with the appropriate constructor, to create whichever type of object we actually need; that's the job of the next two statements.

Once we have created those objects, we can call Write to display both a StockItem and a DatedStockItem, even though the display methods for those two types are actually different. The reason, of course, is that there are actually two different versions of Write, one for StockItems and one for DatedStockItems. The Java interpreter will determine which one of these polymorphic Write methods to call at run time, based on the actual type of the object being displayed.

To use the debugger for this program, follow the instructions in the section titled "Using the debugger" in the file "\readme.txt" on the CD in the back of the book. These instructions assume that you've installed the examples on drive C:, so that the location of this program is program is "c:\whosj\code\polytest2".

Susan had some questions about this program.

> **Susan**: Why are you using new here?

> **Steve**: We always have to use new to create an object of any user-defined type, to allocate the memory for the object.

> **Susan**: Why does Write need to be different for each class?

> **Steve**: Because each class has different fields that have to be written.

Problem
Algorithms
Java
Interpreter
Hardware

Let's look at some diagrams that show how this polymorphic method call works, using the simplified versions of StockItem and DatedStockItem that we used in our previous discussion. First, Figure 8.11 illustrates the method call to the StockItem version of Write.

Step **(1)** gets the mtable pointer from the StockItem object to which x[0] refers. Step **(2)** gets the address of the Write method from that mtable. Then step **(3)** uses that address to call the StockItem version of Write. At the end of that method, it returns to the next statement in the main program. So the net result of the call illustrated in Figure 8.11 is that the StockItem version of Write is called, which is what we want in this situation.

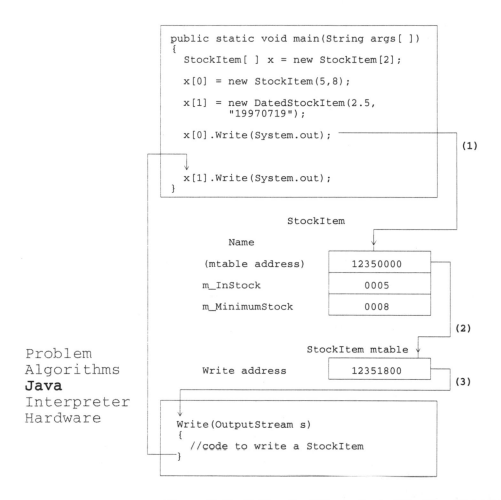

Figure 8.11: Calling the Write method of StockItem through a StockItem reference

Now let's see what happens when the second call to Write is executed in Figure 8.11.

Step **(1)** gets the mtable pointer from the DatedStockItem object to which x[1] refers. Step **(2)** gets the address of the Write method from that mtable. Then step **(3)** uses that address to call the DatedStockItem version of Write. At the end of that method, it returns to the next statement in the main program. So the net result of the call illustrated in Figure 8.11 is that the DatedStockItem version of Write is called, which is what we want in this situation.

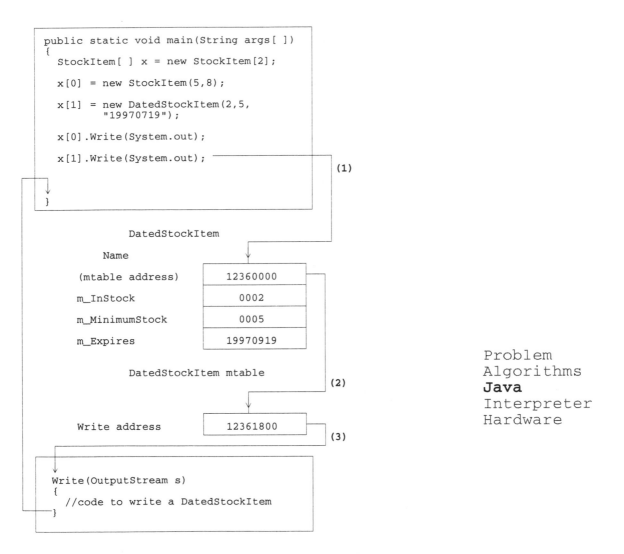

Figure 8.12: Calling the Write method of DatedStockItem through a StockItem reference

Susan had another question about polymorphism and its application.

Susan: So polymorphism is necessary only when using arrays, otherwise inheritance will do?

Steve: Not exactly. Polymorphism is needed whenever we want to be able to decide at run time rather than at compile time what the actual type of an object will be. Usually this is when we have lots of objects to deal with, in which case we would be using arrays or some similar means of keeping track of all those objects. However, sometimes there are only a few objects that can be of various types depending on exactly what the program is doing, and there we would still need polymorphism.

That explains how we can write out an object from our application without having to worry whether it is a StockItem or a DatedStockItem. However, this simple example might understate the importance of polymorphism. How important is it really?

Maintenance Required

Polymorphism is crucial to the maintainability of large systems. The problem is that without polymorphism, the application programmer has to keep track of all the possible variations on the basic types of objects the program uses. That is, in the absence of polymorphism, a scenario like the following one would be almost certain to develop during the lifespan of a large program.

Problem
Algorithms
Java
Interpreter
Hardware

1.   The program would start out with two types of stock items, StockItem and DatedStockItem. Therefore, whenever it was necessary to write one of these data items to a file, the application programmer would need an if statement that said, "If it's a StockItem, call the Write method for that type. Otherwise, call the Write method for a DatedStockItem."

2.   Sometime later, another type of stock item would be needed, say a DrugStockItem, which needs special permission to sell or reorder it. The programmer now has to change the if statement to say, "If it's a StockItem, call the Write method for that type. Otherwise, if it's a DatedStockItem, call the Write method for DatedStockItem. Otherwise, call the Write method for DrugStockItem."

That doesn't sound so bad, does it? Actually, it is very serious. The difficulty is that this sort of change must be made everywhere in the program, and must be made correctly in every case. To see this, consider what would happen if the programmer missed a place where the change in step 2 was needed. The Write method for DatedStockItem would be called whenever the actual type was DrugStockItem! The problem is the "otherwise" clause in the first version of the program, which makes the assumption that if the item in question isn't a StockItem, then it must be a DatedStockItem.

Would the program work properly if it were written to say "if it's a StockItem, do this; if it's a DatedStockItem, do that"? No, because then if the object weren't either of those types, it wouldn't do anything! Whether that would be better or worse than doing the wrong thing depends on the exact situation, but in any event it's clear that neither of these behaviors is correct.

By contrast, with polymorphic classes, the application programmer doesn't need any if statements to select the correct Write method, but just calls Write for each object that needs to be written to the file. The determination of which method to call is made by the compiler rather than the application programmer. Therefore, adding a new class derived from StockItem would not affect the application program at all; so long as the new class is properly implemented, the application program could simply use it without even being recompiled. This goes a long way toward preventing the type of maintenance nightmare that is facing every large organization in the form of the Year 2000 problem.

Begin at the Beginning

Now let's look at the implementation of Write for StockItem (Figure 8.13) and for DatedStockItem (Figure 8.14).

Problem
Algorithms
Java
Interpreter
Hardware

The main thing that might not be obvious about the StockItem.Write method is why StockItem.Write writes the "0" out as its first action. We know that there's no date for a StockItem, so why not just write out the data that it does have?

```
void Write(OutputStream s)
{
    RWVar.println(s,0);
    RWVar.println(s,m_Name);
    RWVar.println(s,m_InStock);
    RWVar.println(s,m_Price);
    RWVar.println(s,m_MinimumStock);
    RWVar.println(s,m_MinimumReorder);
    RWVar.println(s,m_Distributor);
    RWVar.println(s,m_UPC);
}
```

Figure 8.13: StockItem.Write (from code\Itemtst22\StockItem.java)

```
void Write(OutputStream s)
{
    RWVar.println(s,m_Expires);
    RWVar.println(s,m_Name);
    RWVar.println(s,m_InStock);
    RWVar.println(s,m_Price);
    RWVar.println(s,m_MinimumStock);
    RWVar.println(s,m_MinimumReorder);
    RWVar.println(s,m_Distributor);
    RWVar.println(s,m_UPC);
}
```

Figure 8.14: DatedStockItem.Write (from code\Itemtst22\DatedStockItem.java)

Because when we read the data back in, we'll need to be able to tell a StockItem from a DatedStockItem. Since "0" is not a valid date, we will use it to mean that the following data belong to a StockItem, not a DatedStockItem. When we read data from the inventory file to create our StockItem and DatedStockItem objects, any object whose data begins a "0" will become a StockItem, whereas any object whose data starts with a valid date will become a DatedStockItem.

Problem
Algorithms
Java
Interpreter
Hardware

This is also why the DatedStockItem Write method can't just handle its new field and then call StockItem.Write to do the rest of the work; StockItem.Write writes its own "0" value for the "date", so this would produce the wrong output. Of course, it would be possible (and desirable) to handle the common part of this task via another (private or protected) method that both the StockItem and DatedStockItem Write methods called, but for now this solution is good enough.

Now that we can write the data out, how do we read it back in? The main problem is that we can't create an item until we know which type it actually is. That's handled by the next method we're going to tackle: the Read method in the Inventory class.

Why do we have to use a method in the Inventory class rather than one in StockItem? Because we don't know whether we're creating a StockItem or a DatedStockItem until we look at the data being read from the file. If there is an "expiration date" of 0, then it must be a StockItem; otherwise, it must be a DatedStockItem. However, we can't call a constructor until we know what type of object we want to construct! Therefore, we need a method that will figure out the type of object to construct and call the constructor for StockItem or DatedStockItem, whichever is appropriate. Since the Inventory class is the manager for the StockItem and DatedStockItem objects used in our application program, its Read method (Figure 8.15) is a good place to create those objects.

```
protected static StockItem Read(InputStream s)
{
    DataInputStream dis = new DataInputStream(s);
    String tempInStock;
    String tempPrice;
    String tempMinimumStock;
    String tempMinimumReorder;
    String Name;
    String Distributor;
    String UPC;
    int InStock;
    int Price;
    int MinimumStock;
    int MinimumReorder;
    String Expires;
    StockItem Result;

    try
        {
        Expires = dis.readLine();
        Name = dis.readLine();
        tempInStock = dis.readLine();
        tempPrice = dis.readLine();
        tempMinimumStock = dis.readLine();
        tempMinimumReorder = dis.readLine();
        Distributor = dis.readLine();
        UPC = dis.readLine();
        }
    catch (IOException e)
        {
        System.out.println(e);
        return null;
        }

    if (UPC == null)
        return null;

    InStock = Integer.parseInt(tempInStock);
    Price = Integer.parseInt(tempPrice);
    MinimumStock = Integer.parseInt(tempMinimumStock);
    MinimumReorder = Integer.parseInt(tempMinimumReorder);
```

```
Problem
Algorithms
Java
Interpreter
Hardware
```

Figure 8.15: The Inventory.Read method (from code\itemtst22\Inventory.java)

```
    if (Expires.equals("0"))
        {
        Result = new StockItem(Name, InStock, Price, MinimumStock,
            MinimumReorder, Distributor, UPC);
        }
    else
        {
        Result = new DatedStockItem(Name, InStock, Price, MinimumStock,
            MinimumReorder, Distributor, UPC, Expires);
        }

    return Result;
}
```

Figure 8.15 continued

This starts out reasonably enough with the header indicating that it is a protected static method, which means that we can use it in either the Inventory class or any of its descendants (if any), and that we don't need a particular Inventory object to call it. Since its job is to return a StockItem or DatedStockItem that we can stick into any Inventory object, this makes sense. However, what about the return type, which is StockItem? We don't know whether we are actually going to create a StockItem or a DatedStockItem; that's why we have to use a method in Inventory rather than in StockItem or DatedStockItem. So how can the return value be a StockItem?

Problem
Algorithms
Java
Interpreter
Hardware

Blind Date

That was a trick question. The return value isn't an object; it's a *reference* to a StockItem. Because a reference to a base class can actually refer to any object of that type or any of its descendants, either a StockItem or a DatedStockItem can be referred to by references of type StockItem.

The code itself is pretty simple. We read each data item from the file and convert each one that represents a numeric value from its String form to a numeric form via the Integer.parseInt method. Then we check whether the Expires value is equal to "0". If it is, this must be a regular StockItem; otherwise, it must be a DatedStockItem, and we create the appropriate type of object via its normal constructor and assign it to the Result StockItem reference. That reference is then returned to the user.

Now that we've seen all the pieces, let's take a look at how they all fit together. Figure 8.16 shows the main program that reads DatedStockItems and StockItems from a file and displays them.

```java
import WAJ.*;
import java.io.*;

public class Itemtst22
{
    public static void main( String args[ ] )
    {
        FileInputStream ShopInfo;

        FileOutputStream ReorderInfo;

        Inventory MyInventory = new Inventory();

        try
        {
            ShopInfo = new FileInputStream("shop22.in");
        }
        catch (IOException e)
        {
            System.out.println("Can't open file \"shop22.in\"");
            return;
        }

        MyInventory.LoadInventory(ShopInfo);

        try
        {
            ReorderInfo = new FileOutputStream("shop22.reo");
        }
        catch (IOException e)
        {
            System.out.println("Can't open file \"shop22.reo\"");
            return;
        }

        MyInventory.ReorderItems(ReorderInfo);

    }
}
```

Problem
Algorithms
Java
Interpreter
Hardware

Figure 8.16: Test program for DatedStockItem and StockItem
(code\itemtst22\itemtst22.java)

To use the debugger for this program, follow the instructions in the section titled "Using the debugger" in the file "\readme.txt" on the CD in the back of the book. These instructions assume that you've installed the examples on drive C:, so that the location of this program is "c:\whosj\code\itemtst22".

By the way, the ability to use an object of a derived class wherever an object of its base class is specified is also the explanation of the somewhat cryptic note in Chapter 6 mentioning that a catch statement can actually catch any exception of a type that is of either the class specified in its argument list or of any derived class of that class. Of course, this applies not only to the argument list of a catch statement but to all other argument lists as well.

Exercises

Problem
Algorithms
Java
Interpreter
Hardware

1. Rewrite the DrugStockItem class that you wrote in Chapter 6 as a derived class of DatedStockItem, so that DrugStockItem objects can be used in place of StockItem objects or DatedStockItem objects, just as you can use DatedStockItem objects in place of StockItem objects.

2. Modify the Manager class that you wrote in Chapter 7 so that the CalculatePay method in that class has an argument specifying the number of hours worked. The implementation of CalculatePay in the Manager class will fire the manager if the number of hours is less than 50, but will otherwise ignore the argument, while the Hourly implementation of CalculatePay will continue to use the argument as it did previously. Because the CalculatePay methods in these two classes now have the same arguments, objects of these classes can be treated as though they were of the same class; therefore, this is an example of inheritance for re-implementation.

3. Write an essay comparing the advantages and disadvantages of the two approaches to inheritance in the previous exercise and the corresponding exercise in Chapter 7.

Review

We started out this chapter with a DatedStockItem class that was derived from the StockItem class, with the addition of an expiration date field. While this was a fine solution to the problem of creating a class based on the StockItem class without having to rewrite all the previously functioning code in the latter class, it didn't explain how we could mix objects that might or might not have expiration dates in the same array.

Because Java allows us to assign an object of a derived type to a reference of its base class, creating an array of StockItem references allows us to create both StockItems and DatedStockItems and assign them to various elements of the StockItem array. The correct method is always called in this situation because when the compiler sees a call to the Reorder method, it will generate code that will call the appropriate version of that method for the actual type of the object being referred to. In this case, StockItem.Reorder will be called if the actual object being referred to through a StockItem reference is a StockItem, and DatedStockItem.Reorder will be called if the actual object being referred to through a StockItem reference is a DatedStockItem. This is exactly the behavior that we need to make our StockItem objects and DatedStockItem objects do the right thing when we call them through a StockItem reference.

To make this run time determination of which method will be called, the compiler has to add something to every object, namely a reference to an *mtable*, which is short for "method address table". An mtable effectively contains the addresses of all the methods that can be called in the current class, which includes methods defined in any of its ancestors. The code that the compiler generates for a method call uses this mtable to look up the actual address of the method to be called at run time.

After going over some examples showing how this works in the context of our example program that assigns a StockItem to one element of a StockItem array and a DatedStockItem to another element of the same array, we discussed why polymorphism is important to maintainability of large systems.

Finally, we looked at the implementation of the Write and Read methods for the StockItem and DatedStockItem classes. While Write is fairly simple, because the type of the object to be written is already known when we're writing it, the same is not true of Read. In fact, Read can't even be a method of StockItem or DatedStockItem, because we don't know which of those types we have until we have already read the data for the object. Therefore, we had to put this Read method in the Inventory class, which is responsible for managing StockItem and DatedStockItem objects in our example programs.

Problem
Algorithms
Java
Interpreter
Hardware

Appendix A

Tying up Loose Ends

Where Am I, Anyway?

Now that you've reached the end of this book, there are some questions that have probably occurred to you. For example,

1. Am I a programmer now?
2. What am I qualified to do?
3. Where do I go from here?
4. Is that all there is to Java?

The answers to the first three of these questions, as usual with such open-ended topics, is "It all depends". Of course, I can give you some general answers; let's start with questions 1 and 2.

Yes, in the broadest sense, you are a programmer. You've read a fair amount of code and written some programs yourself. But, of course, this doesn't mean that you're a professional programmer. As I said way back at the beginning, no book can turn a novice into a professional programmer. Being a professional in any field takes a lot of hard work, and although you've undoubtedly worked hard in understanding this book, you've just begun the exploration of programming.

Questions 3 and 4 are also closely related. You now have enough background that you should be able to get some benefit from a well-written book about Java that assumes you are already acquainted with programming; that would be a good way to continue. As for whether we've covered everything about Java, the answer is unequivocal: absolutely not. I would estimate that we have examined perhaps 10% of the very large and complicated Java language;

however, that 10% is the foundation for the rest of your learning in this subject. Most books on Java try to cover every aspect of the language and, as a result, cannot provide deep coverage of fundamentals; I've worked very hard to ensure that you have the correct tools to continue your learning.

Tying up Loose Ends

I've skipped over some topics because they weren't essential to the discussion. However, since they are likely to be covered in any other book that you might read on programming in Java, I'll discuss them here briefly. This will ensure that they won't be completely foreign to you when you encounter them in your future reading.

Reference Substitution

```
Problem
Algorithms
Java
Interpreter
Hardware
```

Whenever you are asked for a reference of a particular class, you can provide a derived class reference instead. This is very similar to the rule that a reference of a given class can refer to objects of that class or any of its derived classes, but it's not identical: this rule allows us to supply a reference to a DatedStockItem, for example, where an argument list specifies a reference to a StockItem. The old rule, by contrast, would allow a StockItem reference to refer to a DatedStockItem object.

Command Line Arguments

The by-now-familiar line public static void main(String args[ ]) has another function besides specifying where every Java program starts. The expression String args[ ] is the argument to the main function. What it contains is the Strings that were typed in on the command line when the program was run. For example, if you ran the Average program from Chapter 5 by changing to the "\whosj\code\func1" directory and typing jview Average 14 22, then the value of the String args[0] would be "14" and the value of the String args[1] would be "22". The way that program is currently written, any values typed on the command line are ignored. However, if we wanted the Average program to take input from its command line arguments and convert them to ints, then we could change it to use those values from the command line rather than prompting the user to type them in after the program started running.

Operator Precedence

You may recall from high school arithmetic that an expression like 5 + 3 * 9 is calculated as though it were written 5 + (3 * 9), not (5 + 3) * 9; that is, you have to do the * before the +, so that the correct result is 32, not 72, as it would be under the latter interpretation. The reason for performing the operations in the former order is that multiplication has a higher *precedence* than addition. Well, every operator in Java also has a precedence that determines the order of application of each operator in an expression with more than one operator. This seems like a good idea at first glance, since after all, arithmetic does follow precedence rules like the one we just saw. Unfortunately, Java is just a little more complicated than arithmetic, and so its precedence rules are not as simple and easy to remember as those of arithmetic. In fact, there are 13 different levels of precedence, which no one can remember. Therefore, everyone[1] ends up using parentheses to specify what order was meant when the expression was written; of course, if we're going to have to use parentheses, then why do we need the precedence rules in the first place?

Problem
Algorithms
Java
Interpreter
Hardware

Other Native Data Types

We've confined our use of native data types to short, char, int and boolean (and float in some of the exercises). As I mentioned in Chapter 6, there are other native types; you'll be seeing them in other programs and in other textbooks, so I should tell you about them now. By the way, I haven't avoided them because they're particularly difficult to use; the reason is simply that they weren't necessary to the task at hand, which was teaching you how to program, using Java. Now that we have accomplished that task, you might as well add them to your arsenal of tools. These other native types are

1. double
2. long
3. byte

---

1. At least, everyone who is sensible.

As we've already seen in some of the exercises, the float types are used to store values that can contain fractional parts (so-called *floating-point* numbers), rather than being restricted to whole numbers as in the case of short and the other integral types. Of course, this raises two questions: First, why don't we use this type all the time, if it's more flexible? Second, why do we need double as well as float? These questions are related, because the main difference between float and double is that a float is 4 bytes long and a double is 8 bytes long; therefore, a double can store larger values and maintain higher accuracy. However, it also uses up twice the amount of memory of a float, which may not be important when we're dealing with a few values but is quite important if we have an array of thousands or tens of thousands of elements.

A long is like an int, except longer. It can handle very large integer values, from −9223372036854775808 to 9223372036854775807. If we have whole numbers that are too big to fit into an int, a long would do the trick. On the other hand, if we need values with fractional parts, a double or float would be appropriate.

The byte, as its name indicates, is used to hold one byte of data, which can be useful when exchanging information with the external world, where characters are often one byte in length rather than two as in Java.

Problem
Algorithms
Java
Interpreter
Hardware

The Vector

We've used arrays to good effect in our programs, but they have some drawbacks, the primary one being that you have to know exactly how large an array is before you create it. While this is often a reasonable restriction, there are times when it would be very handy to be able to create a collection of objects without having to know how many there will be in the collection before adding them. This is possible in Java by using a Vector, which is similar in some ways to an array except that it will grow as required to accommodate new elements. Unfortunately, Vectors also have some serious drawbacks, primarily the inability to use the normal indexing operator [ ] to select an element. Because Java is too simple to have operator overloading, you have to use an elementAt method to retrieve values from a Vector and an addElement method to add an element.

The interface

We've already seen how to create a new class that has the behavior of a preexisting class with some added features: *inheritance*. However, what if we want to create a new class that has the behavior of more than one existing class? Java doesn't allow **multiple inheritance**, in which one class is derived from more than one existing class. However, there is a way to solve this problem, by using an interface, which is quite similar to a class, with two important exceptions. First, it has no implementation; instead, it must be implemented separately by every class that wants to display its behavior. Second, it is legal in Java to implement several interfaces in a single class. This provides many of the advantages of multiple inheritance without all of the complexity of that facility.

Threads

Many programming languages support only sequential execution, in which only one statement in a program can be executed at any given time, and it appears to the programmer that a particular method runs from beginning to end without interruption. However, in Java it is possible to write a program as a collection of independent *threads*, each of which can be thought of as executing at the same time as the others. Of course, if you have only one CPU in your computer, only one instruction can really be executing at a given time, but the statements in a given thread can execute without waiting for statements in another thread to finish. Writing programs that use threads correctly can be difficult, but Java has a number of facilities that will help you keep the threads in your programs untangled.

```
Problem
Algorithms
Java
Interpreter
Hardware
```

Standard packages

Besides all of the features of the Java language itself, there are quite a few standard packages that supply facilities not built into the language. Unfortunately, these are far too large and complicated to discuss here: I recommend that you get a copy of *Java in a Nutshell*, by David Flanagan, published by O'Reilly & Associates. Although this book will not teach you Java, and contains some dubious statements about the nature of the language and its relationship to C and C++, it is nevertheless the best reference book on the Java language that I have found.

Applets

Finally, I should mention that Java can be used to write *applets*, which are small programs that run inside a WWW browser such as Netscape Navigator™ or Internet Explorer™. This book doesn't discuss applets, because I believe that it makes more sense to learn how to use the Java language before you try to use it to write interactive programs such as applets. However, you shouldn't have any trouble finding a book that will teach you how to write applets, now that you have a pretty good understanding of the basics of the Java language.

```
Problem
Algorithms
Java
Interpreter
Hardware
```

Appendix B

Java Q&A

Questions and Answers

If you are a C++ programmer, you may have a lot of questions about the similarities and differences between that language and Java. If you're not a C++ programmer, you may still have a lot of questions about some of the finer points of the language. In this Appendix, I'll try to answer some of the more frequently asked questions to your satisfaction, whichever category you fall in. Note: some of these answers are quite different from the ones that diehard Java supporters might give you. If you want the party line, you can find it in virtually any other book on Java, but not here.

Before we begin with the "frequently asked questions", let's hear what Susan has to say about the relationship between Java and C++, as well as how you can decide whether Java is right for you.

> **Susan**: Some of these things may be considered minor nit picking. For one, compared to C++, Java looks too busy on the page. The operators that control input and output are unnecessarily wordy. I would think that they would be very annoying to type many times in a large program.
>
> On a more serious level, I very much disliked the idea of exception handling (or error checking, which I found easier to understand). This may very well be an improvement over C++ in terms of a less error prone program, but it seems to add unnecessary "busy-ness" to the code and is just one more thing to think about when you're starting out.
>
> The method of adding variable values to strings was a bit of a surprise. I find it understandable if not a little silly. Yet, it works so I won't complain.
>
> The idea of practically everything being a reference is also a little hard to swallow, especially for a language that claims it does not employ pointers, when it seems that in reality, almost everything is a pointer.

On a more positive note, the hardest concept that I have had to deal with in both languages is polymorphism, which I found to be much easier to learn in Java than in C++. With the flexibility and usefulness of this object-oriented facility, it is good to see it put in a form that will be faster and easier for more people to learn and use.

My final comment is an opinion that I share with Steve, whose expertise in programming I tend to trust: Java is just another language. It is no better nor worse than other languages. We have different languages to suit different needs and this language came along to fill gaps where there were needs. Is this the end-all language that everyone will be using to the exclusion of others? No, it is simply more useful in doing some things than other languages. It can't hold up to C++ in major programming endeavors. However, it seems fine for its main intention, the making of applets for Internet usage. The excitement and fervor surrounding this language in my opinion is due primarily to the excitement and fervor of the Internet. As with other languages, Java has its place, but how you plan on using it should guide your decision on whether it is the right language for you.

Equality Now?

```
Problem
Algorithms
Java
Interpreter
Hardware
```

Q: The following code (Figure B.1) doesn't work. The result is always "Please answer with either yes or no", no matter what I type. What's wrong?

```java
import WAJ.*;

public class Equality
{
  public static void main( String args[ ] )
  {
    String answer;

    System.out.print("Are we having fun yet? (yes/no):  ");
    answer = RWVar.readString(System.in);

    if (answer == "yes")
        System.out.println("Your answer is correct");
    else if (answer == "no")
        System.out.println("Your answer is erroneous");
    else
        System.out.println("Please answer with either yes or no.");
  }
}
```

Figure B.1: Equality testing program (code\equality\equality.java)

A: The problem is that you can't use != or == to compare two Strings for equality, because those comparisons test whether the two Strings refer to the same actual object rather than whether they have the same contents. Instead, you have to use equals, as in Figure B.2.

```
import WAJ.*;

public class Equal2
{
    public static void main( String args[ ] )
    {
        String answer;

        System.out.print("Are we having fun yet? (yes/no): ");
        answer = RWVar.readString(System.in);

        if (answer.equals("yes"))
            System.out.println("Your answer is correct");
        else if (answer.equals("no"))
            System.out.println("Your answer is erroneous");
        else
            System.out.println("Please answer with either yes or no.");
    }
}
```

Problem
Algorithms
Java
Interpreter
Hardware

Figure B.2: Corrected equality testing program (code\Equal2\Equal2.java)

To use the debugger for either of these programs, follow the instructions in the section titled "Using the debugger" in the file "\readme.txt" on the CD in the back of the book. These instructions assume that you've installed the examples on drive C:, so that the location of the first program is "c:\whosj\code\equality" and the location of the second program is "c:\whosj\code\basic08".

Q: I want to know whether the Strings have the same contents; I don't care whether they refer to the same object. How do I make == do the sensible thing and compare the contents of the Strings?

A: The difficulty is that it's impossible for the compiler to know exactly what == should do for a user-defined variable. This means that in order to make == work correctly for such variables, we would have to write our own version of == for that type of variable.

However, Java is a simple language, without a lot of frills like letting the class designer define what == means. If you want to know whether two Strings have the same content, you have to use equals; to compare two objects of other types that you define, you have to write your own equals method.[1] Of course, if you use == when you meant to use equals, your program will still compile; you'll just get the wrong answer. So don't do that!

By the way, according to the authors of *The Java Programming Language*, one of whom was the originator of the language, "Using equality operators on String objects does not work as expected. Given String objects str1 and str2, str1==str2 tests whether str1 and str2 refer to the same String object. It does *not* test whether they have the same contents. Content equality is tested using String.equals, described in Chapter 8." (p. 116, emphasis in the original)

For C++ programmers: In C++, of course, you *can* use != and == to compare the values of two strings (or objects of another class), so long as the designer of the class has written versions of != and == for that purpose. However, that requires *operator overloading*, which is much too complex for a simple language like Java.[2]

Input and Output

Problem
Algorithms
Java
Interpreter
Hardware

Q: How can I read a number from the keyboard with standard Java functions, rather than having to use the WAJ package to do that?

A: Okay, you asked for it. Figure B.3 is the simplest method I could come up with to read an int from the keyboard.

Q: Why is this so complicated?

A: Remember, Java is a simple language; it doesn't have all the complicated stuff built into it that many other languages do. This means that you often have to know a great deal about the language in order to do the simplest things. Let's see what we need to know to write this function:

1. How to create a DataInputStream from an InputStream, so that we can read data from the input source (the keyboard, in this case).
2. How to cause any waiting output to be sent to the screen before we try to read data (the flush method).

---

1. Which is obviously *much* simpler than writing your own == method!

2. Except when the designers of Java really wanted to use it, as they did with the + method for Strings. But that doesn't count.

3. How to use exception handling to deal with possible errors when trying to read data from the keyboard.[3]
4. How to read a String from a DataInputStream.
5. How to use the parseInt method of the Integer class to convert the String we've read to an int.

See how simple that was?

```
static public int readInt(InputStream in)
    {
    String templine;
    int result;
    DataInputStream dis = new DataInputStream(in);
    System.out.flush();

    try
        {
        templine = dis.readLine();
        result = Integer.parseInt(templine);
        }
    catch (IOException ioe)
        {
        System.out.println(ioe.toString());
        System.out.println("Unable to get int data.");
        return 0;
        }

    return result;
    }
```

Problem
Algorithms
Java
Interpreter
Hardware

Figure B.3: Reading an int from the keyboard (from
code\WAJ\WAJ\RWvar.java)

Q: I don't believe it. I've heard that you can just read a number from the keyboard by using readInt (as in Figure B.4), rather than going through all that malarkey.

(To use the debugger for this program, follow the instructions in the section titled "Using the debugger" in the file "\readme.txt" on the CD in the back of the book. These instructions assume that you've installed the examples on drive C:, so that the location of this program is "c:\whosj\code\testinput".)

---

3. See the "Exceptional Opportunities" section for some more details on exception handling.

```java
import java.io.*;

public class Testinput
{
  public static void main(String args[ ]) throws IOException
  {
    DataInputStream d = new DataInputStream(System.in);
    int i;
    int j;

    System.out.print("Enter the first number: ");
    System.out.flush();
    i = d.readInt();

    System.out.print("Enter the second number: ");
    System.out.flush();
    j = d.readInt();

    System.out.println("The first number is: " + i);
    System.out.println("The second number is: " + j);
    System.out.println("The sum is: " + (i+j));
  }
}
```

Problem
Algorithms
Java
Interpreter
Hardware

Figure B.4: Test input program (code\testinput\testinput.java)

A: First of all, that code doesn't look very simple. However, a more significant problem is that it won't work properly. Here's the result of running that program:

Enter the first number: 1000
Enter the second number: 2000
The first number is: 825241648
The second number is: 171061296
The sum is: 996302944

The problem is that readInt doesn't work the way you would expect. Rather than interpreting the characters read from the keyboard as digits of a decimal number as my RWVar.readInt method does, the readInt method of the DataInputStream class uses the byte value of each character from the keyboard as one byte of the resulting int. In this case, the value of i is calculated as the number created by taking the character '1' as the first byte of the number and the three occurrences of the character '0' as the other three bytes of the number. Since '1' has the value 49 and '0' has the value 48, the entire value of i can be calculated as 256*256*256*49 + 256*256*48 + 256*48 + 48, which comes out to 825241648. What about j; surely "2000" should give a higher value than "1000"! However, the actual value is the result of combining the value of the next character typed in, which is the *newline* character that ended the line where the "1000" was typed in, with the next three characters, which are the '2' and two '0's. The newline has a value of 10, so combining this with the '2' (value 50) and the first two '0's (value 48) allows us to calculate the value of j as 256*256*256*10 + 256*256*50 + 256*48 + 48, or 171061296.

For C++ programmers: In C++, of course, you can just say cin >> x; and the data will be read in the format that you expect for a variable of whatever type x might be, but providing that facility requires *operator overloading*.

Exceptional Opportunities

Q: Why do I get the error message "error J0122: Exception 'IOException' not caught or declared by 'String IOTest1.readInfo()'" when I try to compile the program in Figure B.5?

Problem
Algorithms
Java
Interpreter
Hardware

```java
import java.io.*;

public class IOTest1
{
  public static void main(String args[ ])
    {
    String text;

    System.out.println("What do you say? ");

    text = readInfo();
    System.out.println("You said: " + text);
    }

  static String readInfo()
    {
    String templine;
    DataInputStream dis = new DataInputStream(System.in);

    templine = dis.readLine();
    return templine;
    }
}
```

Figure B.5: Test input/output program (code\IOTest1\IOTest1.java)

A: The compiler is telling you that your readInfo method has to deal with the possibility that you might not be able to read a line from the keyboard for some reason; if that should occur in your method, the readLine method would throw an *exception*. You have the choice of either stating that you aren't going to worry about the exception, thus pawning it off to the method that calls the method you're writing (which in this case is main), or doing the *exception handling* yourself. If an exception does occur and no method currently in use wants to handle the exception, the program will terminate. If that's what you want to happen, all you have to do is add the expression throws IOException to the declarations of your readInfo method and your main method, resulting in the program in Figure B.6.

```java
import java.io.*;

public class IOTest2
{
  public static void main(String args[ ]) throws IOException
    {
      String text;

      System.out.print("What do you say? ");
      System.out.flush();

      text = readInfo();
      System.out.println("You said: " + text);
    }

  static String readInfo() throws IOException
    {
      String templine;
      DataInputStream dis = new DataInputStream(System.in);

      templine = dis.readLine();
      return templine;
    }
}
```

Problem
Algorithms
Java
Interpreter
Hardware

Figure B.6: Test input/output program (code\IOTest2\IOTest2.java)

To use the debugger for this program, follow the instructions in the section titled "Using the debugger" in the file "\readme.txt" on the CD in the back of the book. These instructions assume that you've installed the examples on drive C:, so that the location of this program is "c:\whosj\code\iotest2".

Q: What's an exception?

A: It's an unexpected event that occurs during the execution of a program, or in other words, an error. What makes it different from other kinds of errors is that it isn't predictable because it may arise from causes outside the program. Examples are missing files, attempts to divide by zero, and other events that aren't caused by errors in the program itself.

Q: Why does Java force you to handle exceptions when reading data (e.g., readLine()) but not when writing (e.g., println())? How does Java decide when it does and doesn't require exception handling?

A: If you find the distinction between these categories far from obvious, you're not alone. I consider the division into checked and unchecked exceptions fairly arbitrary; you just have to look up which is which, or let the compiler tell you when you've called a method that might throw a checked exception.

In general, it's a good idea to handle exceptions as soon as you can, because that will allow you to give better error messages to the user of the method. Figure B.8 shows how to do that; its output, assuming you type in "Hello", is:

Problem
Algorithms
Java
Interpreter
Hardware

```
What do you say? Hello
You said: Hello
```

Figure B.7: Output of first test input/output program with exception handling

To use the debugger for this program, follow the instructions in the section titled "Using the debugger" in the file "\readme.txt" on the CD in the back of the book. These instructions assume that you've installed the examples on drive C:, so that the location of this program is "c:\whosj\code\except1".

```java
import java.io.*;
public class Except1
{
  public static void main(String args[ ])
      {
      String text;

      System.out.print("What do you say? ");
      System.out.flush();

      text = readInfo();
      System.out.println("You said: " + text);
      }

   static String readInfo()
      {
      String templine;
      DataInputStream dis = new DataInputStream(System.in);

      try
         {
         templine = dis.readLine();
         }
      catch (IOException ioe)
         {
         System.out.println();
         System.out.println("*****");
         System.out.println(ioe.toString());
         System.out.println("Unable to get keyboard data.");
         System.out.println("*****");
         return "";
         }

      return templine;

      }
}
```

Problem
Algorithms
Java
Interpreter
Hardware

Figure B.8: Test input/output program with exception handling
(code\Except1\Except1.java)

Q: What could go wrong when you're just trying to read a String from System.in? There must be some reason that you have to catch exceptions in this case, but I haven't been able to make it throw an exception.

A: The program in Figure B.9 shows how to cause an exception to be thrown when trying to read from System.in. Note that in this case you have to specify that main can throw IOException, because the close method can theoretically cause that to happen.

```java
import java.io.*;
public class Except2
{
  public static void main(String args[ ]) throws IOException
    {
    String text;

    System.out.print("What do you say? ");
    System.out.flush();

    System.in.close();

    text = readInfo();
    System.out.println("You said: " + text);
    }

  static String readInfo()
    {
    String templine;
    DataInputStream dis = new DataInputStream(System.in);

    try
      {
      templine = dis.readLine();
      }
    catch (IOException ioe)
      {
      System.out.println();
      System.out.println("*****");
      System.out.println(ioe);
      System.out.println("Unable to get keyboard data.");
      System.out.println("*****");
      return "";
      }

    return templine;

    }
}
```

Problem
Algorithms
Java
Interpreter
Hardware

Figure B.9: Second test input/output program with exception handling
(code\Except2\Except2.java)

The result of running this program is:

What do you say?
*****

java.io.IOException: read error
Unable to get keyboard data.
*****

You said:

Figure B.10: Output of second test input/output program with exception handling

The reason the main program displays "You said:" is that it doesn't know that the exception has occurred in the readInfo method. Depending on your viewpoint, this is either an advantage or a disadvantage of handling the exception at the lowest level and not telling the calling method about it.

To use the debugger for this program, follow the instructions in the section titled "Using the debugger" in the file "\readme.txt" on the CD in the back of the book. These instructions assume that you've installed the examples on drive C:, so that the location of this program is "c:\whosj\code\except2".

Problem
Algorithms
Java
Interpreter
Hardware

For C++ programmers: In C++, of course, you don't have to declare what exceptions your functions can throw, although you are permitted to do so (and also to declare that it won't throw any). I don't particularly mind the extra rigor of Java, although I'm not convinced that it is of significant benefit.

In Resplendent Array

Q: When trying to use an element of an array of StockItems I get a run-time error that says "ERROR: java.lang.NullPointerException". What's wrong with this picture (Figure B.11)?

A: The problem is that when you create an array of a user-defined type, you're really not creating an array of objects, but an array of references to objects of that type. Until you set a reference to refer to some particular object, you can't use it. In the present example, we can use new to initialize each reference before using it. Figure B.12 is the corrected program.

```
class Test
{
int x;
}

class ArrayTest1
{
   public static void main(String args[ ])
   {
      int i;
      Test TestArray[ ] = new Test[100];

      for (i = 0; i < 100; i ++)
         {
         TestArray[i].x = i;
         }

      System.out.println("We made it!");
   }

}
```

Figure B.11: A sample program for arrays
(code\ArrayTest1\ArrayTest1.java)

```
class Test
{
int x;
}

class ArrayTest2
{
   public static void main(String args[ ])
   {
      int i;
      Test TestArray[ ] = new Test[100];

      for (i = 0; i < 100; i ++)
         {
         TestArray[i] = new Test();
         TestArray[i].x = i;
         }

      System.out.println("We made it!");
   }

}
```

Problem
Algorithms
Java
Interpreter
Hardware

Figure B.12: A sample program for arrays
(code\ArrayTest2\ArrayTest2.java)

To use the debugger for this program, follow the instructions in the section titled "Using the debugger" in the file "\readme.txt" on the CD in the back of the book. These instructions assume that you've installed the examples on drive C:, so that the location of this program is "c:\whosj\code\ArrayTest2".

For C++ programmers: A Java array of references is more like a C++ array of pointers rather than one of objects, because Java references are pretty much the same as C pointers except that you can't do arithmetic with them (a restriction that doesn't bother me at all). You'll have to watch out for this difference between Java and C++ when writing Java programs, or they will fail mysteriously with "Null pointer exceptions".[4]

Getting into an Argument

Q: How do arguments work in Java? Are they copies of the variables in the calling method (*pass by value*) or are they merely different names for the corresponding variables in the calling method (*pass by reference*)?

Problem
Algorithms
Java
Interpreter
Hardware

A: As is usually the case in Java, the answer is simple: Pass by value, with an explanation. Variables of primitive types are always passed by value. Variables of reference types are also passed by value; however, the meaning of passing a reference variable by value is not quite as obvious as it might appear. For example, consider the program in Figure B.13, in which the SetName method of a StockItem argument is called, and another StockItem argument is set to a new value. The output of this program is:

Name: New first item name
Name: Second item

To use the debugger for this program, follow the instructions in the section titled "Using the debugger" in the file "\readme.txt" on the CD in the back of the book. These instructions assume that you've installed the examples on drive C:, so that the location of this program is "c:\whosj\code\Arg1".

---

4. What happened to the claim that Java doesn't have pointers?

```
import WAJ.*;

public class Arg1
{
    public static void main( String args[ ] )
    {
        StockItem item1;
        StockItem item2;

        item1 = new StockItem("First item");
        item2 = new StockItem("Second item");

        Argtest(item1, item2);

        item1.Display();
        item2.Display();
    }

    static void Argtest(StockItem first, StockItem second)
    {
    first.SetName("New first item name");
    second = new StockItem("New second item");
    }
}

class StockItem
{
private String m_Name;

StockItem()
{
    m_Name = "";
}


StockItem(String Name)
{
    m_Name = Name;
}

void Display()
{
    System.out.print("Name: ");
    System.out.println(m_Name);
}

void SetName(String Name)
{
    m_Name = Name;
}
}
```

Problem
Algorithms
Java
Interpreter
Hardware

Figure B.13: How arguments work (code\Arg1\Arg1.java)

Q: I don't get it. Why was the first one changed but not the second?

A: The first StockItem was changed because copying a reference variable produces another reference variable that refers to the same object that the original one did. Therefore, first in Argtest refers to the same object that item1 did in main, and calling the SetName method on first changes the name in item1.

The second StockItem argument, second, also started out as a copy of the corresponding reference variable in main, which in this case was item2. However, once we assigned second a new value in the line second = new StockItem("New second item");, second no longer referred to the same StockItem object that item2 did, but to a new StockItem object that was unrelated to the one that item2 refers to. Therefore, item2 remains unchanged after the return to main.

Q: What about using arguments to return values from a method?

A: Because arguments are always passed by value, assigning a new value to an argument affects only the argument, not the calling method's variable. However, as we saw in the previous example, the object that a calling program's reference variable refers to *can* be changed by calling a method on that same object through the argument in the called method. In the example, although you can't make item1 refer to a different object by assigning a new object to first, you *can* change the contents of the object to which both item1 and first refer.

Problem
Algorithms
Java
Interpreter
Hardware

For C++ programmers: Java has no way to specify that you want to pass a variable by reference rather than by value. However, an argument of reference type allows you to change the object to which the calling method's reference variable refers.[5] Thus, "pass by value" in Java, when applied to a reference type, has all the hazards of "pass by reference" in C++, but is more complex semantically.

Semifinalist

Q: How can I make sure that all of the resources (other than memory) used in my objects are released when I'm finished using the objects?

---

5. This assumes that there are methods that will change the object. Some classes, notably String, have no such methods, so references to such classes are safe to use as arguments.

A: That's easy: you just write a method that frees the resources and remember to call it whenever you need to.

Q: Yes, but what if someone has copied a reference to the object and it's still in use?

A: Then don't free the resources until the object isn't being used.

Q: But that's just like saying "Don't forget to delete your objects when you're done with them". If garbage collection is needed to prevent programmers from making that mistake, why won't those same programmers make mistakes about other resources?

A: Well, you can always write a finalize method for your objects. That method will be called before each object is garbage collected. Does that satisfy your requirements?

Q: Sure, as long as I know that the objects will be garbage collected in time to free the resources before I run out of them. When will they be garbage collected?

A: I have no idea. There's no guarantee in Java that the garbage collector will *ever* run, even after the program terminates.

Problem
Algorithms
Java
Interpreter
Hardware

Q: Then what good is the finalize method?

A: You've got me there.

For C++ programmers: As this discussion suggests, the finalize method is *not* the equivalent of C++ destructors. In fact, it doesn't seem to be of any value, since you can't be sure when or *if* it will be called. It would seem fairly simple to change the Java language specification to require that when an object with a finalize method is no longer in use, that object will be garbage collected immediately (after running the finalize method, of course). Unfortunately, that is apparently not feasible as it would make the implementation of the Java interpreter much more complex. Under current and foreseeable circumstances, therefore, there is no automatic way to reclaim resources when an object is no longer in use. This means that Java is unsuitable for projects where you have to be sure that resource deallocation is done in a timely manner without requiring omniscience of the application programmers.

Glossary

Special Characters

< is the "less than" operator, which returns the value true if the *expression* on its left has a lower value than the expression on its right; otherwise, it returns the value false.

= is the *assignment* operator, which assigns the *expression* on its right to the *variable* on its left. Note that assigning one *reference* to another will result in these two references pointing to the same *object*, so changes made to that object via one of the references will be reflected when that object is referred to via the other reference.

> is the "greater than" operator, which returns the value true if the *expression* on its left has a greater value than the expression on its right; otherwise, it returns the value false.

[is the left square bracket; see *square brackets* for usage.

] is the right square bracket; see *square brackets* for usage.

{ is the left curly brace; see *curly braces* for usage.

} is the right curly brace; see *curly braces* for usage.

!= is the "not equals" operator, which returns the value true if the *expression* on its left has a value different from the expression on its right; otherwise, it returns the value false.

&& is the "logical AND" operator. It produces the result true if both of the *expressions* on its right and left are true; if either of those expressions is false, it produces the result false. However, this isn't the whole story. There is a special rule in Java governing the execution of the && operator: If the expression on the left is false, then the answer must be false and the expression on the right is not executed at all. The reason for this *short-circuit evaluation* rule is that in some cases you may want to write a right-hand expression that will only be legal if the left-hand expression is false.

++ is the *increment* operator, which adds 1 to the variable to which it is affixed.

+= is the *add to variable* operator, which adds the *expression* on its right to the variable on its left.

-= is the *subtract from variable* operator, which subtracts the *expression* on its right from the variable on its left.

// is the comment operator; see *comment* for usage.

<= is the "less than or equal to" operator, which returns the value true if the *expression* on its left has the same value or a lower value than the expression on its right; otherwise, it returns the value false.

== is the "equals" operator, which returns the value true if the *expression* on its left has the same value as the expression on its right; otherwise, it returns the value false. Note that the result of comparing two *references* will not tell you whether the *objects* these references point to are equal, but whether the references point to the same object.

>= is the "greater than or equal to" operator, which returns the value true if the *expression* on its left has the same value or a greater value than the expression on its right; otherwise, it returns the value false.

|| is the "logical OR" operator. It produces the result true if at least one of the two *expressions* on its right and left is true; if both of those expressions are false, it produces the result false. However, this isn't the whole story. There is a special rule in Java governing the execution of the || operator: If the expression on the left is true, then the answer must be true and the expression on the right is not executed at all. The reason for this *short-circuit evaluation* rule is that in some cases you may want to write a right-hand expression that will only be legal if the left-hand expression is true.

A

An **access specifier** controls the access of *methods* of other classes to the methods and variables of a given class. The access specifiers used in this book are public, which allows general access to methods and variables; private, which forbids access by *methods* of other classes; and protected, which allows access by methods of *derived* classes.

Access time is a measure of how long it takes to retrieve data from a storage device, such as a hard disk or *RAM*.

Address; see *memory address*.

An **algorithm** is a set of precisely defined steps guaranteed to arrive at an answer to a problem or set of problems. As this implies, a set of steps that might never end is *not* an algorithm.

An **application program** is a program that actually accomplishes some useful or interesting task. Examples include inventory control, payroll, and game programs.

An **application programmer** (or *user*) is a programmer who uses primitive and class variables to write an application program. See also *library designer*.

An **argument** is a value that is supplied by one method (the *calling method*) that wishes to make use of the services of another method (the *called method*). Arguments are *copies* of the values from the *calling method*. In the case of *primitive types*, this means that making changes to an argument will not affect the corresponding variable or value in the calling method.

However, this is not true of arguments of *user-defined* types, because these are actually *references* to the same *objects* used in the calling method. As a result, changes made to arguments of user-defined types in a method *can*, under certain circumstances, affect the objects to which references in the calling method refer.

An **argument list** is a set of *argument* definitions specified in a *method declaration*. The argument list describes the types and names of all the *variables* that the *method* receives when it is called by a *calling method*.

An **array** is a group of *elements* of the same type which we wish to consider a single variable; for example, we can create an array of chars. We can refer to the individual elements by their indexes; so, if we have an array of chars called m_Data, m_Data[i] refers to the ith char in the array.

Assignment is the operation of setting a *variable* to a value. The operator that indicates assignment is the equal sign, =.

An **assignment statement** such as x = 5; is *not* an algebraic equality, no matter how much it may resemble one. It is a command telling the computer to assign a value to a variable. In the example, the variable is x and the value is 5.

B

A **base class** is a class from which one or more other classes are derived. The derived classes inherit all the *fields* and *regular methods* from the base class. See also *inheritance*.

The **base class part** of a *derived* class object is an unnamed component of the derived class object whose fields and methods are accessible as though they were defined in the derived class, so long as they are either public or protected. See also *inheritance*.

A **binary** number system uses only two digits, 0 and 1.

A **bit** is the fundamental unit of storage in a modern computer; the word *bit* is derived from the phrase *bi*nary digi*t*. Each bit, as this suggests, can have one of two states, 0 and 1.

A **block** is a group of *statements* that are considered one logical statement. A block is delimited by the "curly braces", { and }; the first of these symbols starts a block, and the second one ends the block. A block can be used anywhere that a statement can be used, and is treated in exactly the same way as if it were one statement. For example, if a block is the *controlled block* of an if statement, then all of the statements in the block are executed if the condition in the if is true, and none of the statements are executed if the condition in the if is false.

A **boolean** is a type of variable whose range of values is limited to true or false. This is the most appropriate return type for a method that uses its return value to report whether some condition exists.

Brace; see *curly braces*.

A **break statement** is a loop control device that interrupts processing of a *loop* whenever it is executed within the *controlled block* of a *loop control statement*. When a break statement is executed, the flow of control passes to the next statement after the end of the *controlled block*.

A **byte** is the unit in which data capacities are stated, whether in *RAM* or on a disk. In modern computers, a byte consists of eight *bits*.

A **byte-code instruction** is one of the fundamental operations that a *Java interpreter* can perform. Some examples of these operations are addition, subtraction, or other arithmetic operations; other possibilities include operations that control what instruction will be executed next. All Java programs must be converted into byte-code instructions by a *compiler* before they can be executed by the Java interpreter.

A **byte-code** program is a program in a form suitable for execution by the Java interpreter.

C

A **cache** is a small amount of fast memory where frequently used data are stored temporarily.

Call; see *method call*.

A **called method** is a *method* that starts execution as the result of a *method call*. Normally, it will return to the *calling method* via a return *statement* when finished.

A **calling method** is a *method* that suspends execution as a result of a *method call*; the *called method* begins execution at the point of the method call.

A **char** is a type of variable that can represent one character of text. It occupies two bytes of RAM. The char is sometimes considered an *integer variable* type and can be used for arithmetic, but this is not commonly done.

In case you were wondering how to pronounce this term, the most common pronunciation has an *a* like the *a* in "married", whereas the *ch* sounds like *k*. Other pronunciations include the standard English pronunciation of "char", as in over-cooking meat, and even "car" as in "automobile".

A **checked exception** is an *exception* that the design of Java assumes can happen only at certain reasonably predictable places in your program; therefore, you are required to let the callers of your methods know about the possibility of its occurring if you don't handle it yourself. An example of a condition that can cause a checked exception is trying to open a nonexistent file for reading. See also *unchecked exception*.

Child class; see *inheritance*, *derived* class.

A **class** is a user-defined type; for example, StockItem is a class.

A **class definition** tells the compiler what facilities the class supplies and how to implement those facilities. A class definition is found in a source-code file, which has the extension .java.

A **class implementation** is the code that is responsible for actually doing the things that the objects of the class are supposed to do. See also class *interface*.

A **class interface** is the set of operations that objects of that class can perform, as contrasted with the implementation of those operations.

class scope describes the visibility of *fields*; that is, *variables* that are defined within a class rather than within a *method*. Such variables can be accessed by any method of that class; their accessibility to methods outside the class is controlled by the *access specifier* specified when they were defined in the class *interface*.

A **comment** is a note to yourself or another programmer; it is ignored by the compiler. The symbol // marks the beginning of a comment; the comment continues until the end of the line containing the //. For those of you with BASIC experience, this is just like REM (the "remark" keyword); anything after it on a line is ignored.

Compilation is the process of translating *source code* into a *byte-code program*, which is composed of *byte-code instructions* along with the data needed by those instructions.

A **compiler** is a program that performs the process of *compilation*.

Compile time means "while the *compiler* is compiling the *source code* of a program".

A **constructor** is a *method* that creates new *objects* of a (particular) class type. All constructors have the same name as the class for which they are constructors; therefore, the constructors for the StockItem class also have the name StockItem.

A **continuation expression** is the part of a for *statement* computed before every execution of the *controlled statement*. The statement controlled by the for will be executed if the result of the computation is true, but not if it is false; see the entry for the for statement for an example.

A **controlled block** is a *block* under the control of a *loop control statement* or an if or else statement. The controlled block of a loop control statement can be executed a variable number of times, whereas the controlled block of an if or else statement is executed either once or not at all.

Controlled statement; see *controlled block*.

CPU is an abbreviation for Central Processing Unit. This is the "active" part of your computer, which executes the *machine instructions* that make the computer do useful work.

The **curly braces** { and } are used to surround a *block*. The *compiler* treats the *statements* in the block as one statement.

D

Data are the pieces of information that are operated on by programs. The singular of "data" is "datum"; however, the word "data" is commonly used as both singular and plural.

A **debugger** is a program that controls the execution of another program, so that you can see what the latter program is doing. The Visual J++ compiler on the CD-ROM in the back of this book includes a debugger.

A **default constructor** is a *method* that is used to create an *object* when no initial value is specified for that object. For example, StockItem() is the default constructor for the StockItem class.

A **derived** class is one that inherits methods and fields from a *base* class. See also *inheritance*.

A **digit** is one of the characters used in any positional number system to represent all numbers starting at 0 and ending at one less than the base of the number system. In the decimal system, there are ten digits, 0 through 9, and in the hexadecimal system there are sixteen digits, 0 through 9 and a through f.

A **double** is a type of *floating-point variable* that can represent a range of positive and negative numbers of magnitude from approximately 4.940656e–324 to approximately 1.79769e+308 (and 0), with approximately 16 digits of precision.

Dynamic type checking refers to the practice of checking the correct usage of *variables* of different types during execution of a program rather than during *compilation*; see the *type system* entry for further discussion.

Dynamic typing means delaying the determination of the exact type of a *variable* until *run time* rather than fixing that type at *compile time* as in *static typing*. This is the typing mechanism used for *user-defined data types* in Java. Please note that dynamic typing is not the same as *dynamic type checking*; Java has the former but not the latter. See the *type system* entry for further discussion.

E

An **element** is one of the *variables* that makes up an *array*.

The keyword **else** causes its *controlled block* to be executed if the condition in its matching *if* statement turns out to be false at run time.

An **empty stack** is a *stack* that currently contains no values.

Encapsulation is the concept of hiding details inside a class *implementation* rather than exposing them in the class *interface*. This is one of the primary organizing principles that characterize object-oriented programming.

An **end user** is the person who actually uses an *application program* to perform some useful or interesting task. See also *application programmer*, *library designer*.

An **exception** is an unexpected event that occurs during the execution of a program, or in other words, an error. The idea behind exception handling can be expressed by the old saying: "Hope for the best, but prepare for the worst." In other words, rather than trying to handle every possible error condition in the normal flow of a program, we assume that everything will work all right. If it doesn't, we have a fallback plan to handle the error.

An **expression** is one of the units of which a *statement* is made. It is made up of one or more *tokens*. In the statement i = k + 3;, "k + 3" is an expression composed of the three tokens k, +, and 3.

F

The keyword **false** is a predefined value, representing the result of a conditional expression whose condition is not satisfied. For example, in the conditional expression x < y, if x is not less than y, the value of the expression will be false. See also boolean.

A **fence post error** is a logical error that causes a loop to be executed one more or one less time than the correct count. A common cause of this error is confusing the number of *elements* in an *array* with the *index* of the last *element*. The derivation of this term is by analogy with the problem of calculating the number of fence sections and fence posts that you need for a given fence. For example, if you have to put up a fence 100 feet long, and each section of the fence is 10 feet long, how many sections of fence do you need? Obviously, the answer is 10. Now, how many fence posts do you need? 11. The confusion caused by counting fence posts when you should be counting segments of the fence (or vice versa) is the cause of a fence post error.

To return to a programming example, if you have an array with 11 elements, the index of the last element is 10, not 11. Thus, confusing the number of elements with the highest index has much the same effect as the fence post problem.

This sort of problem is also known, less colorfully, as an *off-by-one* error.

A **field** is a *variable* that is part of the definition of a class. It is viewed as "belonging" to the class.

A **float** is a type of *floating-point variable* that can represent a range of positive and negative numbers of magnitude from approximately 1.401298e–45 to approximately 3.40282e+38 (and 0), with approximately 6 digits of precision.

A **floating-point variable** is a Java approximation of a mathematical "real number". Unlike mathematical real numbers, Java floating-point variables have a limited range and precision, depending on their types; see the individual types, float and double, for details.

A **for statement** is a *loop control statement* that causes its *controlled block* to be executed while a specified logical expression (the *continuation expression*) is true. It also provides for a *starting expression* to be executed before the first execution of the controlled statement, and a *modification expression* to be executed after every execution of the controlled statement. For example, in the for statement for (i = 0; i < 10; i ++), the initialization expression is i = 0, the continuation expression is i < 10, and the modification expression is i ++.

H

Hardware refers to the physical components of a computer, the ones you can touch. Examples include the keyboard, the monitor, the printer.

The **heap** is the area of memory where *objects* are stored.

Hex is an abbreviation for *hexadecimal*.

A **hexadecimal** number system has 16 digits, 0–9 and a–f.

I

An **identifier** is a user-defined name; both *method* names and *variable* names are identifiers. Identifiers must not conflict with *keywords* such as if and for; for example, you cannot create a method or a variable with the name for.

An **if statement** is a *statement* that causes its *controlled block* to be executed if the *logical expression* specified in the if statement is true.

Implementation; see class *implementation*.

To **increment a *variable*** means to add 1 to its value. This can be done in Java by using the increment operator, ++.

An **index** is an expression used to select one of a number of *elements* of an *array*. It is enclosed in *square brackets* ([ ]). For example, in the expression a[i+1], the index is the expression i+1.

An **index variable** is a *variable* used to hold an *index*.

Inheritance is the definition of one class as a more specific version of another class which has been previously defined. The newly defined class is called the *derived* class (or sometimes the child class or the *subclass*), whereas the previously defined class is called the *base* class (or sometimes the *parent* class or the *superclass*). This book uses the terms "base" and "derived". The derived class inherits all of the *fields* and *regular methods* from the base class. Inheritance is one of the primary organizing principles of object-oriented programming.

Initialization is the process of setting the initial value of a *variable*. It is very similar to *assignment* but is not identical: Initialization is done only once for each variable, when that variable is created, whereas assignment can be done as many times as desired.

Input refers to the process of reading data into the computer from the outside world, or sometimes the process of providing data for a *called method* to operate on. A very commonly used source of input for simple programs is the keyboard.

Instruction; see *byte-code instruction*, *machine instruction*.

An **int** (short for *integer*) is a type of *integer variable* that can represent a whole number in the range -2147483648 (-2^{31}) to 2147483647 ($2^{31}-1$). It is 4 bytes long.

An **integer variable** is a Java representation of a whole number. Unlike mathematical integers, Java integers have a limited range, depending on their types; see the individual types short, int, and long for details. The char type is also sometimes considered an integer variable, but is not generally used for arithmetic.

I/O is an abbreviation for "input/output". This refers to the process of getting information into and out of the computer or a particular *method* in a program; see *input* and *output* for more details.

J

The **Java interpreter** is the program that controls the execution of Java programs. A Java program is actually a set of instructions to be used by the Java interpreter, describing the actions that would be taken by a hypothetical specialized computer that would solve the problem our program is designed to solve. When the Java interpreter is executed, it performs the actions specified by your Java program.

java.io is the name of the *package* that tells the *compiler* how to compile code that uses predefined *variables* like System.out and their methods such as println.

The **Java program counter** is a *variable* in the *Java interpreter* that holds the address of the next *byte-code instruction* to be executed. During a *method call*, a call byte-code instruction *pushes* the contents of the program counter on the *stack* so that the *called method* can return to the *calling method* when it is finished executing.

K

A **keyword** is a word defined in the Java language, such as if and for. It is illegal to define an *identifier* such as a *variable* or *method* name that conflicts with a keyword; for example, you cannot create a method or a variable with the name for.

L

A **library designer** is a programmer who creates classes for *application programmers* to use in writing *application programs*.

A **literal** value doesn't have a name, but represents itself in a literal manner. Some examples are 'x' (a char literal having the ASCII value that represents the letter *x*), and 5 (a numeric literal with the value 5).

Local scope describes the visibility of *variables* that are defined within a *method*; such variables can be accessed only by code in that method.[1]

A **logical expression** is an expression that takes on the value true or false, rather than a numeric value. Some examples of such expressions are: x > y, which will be true if x has a greater value than y, and false otherwise; and a == b, which will be true if a has the same value as b, and false otherwise; see also boolean.

A **long** is a type of *integer variable* that contains 64 bits (8 bytes) of data and therefore can represent a whole number in the range -9223372036854775808 (-2^{63}) to 9223372036854775807 ($2^{63}-1$).

A **loop** is a means of executing a *controlled block* a (possibly variable) number of times, depending on some condition. The

---

1. In fact, a variable can be declared in any *block*, not just in a *method*; in that case, its scope is from the point where it is declared until the end of the block where it is defined. However, in this book all local variables have method scope, so this distinction is not critical here and omitting it simplifies the discussion.

statement that controls the controlled block is called a *loop control statement*. This book covers the while and for loop control statements; see those headings for details.

A **loop control statement** is a *statement* that controls the *controlled block* in a *loop*.

M

Machine address; see *memory address*.

A **machine instruction** is one of the fundamental operations that a *CPU* can perform. Some examples of these operations are addition, subtraction, or other arithmetic operations; other possibilities include operations that control what instruction will be executed next.

A **memory address** is a unique number identifying a particular *byte* of *RAM*.

A **method** is a section of code defined in a class, and is viewed as belonging to that class. A method has a name, optional *arguments*, and a *return type*. The name makes it possible for one method to start execution of another one via a *method call*; the arguments are used to provide input for the method, and the return type allows the method to provide output to its *calling method* when the return *statement* causes the calling method to resume execution; see Figure 5.2 for a diagram illustrating a method call and return.

A **method call** (or *call* for short) causes execution to be transferred temporarily from the current *method* (the *calling method*) to the one named in the method call (the *called method*). Normally, when a called method is finished with its task, it will return to the calling method, which will pick up execution at the statement after the method call.

A **method declaration** is the first line of a *method*. It tells the compiler some vital statistics of the method. The method declaration consists of three required parts: a *return type*, the method's name, and an *argument list*. There are also several optional parts called qualifiers which provide the compiler with more details about the method being declared. In this book, we use the static qualifier.

Method overloading is the Java facility that allows us to create more than one *method* with the same name. So long as all such methods have different *signatures*, we can write as many of them as we wish, and the compiler will be able to figure out which one we mean.

A **modification expression** is the part of a for *statement* executed after every execution of the *controlled block*. It is often used to *increment* an *index variable* to refer to the next *element* of an *array*; see the entry for the for statement for an example.

N

A **nanosecond** is one-billionth of a second.

The **new** operator is used to allocate memory for *objects*.

Non-display character; see *non-printing* character.

A **non-numeric variable** is a *variable* that is not used in calculations like adding, multiplying, or subtracting. Such variables might represent names, addresses, telephone numbers, bank account numbers, or drivers license numbers. Note that just because something is called a *number* or even is composed entirely of the digits 0–9, does not make it a *numeric variable* by our standards; the question is how the item is used. No one adds, multiplies, or subtracts drivers license numbers, for example; they serve solely as identifiers, and could just as easily have letters in them, as indeed some of them do.

A **non-printing character** is used to control the format of our displayed or printed information, rather than to represent a particular letter, digit, or other special character. The *space* ( ) is one of the more important nonprinting characters.

A **null reference** is a *reference* that isn't pointing to anything at the moment.

A **numeric variable** is a *variable* representing a quantity that can be expressed as a number, whether a whole number (an *integer variable*) or a number with a fractional part (a *floating-point variable*), and which can be used in calculations such as addition, subtraction, multiplication, or division. The integer variable types in

Java are short, int, and long; each of these types can represent both negative and positive values (and 0).

The floating-point variable types are float and double, which differ in their range and precision. Like the integer variable types, the floating-point types can represent either positive or negative numbers as well as 0; see the individual headings, float and double, for details on range and precision.

O

An **object** is a programming construct that represents a specific item of user-defined data that we wish to keep track of in a program. Note that an object is similar to a variable in that it represents an item of data. However, unlike a variable, we cannot use an object directly but must refer to it via a *reference*.

Object-oriented programming is an approach to solving programming problems by creating *objects* to represent the entities being handled by the program, rather than relying solely on *primitive* data types. This approach has the advantage that you can match the language to the needs of the problem you're trying to solve. For example, if you were writing a nurse's station program in Java, you would want to have objects that represented nurses, doctors, patients, various sorts of equipment, and so on. Each of these objects would display the behavior appropriate to the thing or person it was representing.

Off-by-one error; see *fence post error*.

An **operating system** is a program that deals with the actual hardware of your computer; it supplies the lowest level of the software infrastructure needed to run a program. As this is written, MS-DOS (which is also the basis for Windows 95) is by far the most common operating system for Intel CPUs. It is followed by OS/2, Linux, and Windows NT, not necessarily in that order.

An **operator** is one of the facilities of Java that is built into the language rather than being added on later, and therefore can have a name that does not conform to the rules for *identifiers*. Examples are +, -, and =.

Output refers to the process of sending data from the computer to the outside world, or sometimes the process of returning data from a *called method* to its *calling method*. The most commonly used destination for program output is the screen.

Overloading: see *method overloading*.

A method in a derived class is said to **override** a base class method if the derived class method has the same *signature* (name and argument types) as the base class method. The derived class method will be called instead of the base class method when the method is called for an object of the derived class. A method in a derived class with the same name but a different signature from a method in the base class does *not* override the base class method. Instead, both the derived class method and the base class method are available for use with objects of the derived class.[2]

P

A **package** contains the *source code* and *byte code* belonging to several *source-code files*, in a form that the *interpreter* can search when it needs to find general-purpose methods.

Parent class; see *inheritance*.

Polymorphism is the major organizing principle in Java that allows us to implement several classes with the same class *interface* and treat objects of all these classes as though they were of the same class. This is the Java mechanism for *dynamic typing*. The word "polymorphism" is derived from the Greek words "poly", meaning "many", and "morph", meaning "form". In other words, the same behavior is implemented in different forms.

Pop means "remove the top value from a *stack*".

A **primitive** data type (also sometimes known as a "native" data type) is one that is defined in the Java language, as opposed to a *user-defined data type* (class). In Java, it is impossible to create user-defined data types that behave in the same way as primitive types.

---

2. C++ programmers should note this significant difference between the handling of inheritance in C++ and Java.

print: see System.out.print.

println: see System.out.println.

The keyword **private** is an *access specifier* that allows access only by *methods* of the same class to a specified *field* or *method*.

A **program** is a set of instructions specifying the solution to a set of problems, along with the data used by those instructions.

Program counter: see *Java program counter*.

Programming is the art and science of solving problems by the following procedure:

1. Find or invent a general solution to a set of problems.
2. Express this solution as an *algorithm* or set of algorithms.
3. Translate the algorithm(s) into terms so simple that a stupid machine like a computer can follow them to calculate the specific answer for any specific problem in the set.

Warning: This definition may be somewhat misleading since it implies that the development of a program is straightforward and linear, with no revision. This is known as the "waterfall model" of programming, since water going over a waterfall follows a preordained course in one direction. However, real-life programming doesn't usually work this way; rather, most programs are written in an incremental process as assumptions are changed and errors are found and corrected.

The keyword **protected** is an *access specifier*. When present in a *base* class definition, it allows *derived* class methods access to *fields* and *methods* in the base class part of a derived class object, while preventing access by other methods outside the base class.

The keyword **public** is an *access specifier* that allows *methods* of other classes access to *methods* and *fields* of its class.

Push means "add another value to a *stack*".

R

RAM is an acronym for Random Access Memory. This is the working storage of a computer, where data and programs are stored while we're using them.

A **reference** is a variable that refers to an object and thus allows us to use that object.

A **register** is a storage area that is on the same chip as the *CPU* itself. Programs use registers to hold data items that are actively in use; data in registers can be accessed within the time allocated to instruction execution, rather than the much longer times needed to access data in *RAM*.

A **regular method** is any method that is *not* a constructor. A *derived* class inherits all regular methods from its *base* class.

A **retrieval method** is a *method* that retrieves data, which may have been previously stored by a *storage method* or may be generated when needed by some other process such as calculation according to a formula.

A **return address** is the *memory address* of the next *byte-code instruction* in a *calling method*. It is used during execution of a return *statement* in a *called method* to transfer execution back to the correct place in the calling method.

A **return statement** is used by a *called method* to transfer execution back to the *calling method*. The return statement can also specify a value of the correct *return type* for the called method; this value is made available to the calling method to be used for further calculation. An example of a return statement is return 0;, which returns the value 0 to the calling method.

A **return type** tells the *compiler* what sort of data (if any) a *called method* returns to the *calling method* when the called method finishes executing. If no data is to be returned from the called method, the return type is specified as void.

ROM is an abbreviation for Read-Only Memory. This is the permanent internal storage of a computer, where the programs needed to start up the computer are stored. As this suggests, ROM does not lose its contents when the power is turned off, as contrasted with *RAM*.

Run time means "while a (previously compiled) program is being executed".

S

A **scalar** *variable* has a single value (at any one time); this is contrasted with an *array*, which contains a number of values, each of which is referred to by its *index*.

The **scope** of a *variable* is the part of the program in which the variable can be accessed. The two scopes in Java are *local* and *class*; see the entry for each specific scope for more details.

A **selection sort** is a sorting algorithm that selects the highest (or lowest) *element* from a set of elements (the "input list"), moving that selected element to another set of elements (the "output list"). The next highest (or lowest) element is then treated in the same manner; this operation is repeated until as many elements as desired have been moved to the output list.

A **short** is a type of *integer variable* that can represent a whole number in the range −32768 to 32767. It is two bytes long.

The **short-circuit evaluation rule** governs the execution of the || and the && operators. See || and && for details.

A **side effect** is any result of calling a *method* that persists beyond the execution of that method, other than providing a return value. For example, writing data to a file is a side effect.

The **signature** of a *method* consists of its name and the types of its *arguments*. Every method is uniquely identified by the combination of its signature and the class to which the method belongs, which is what makes it possible to have more than one method with the same name; this is called *method overloading*.

Software refers to the nonphysical components of a computer, the ones you cannot touch. If you can install it on your hard disk, it's software. Examples include a spreadsheet, a word processor, or a database program.

Source code is a program in a form suitable for reading and writing by a human being.

A **source-code file** contains *source code* statements that are turned into *byte-code instructions* by the Java *compiler*. Source-code files have the extension *.java*.

The **space** character ( ) is one of the *non-printing characters* (or *non-display characters*) that control the format of displayed or printed information.

The **square brackets**, [and], are used to enclose an *array index*, which selects an individual *element* of the *array*.

A **stack** is a data structure with characteristics similar to a spring-loaded plate holder such as you might see in a cafeteria. The last plate deposited on the stack of plates will be the first one to be removed when a customer needs a fresh plate; similarly, the last value deposited (*pushed*) onto a stack is the first value retrieved (*popped*).

The **stack pointer** is a *dedicated register*. The stack pointer is used to keep track of the most recently *pushed* value on the *stack*.

A **starting expression** is the part of a for *statement* executed once before the *controlled block* of the for statement is first executed. It is often used to initialize an *index variable* to 0, so that the index variable can be used to refer to the first element of an *array*; see the entry for the for statement for an example.

A **statement** is a complete operation understood by the Java compiler. Each statement is ended with a semicolon (;).

A **static method** is a method that can be called without reference to an object of its class. Because such a method call is not connected with any particular object of its class, a static method cannot refer to fields of the class.

Static type checking refers to the practice of checking the correct usage of variables of different types during compilation of a program rather than during execution. Java uses static type checking; see the *type system* entry for further discussion. Note that this has no particular relation to the keyword static.

Static typing means determining the exact type of a variable when the program is compiled. It is the typing mechanism used for *primitive* variables in Java. Note that this has no particular relation to the keyword static, and also that it is not the same as *static type checking*; see the *type system* entry for further discussion.

Stepwise refinement is the process of developing an *algorithm* by starting out with a "coarse" solution and "refining" it until the steps are within the capability of the Java language.

Storage; syn. *memory*.

A **storage class** is the characteristic of a *variable* that determines how and when a *memory address* is assigned to that variable. In Java, *primitive* variables are usually stored on the *stack*, while *user-defined data types* always store their data on the heap. Please note that the term *storage class* has nothing to do with the Java term class.

A **storage method** is a *method* that stores data for later retrieval by a *retrieval method*.

Subclass: syn. *derived* class.

The keyword **super** refers to the *base* class of the current class. One use of this keyword is to specify which *base* class *constructor* a *derived* class *constructor* wishes to call to initialize the *base* class *part* of the derived class. Another use of this keyword is to call a method in the base class from a derived class method, when the base class method has the same name as a method in the derived class. In such a case, if we didn't use the super keyword the derived class method would be called rather than the base class method.

Superclass: syn. *base* class.

System.out.print is a *method* that displays its argument on the screen.

System.out.println is a *method* that displays its argument on the screen and then moves the output position to the next line.

T

A **token** is a part of a program that the *compiler* treats as a separate unit. It's analogous to a word in English; a *statement* is more like a sentence. For example, StockItem is a token, as is (. On the other hand, x = 5; is a statement.

The keyword **true** is a predefined value representing the result of a conditional expression whose condition is satisfied. For example, in the conditional expression x < y, if x is less than y, the value of the expression will be true.

The **type** of a class variable is the class to which it belongs. The type of a primitive variable is one of the predefined variable types in Java; see *integer variable*, *floating-point variable*, and boolean for details on the primitive types.

The **type system** refers to the set of rules that the compiler uses to decide what uses are legal for a variable of a given *type*. In Java, these determinations are made by the compiler (*static type checking*). This makes it easier to prevent type errors than it is in languages where type checking is done during execution of the program (*dynamic type checking*).

Please note that Java has both *static type checking* and *dynamic typing*. This is possible because the set of types that is acceptable in any given situation can be determined at compile time, even though the exact type of a given variable may not be known until run time.

U

An **unchecked exception** is an *exception* that the design of Java assumes can happen virtually anywhere in your program, so it wouldn't make sense to force you to specify that your methods can throw such an exception. Examples of conditions that cause unchecked exceptions are attempting to use a null reference, trying to access an element of an array that is past the end of the array, and the like. We can handle unchecked exceptions in our methods if we wish, but we don't have to; whether or not we handle them, we don't have to declare that we will throw them, because any method is permitted to throw them. See also *checked exception*.

An **uninitialized variable** is one that has never been set to a known value. Attempting to use such a *variable* is an error that will be caught either at compile time (in most cases) or at run time.

An **unqualified name** is a reference to a *field* or a *method* that doesn't specify which *object* the field belongs to. When we use an unqualified field name in a method, the compiler assumes that the object we are referring to is the object for which that method has been called. When we use an unqualified method name, the compiler assumes that we mean the method of that name in the current class.

The term **user** has several meanings in programming. The primary usage in this book is *application programmer*. However, it can also mean *library designer* (in the phrase *user-defined data type*) or even *end user*.

A **user-defined** data type is one that is, well, defined by the user. In this usage, however, "user" means "someone using language facilities to extend the range of variable types in the language" (i.e., *library designer*). The primary mechanism used to define a user-defined type is the class.

V

A **value argument** is a *variable* of *local scope* created when a *method* begins execution. Its initial value is set to the value of the corresponding *argument* in the *calling method*. Changing a value argument does not affect any variable in the calling method, except in some cases when that value argument is of *reference* type.

A **variable** is a programming construct that represents a specific item of data that we wish to keep track of in a program. Some examples are the weight of a pumpkin or the number of cartons of milk in the inventory of a store.

A **void** return type specifier in a *method declaration* indicates that the method in question does not return any value when it finishes executing.

W

A **while statement** is a *loop control statement* that causes its *controlled block* to be executed while a specified logical expression is true.

Z

Zero-based indexing refers to the practice of numbering the *elements* of an *array* starting at 0 rather than 1. Although it might seem arbitrary to start counting at 0 rather than at 1, there are historical reasons for this decision, stemming from the *assembly language* ancestry of the C language.

Index